handbook for preparing visual media

second edition

Ed Minor

Professor of Communications
California State University, Sacramento

McGraw-Hill
Book Company

New York   St. Louis   San Francisco
Auckland   Bogotá   Düsseldorf   Johannesburg
London   Madrid   Mexico   Montreal
New Delhi   Panama   Paris   São Paulo
Singapore   Sydney   Tokyo   Toronto

Library of Congress Cataloging in Publication Data

Minor, Ed.
    Handbook for preparing visual media.

    Published in 1962 under title: Simplified
techniques for preparing visual instruction materials.
    Includes index.
    1. Visual aids. II. Title.
LB1043.5.M43   1978   371.33′5   77-25459
ISBN 0-07-042407-1

The designer and illustrator was Suzanne Bowen.

To Bertha for understanding,
and believing in me.

ACKNOWLEDGMENTS

In every undertaking there are those who contribute more
than is expected, and to them a very special *mahalo*—to
the late Harvey Frye, my former instructor and the co-
author of our successful book *Techniques for Producing
Visual Instructional Media,* who by touching my life has
helped to make all this possible; to my devoted wife, Bertha,
who has watched me struggle during the last seventeen
years putting into writing that which I felt would help others
better communicate visually; to my young and gifted illustrator and designer, Suzanne Bowen, for putting my
words and thoughts into exciting visual form; to James L.
Bruton and Archie V. Hannon, two truly total typographers,
for their part in this publication; to Dr Paul Snipes and Dr. Ira
Harris and their staffs at the University of Hawaii for making
their resources available to me during the final months of
production; and to my editor, Jean Smith, for giving an
author the ultimate gift—freedom to write, illustrate, and
design his own book.

contents

preface

We live in a visually oriented world in which we are constantly exposed to visual messages that reach us through visual media. Billboards, television, transparencies, posters, charts, and maps are but a few of the forms visual media can take. With the exception of television itself, all types of visual media can be made by a non-artist.

This handbook was written for teachers, librarians, and those who have the desire to create and prepare effective and exciting visual media but feel they lack the skills necessary for such an undertaking. I wrote this handbook with the belief that visual media, such as transparencies, posters, charts, signs, displays, and individualized instructional materials, can be designed and prepared with a basic knowledge of simple graphic production techniques and aids. To serve this purpose, I have developed a simple step-by-step approach adaptable both for the person without skills in art, graphic art, or photography, and for the professional seeking new solutions to visual media production problems. Since I feel that excellence does not imply complexity, I have avoided complicated instructions and terminology, relying instead on several hundred clear, simple illustrations to clarify the techniques described. Designed to be used in an actual working situation, the handbook may be folded back to allow ready implementation of illustrated instructions.

This handbook is divided into seven sections. Section 1, "Visual Media Preparation Guidelines," is a starting point for designing and preparing visual media. The guidelines cover visual media idea sources, design, size standards, color, and lettering as they apply to visual media. Section 2, "Visual Imaging," is perhaps the most exciting of all sections as it can help make one an "instant" artist. This section contains simplified techniques and aids for creating, enlarging, reducing, and modifying images (visuals). Section 3, "Special Effects for Images," covers several effects that can add an exciting dimension to visual media. Color,

pattern and shading, and "motion" effects have been selected for inclusion here. Section 4, "Lettering Made Simple," includes 27 different lettering techniques and aids that can be used to solve any media lettering problem. Section 5, "Mounting and Laminating Images," deals with unique techniques and aids for mounting and laminating visual media. Section 6, "Simple Display Making," contains patterns of attractive easy-to-make display units that can be traced and enlarged to any size. These free-standing and hanging units can be used as display units, posters, signs, or any material requiring a standing or hanging support for display. Section 7, "Transparencies for Study and Display," deals exclusively with the making of large transparencies and 2-by 2-inch slides. Included are 14 techniques for preparing large transparencies, and six techniques for making slides. Instructions for mounting transparencies and slides are also included.

Sections 2, 3, 4, and 5 have a selection chart at the start of the section. These charts are designed to assist the reader in selecting the most appropriate techniques for the visual media being prepared. All of the sections include sources of print and nonprint materials, and sources of equipment and materials.

The INDEX is a total reference in that it can, in addition to serving as a conventional index, be used to locate specific information on techniques, aids, materials, and equipment within the handbook.

The success of preparing effective visual media depends much on an understanding of graphic techniques, materials, and equipment. Skill comes with the doing, as it does with all accomplishments.

Should you not completely understand any of the material between these covers, write me; it will be my pleasure to reply.

Ed Minor

There are several ways to effectively use this handbook. First, remember that the primary intent of the handbook is to assist the non-artist design and prepare his own visual media. Each section has been designed and written to be used independently, or used to support other sections. For example, if you wish only to create a visual or symbol, then Section 2, "Visual Imaging" is all you need to use. However, should you desire to prepare a poster which requires a design, visual, color or texture, and lettering, Sections 1, 2, 3, and 4 are recommended. If you wish to display the poster on a free-standing or hanging support, Section 6, "Simple Display Making" should be used. The handbook can also be an enjoyable reading experience to understand and appreciate how easy it is to put things together to make learning and looking exciting experiences.

The handbook goes one step beyond showing you how to make things. At the end of each section, sources of print and nonprint references are listed, and sources for all the equipment and materials referred to in the section are also listed.

⌐1

VISUAL MEDIA PREPARATION GUIDELINES

- Need an idea for making a poster, chart or sign?
- What's a good size for viewing?
- What size should the artwork be for photographic reproduction?
- What size and style of letters?
- What colors are best to use?

For answers, read this section as a start. Its intent is to provide you with basic guidelines for preparing to create visual media.

⌐2

VISUAL IMAGING

- Want to create your very own visuals (images)—become an "instant" artist?

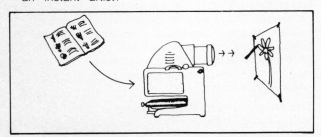

- Need sources of excellent visuals that can be used directly without violating copyright laws?
- Need sources of visuals that can be modified (traced, enlarged, reduced, etc.) for use?
- Want to change a photograph into a pen-and-ink sketch in minutes?

- Want to produce good visuals for stencil and spirit duplication?

This section has the answers. While it won't qualify you as a professional artist, it will help to prepare you to create your own visuals for almost any use. First, take a look at the Visual Imaging Selection Chart on page 11, it will suggest possible solutions to imaging problems.

⌐3

SPECIAL EFFECTS FOR IMAGES

- Want to add opaque or transparent color to images or letters?
- Want to add patterns or shading, the easy way, to images?

- Want to add a "motion" effect to your transparencies?

Here is a section that deals solely to adding special effects to visual media. The Special Effects Selection Chart on page 40 suggests appropriate special effects for various materials.

4

LETTERING MADE SIMPLE

- Need letters 20-inches high?
- Want to do lettering on acetate, glass, or metal?
- Need professional-looking letters for just tracing?

- Want to die-cut your own letters?
- Want to rub-and-transfer printed letters to almost any dry surface?
- Looking for exciting ways to layout your letters?

Lettering for any use can be found in this section. There are 27 lettering techniques and aids included here. First, look at the Lettering Selection Chart on page 54, as it will suggest appropriate lettering for visual media and different surfaces.

5

MOUNTING AND LAMINATING IMAGES

- Want to mount maps, charts, or photographs on cloth?
- Need to mount delicate fabrics on wood or metal?
- Want to mount color photographic prints on cardboard, wood, or metal?

- Want to laminate a glass-like (acetate) on a surface for "write-on" and "wipe-off" use?
- Want to laminate acetate on a surface for protection against weather or constant use?

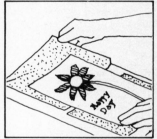

This section has the answers. A look at the Mounting and Laminating Selection Chart on page 94 is recommended as a starting point for selecting an appropriate technique or aid.

6

SIMPLE DISPLAY MAKING

- Need a free-standing or hanging cardboard support for a poster or sign?
- Want to try your hand at making the same type of exciting display units you see in public places?

This section on display making contains patterns of exciting, easy-to-make display units. Most of these units can be made from a single sheet of heavyweight cardboard.

7

TRANSPARENCIES FOR STUDY AND DISPLAY

- Want to turn magazine pictures into "instant" transparencies for projection or display?
- Need to make a quick large transparency or 2-by 2-inch slides for projection?
- Want to make large transparencies or slides with your Xerox or thermocopy machine?
- Want to make 60-second slides from photographic negatives?

This section shows you 14 ways to make larger-size transparencies, and six techniques for making slides. Instructions for mounting and masking transparencies are also included.

visual media preparation guidelines

We live in a world surrounded by visual media: posters, signs, graphs, maps, supergraphics, transparencies, and the list goes on and on. All of these materials can be made by the non-artist. The guidelines that follow have been developed with the non-artist in mind, and are intended to start you off in the right direction for designing and preparing your own visual media. Guideline topics include visual media idea sources, design, size standards, artwork for photo reproduction, color, and lettering.

Idea Sources

Ideas for visual media are everywhere: in magazines, newspapers, brochures, posters, billboards, and catalogs of visual media producers. An equally important source of ideas can come from existing visual media. The value of using these idea sources in preparing your own visual media is that the design and production of these media have been carefully worked out by professionals for the selling of ideas and products. The adaptation of these ideas for use in areas

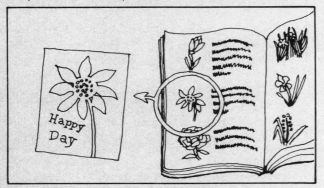

where learning and looking takes place involves only the application of the techniques in this handbook to the materials you wish to make.

Designing Visual Media

Design, as treated in this handbook, is simply the orderly or creative arrangement of images (visuals), color or special effects, and lettering into an effective visual medium such as a chart, poster, transparency, etc. Basic to design is an understanding of visual media as they relate to a particular

communication need. Several highly recommended print and nonprint references are listed at the end of this section. These references deal specifically with the role of visual media in the communication process. Equally important in the matter of design is an understanding of the physical characteristics of visual media; is it a projected or non-projected medium, is it on a transparent or opaque base, etc.

No attempt will be made here to go into the fine points of design, other than suggest to the non-artist to lean heavily on the idea sources discussed earlier in this section for assistance in designing visual media.

Lettering and Visual Media

Lettering is an important element of visual media as it is responsible for getting over the written message. Legible lettering involves three major factors; style, size, and spacing.

STYLE
Usually the thickness (boldness) of a letter style determines the ease with which it can be read. Letters should not be too

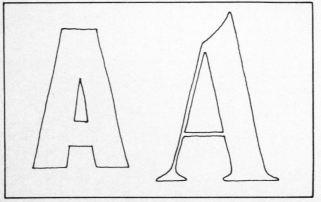

tall and skinny, or too short and squatty. A good rule for body

(line) thickness of a letter is about one-fifth to one-fourth of the letter height. There are, however, exceptions to this rule. Some of the newer and exciting letter styles available today, while not conforming completely to the thickness rule, are acceptable. Use a simple letter without serifs. The letter on the left is an example of this. The letter on the right has serifs as part of its style which complicate legibility.

With most letter styles, *lower case* lettering is easier to read than *upper case* (capital). However, capital letters can be used for headings or titles.

Where possible, don't mix letter styles in the same message. The one exception for use of different styles is for emphasis.

SIZE
It is a proven fact that, in general, audiences will not make any extra effort to read your message. Giving careful consideration to letter size is important when preparing visual

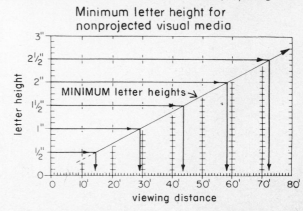

Minimum letter height for nonprojected visual media

media. The chart illustrated here can be used as a guide in the selection of letter size for nonprojected visual media.

For information on letter size for projected media, see page 125 .

SPACING

The spacing of letters could be difficult for some. To make this phase of lettering less difficult, read Letter and Word Spacing, Alignment and Special Effects on page 58 .

Color and Visual Media

The medium, the message, the season or occasion, the location, and the desired visual impact should be considered when selecting colors for visual media. No attempt will be made here to go into the fine and technical points on color. However, some basic considerations for the selection of color, as applied to the preparation of effective visual media, are suggested.

MEANINGS OF COLOR

Colors have meaning and can create the desired mood or atmosphere of your message. Here are some typical meanings of color:

RED—love, hatred, anger, danger

YELLOW—warmth, light, ripe

BLUE—cool, melancholy, depressed

BLACK—strong, formal, neat, rich

GREEN—young, fresh, growing

WHITE—purity, neat, clean

ORANGE—festive, gay, energy

PURPLE—rich, royalty, imperial

Traditional seasonal and holiday colors are:

RED and GREEN—Christmas.

GREEN—St. Patrick's Day.

RED, PURPLE, PINK—Valentine's Day.

BLUES, SILVER—Winter

RED, WHITE and BLUE—Fourth of July.

BROWN, GOLD, YELLOW, ORANGE—Fall.

GREEN, YELLOW, ORANGE—Spring and Summer.

BROWN and ORANGE—Thanksgiving.

COLOR COMBINATIONS

For posters, signs, and similar visual media, the right color combinations can greatly influence their visual impact. When combining colors, consider these suggestions:

1   Dark and light colors in combination give the best contrast.

2   Dark colors next to each other are not recommended.

3   White letters next to a dark background are highly visible from great distances.

4   Limit the color to two or three, so color does not become too obvious to the viewer. Use one dominant color. A good rule to follow is "the smaller the area, the brighter the color should be."

Color combinations also influence legibility. Although various color combinations may harmonize, they may not make the message easy to read. Here are some suggested color combinations for good legibility:

BLACK on YELLOW

BROWN on WHITE

GREEN on WHITE

BLUE on WHITE

BLACK on WHITE

YELLOW on BLACK

WHITE on RED

WHITE on GREEN

RED on YELLOW

Magazines, brochures, newspapers, and package labels are excellent sources of ideas on color and color combinations. For coloring techniques and other visual effects, see Section 3 of this handbook.

Artwork For Photographic Reproduction

If you are going to make photographic 35mm, 2-by 2-inch slides from original artwork, what size should, or can the artwork be? Not just any size, as photography is a science that has certain technical standards it must meet. That is what this bit of information is all about. The artwork must be an acceptable size that can be enlarged or reduced to the size of the final product (slide, filmstrip, poster, etc.). This all sounds complicated, but it's not really.

Let's take one example of an artwork size problem. If you are going to make regular 35mm, 2-by 2-inch photographic slides, the actual image area of the slide is only 22.9mm-by 34.2mm—about the size of a postage stamp. Artwork this size is almost impossible, with the exception of handmade direct image slides (see page 149). This means that the artwork will have to be done in a much larger size—but what size? The artwork can be almost any larger size as long as it

is in proportion to the final size it will be reduced to. There are several methods for arriving at various size proportions that are acceptable. One of the simplest methods for selecting a workable artwork size is the DIAGONAL LINE method.

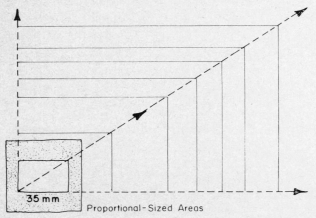

Proportional-Sized Areas

The proportion scale illustrated here graphically explains the DIAGONAL LINE method. The rectangle in the lower left of the illustration is the actual image area of a 35mm, 2-by 2-inch slide. The diagonal line running from the lower left corner up and through the upper right corner can be extended to any length. The vertical lines running from the base horizontal line up to the diagonal line are all possible new widths of the artwork. Matching horizontal lines from the left base vertical line establishes new heights the artwork will be.

Which of the new proportionate sizes to use? The size choice can be influenced by several factors; size of artowrk (clip art, photograph, etc.) to be used, size of lettering, etc. One last consideration in determining the final artwork size is to take into consideration the capability of the camera to copy the size artwork selected. All cameras have a minimum size area it will copy.

Two photographic slide making systems are discussed in Section 7; Kodak Visualmaker Slides and Polaroid Land Projection Transparencies.

Visual Media Size Standards

With the exception of visual media like slides, filmstrips, overhead projection transparencies, and motion picture films, there are very few agreed-upon size standards for other visual media. Size is mainly influenced by the distance from which the material is to be viewed. So as not to make the factor of size difficult to understand, here are suggested sizes for selected nonprojected visual media.

GRAPHIC MATERIALS
Graphic materials include charts, graphs, diagrams, maps, and similar designed visual materials. The guidelines that follow should be helpful in deciding the size these materials should be.

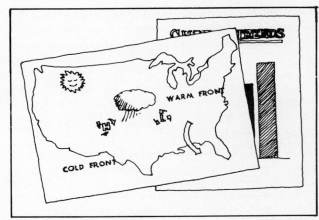

FOR ACROSS-THE-DESK and AROUND-THE-TABLE USE a 15-by 20-inch size with normal margins usually is adequate for up to about 15 people. This size is also recommended for slide, videotape, or motion picture film reproduction.

FOR GROUPS UP TO 40 or 50, the 20-by 30-inch size is recommended.

FOR LARGER GROUPS, the 30-by 40-inch size will serve in rooms or auditoriums of moderate size. For this size, it is advisable to keep the material simple in design.

LONG GRAPHICS, such as long charts, can be made 20-by 45-inch, 20-by 60-inch, etc. Accordion folding is recommended for these.

POSTERS
Posters come in a variety of sizes and shapes. Poster shapes include rectangles, squares, triangles, circles, and assorted odd-shaped forms.

Posters can be almost any size, as long as they can be seen and the message understood. The size of regular poster boards may have some influence on the poster size. Poster

visual media preparation guidelines

boards come in two popular sizes, 22-by 28-inch and 22-by 44-inch sheets. The poster board illustrated can be used as is, or cut into two or four pieces.

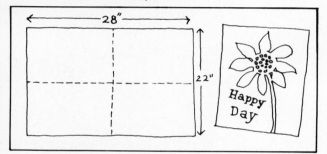

In selecting a functional poster size, the guidelines on Graphic Materials discussed earlier should be of some assistance. The popular contemporary ARGUS posters are 14 by 21 inches, a good size to start with.

SPECIALIZED VISUAL MEDIA

Specialized visual media such as bulletin board and display materials, skill and study drill pieces, matching puzzle sets, etc., all come in a variety of sizes. Catalogs of manufacturers such as TREND, INSTRUCTO, and CHILDCRAFT are excellent resource materials that can do much in assisting you in preparing your own materials.

PROJECTED VISUAL MEDIA

Projected visual media (slides, filmstrips, overhead projection transparencies, etc.) usually require original artwork for same-size reproduction or photographic reproduction. For artwork that is to be photographed for enlargement or reduction, the information that follows should be helpful. For overhead projection transparency artwork, see Transparency Guidelines on page 124.

SOURCES

Selected publications and audiovisual media have been annotated and sourced here to supplement the contents of this section. The figures in parentheses at the end of each entry (08) indicate the coded address source for the procurement of the reference. Complete addresses are listed at the end of this section.

AUDIOVISUAL LITERATURE PACKET (No. U-915), Eastman Kodak.
Pamphlets dealing with materials, equipment, and techniques for filmstrip, slide, and motion-picture planning, production, and presentations. (05)

BASIC TITLING AND ANIMATION (No. S-21), Eastman Kodak, 1962.
Covers planning, equipment, artwork preparation, titling, and techniques of animation basic to the production of an animated film. (05)

Belland, John C., and Sidney Rotenberg: DEVELOPING INSTRUCTIONAL MATERIALS FOR THE HANDICAPPED, National Center on Educational Media for the Handicapped, 1973.
Guidelines for preparing instructional media for the physically handicapped. (016)

Bowman, William J.: GRAPHIC COMMUNICATION, Wiley, 1967.
A complete text that offers a design methodology for translating ideas into visual messages. (023)

Brown, James W., R. B. Lewis, and Fred F. Harcleroad: AV INSTRUCTION: TECHNOLOGY, MEDIA, AND METHODS, 4th ed., McGraw-Hill, 1973.
A total media technology text. Chapters 3 to 15 deal with selecting, using, producing, and evaluating educational media. (013)

Brown, Robert M.: EDUCATIONAL MEDIA: A COMPETENCY-BASED APPROACH, Charles E. Merrill, 1973.

Two of the ten modules in the book deal with basic production techniques to assist readers in producing instructional media to fit into their instructional design. (015)

Bullard, John R., and Calvin E. Mether: AUDIOVISUAL FUNDAMENTALS, William C. Brown, 1974.
Equipment operation manual with "hands-on" instructions for producing simple visual media. (03)

Bullough, Robert V.: CREATING INSTRUCTIONAL MATERIALS, Merrill, 1974.
A text covering the fundamentals of producing slides, films and audiotapes. (15)

Calder, Clarence R.: TECHNIQUES AND ACTIVITIES TO STIMULATE VERBAL LEARNING, MacMillan, 1970.
Part II of this book gives techniques for creating instructional materials. (012)

DESIGNING INSTRUCTIONAL VISUALS, University of Texas at Austin, 1968.
Deals with design requirements for producing instructional visuals. (019)

Erickson, Carlton, and David H. Curl: FUNDAMENTALS OF TEACHING WITH AUDIOVISUAL TECHNOLOGY, 2d ed., MacMillan, 1972.
A complete book on the creative use of instructional media. One chapter deals with producing audiovisual media. (12)

Frye, Roy A.: GRAPHIC TOOLS FOR TEACHERS, 4th ed., Graphic Tools for Teachers, 1975.
How-to-do-it details for teacher production of lettering, mounting, laminating, layout, etc. (08)

Turner, Ethel M.: TEACHING AIDS FOR ELEMENTARY MATHEMATICS, Holt, 1966.
Specific instructions for constructing and using seventy-nine elementary mathematics teaching aids. (011)

Halas, John: FILM AND TV GRAPHICS, Hastings House, 1967.
Design and preparation of graphics for motion-picture and television production. (010)

Jensen, Mary, and Andrew Jensen: AUDIOVISUAL IDEAS FOR CHURCHES, Augsburg Publishing House, 1974.
A publication written mainly for the producer of audiovisual media for churches. (02)

Kemp, Jerrold E. : PLANNING AND PRODUCING AUDIOVISUAL MATERIALS, 3d ed., Thomas Y. Crowell, 1975.
A total text on planning and producing instructional media. Contains step-by-step instructions from concept to presentation of audiovisual media. (04)

Kinder, James S.: USING INSTRUCTIONAL MEDIA, Van Nostrand Reinhold, 1973.
A basic text dealing with the selection, preparation, and utilization of audiovisual materials. (021)

Langford, Michael J.: VISUAL AIDS AND PHOTOGRAPHY IN EDUCATION, Hastings House, 1973.
A manual on the production of instructional media containing step-by-step instructions. (010)

LEGIBILITY: ARTWORK TO SCREEN (No. S-24), Eastman Kodak, 1974.
Legibility guidelines for the preparation of artwork for projection. (05)

LOCAL PRODUCTION TECHNIQUES, University of Texas at Austin, 1967.
A handbook for assisting classroom teachers in the design and preparation of simple instructional materials. (019)

MacLinker, Jerry: DESIGNING INSTRUCTIONAL VISUALS: THEORY, COMPOSITION, AND IMPLEMENTATION, University of Texas at Austin, 1968.
Deals with visual media design for instructional use. (019)

Minor, Ed, and Harvey Frye: TECHNIQUES FOR PRODUCING VISUAL INSTRUCTIONAL MEDIA, McGraw-Hill, 1977.
A total text for preparing visual media. The first two sections deal with planning and designing visual media. (013)

Rowe, Mack R., et al: THE MESSAGE IS YOU: GUIDELINES FOR PREPARING PRESENTATIONS, AECT, NEA, 1971.
A well-developed set of guidelines for the design and preparation of visual media by leading visual media designers. (01)

Tierney, Joan D.: AN AUTO-TUTORIAL COURSE IN BASIC GRAPHICS, Joan D. Tierney Enterprises, 1975
A thirty-lesson autotutorial course in basic graphics covering color and design, organization of space, selection of ideas, etc, (020)

Wittich, Walter A., and Charles F. Schuller: INSTRUCTIONAL TECHNOLOGY: ITS NATURE AND USE, 5th ed., Harper & Row, 1973.
A complete instructional technology text for classroom teachers and professional users of instructional media. Several chapters include instructions for preparing instructional media. (09)

Addresses

01 - AECT, NEA, 1201 16th St., NW, Washington, DC 20036
02 - AUGSBURG PUBLISHING HOUSE, 426 S. Fifth St., Minneapolis, MN 55415

03 - WILLIAM C. BROWN BOOK CO., 135 S. Locust St., Dubuque, IA 52001
04 - THOMAS Y. CROWELL CO., College Division, Dept. JG, 666 Fifth Ave., New York, NY 10019
05 - EASTMAN KODAK CO., 343 State St., Rochester, NY 14650
06 - EDUCATIONAL FILMSTRIPS, Box 1401, Huntsville, TX 77340
07 - EDUCATIONAL MEDIA LABS, 4101 S. Congress Ave., Austin, TX 78745
08 - GRAPHIC TOOLS FOR TEACHERS, Mapleville, RI 02839
09 - HARPER & ROW PUBLISHERS, INC., 10 E. 53rd St., New York, NY 10022
010 - HASTING HOUSE PUBLISHERS, INC., 151 E. 50th St., New York, NY 10022
011 - HOLT, RINEHART & WINSTON, INC., 383 Madison Ave., New York, NY 10017
012 - MACMILLAN COMPANY, 866 Third Ave., New York, NY 10022
013 - McGRAW-HILL BOOK CO., 1221 Avenue of the Americas, New York, NY 10020
014 - McGRAW-HILL FILMS, 1221 Avenue of the Americas, New York, NY 10020
015 - CHARLES E. MERRILL PUBLISHING CO., 1300 Alum Creek Rd., Columbus. OH 43216
016 - NATIONAL CENTER ON EDUCATIONAL MEDIA AND MATERIALS FOR THE HANDICAPPED, 220 W. 12th Ave., Columbus, OH 43210
017 - PITMAN PUBLISHING CORP., 6 East 43rd St., New York, NY 10017
018 - SCOPE, Dowling College, Oakdale, NY 11769
019 - THE UNIVERSITY OF TEXAS at Austin, Instructional Media Center, Drawer W., University Station, Austin, TX 78712
020 - JOAN DE TIERNEY ENTERPRISES, 26 Melbourne Ave., Westmont, Que., H3Z 1H7 Canada
021 - VAN NOSTRAND REINHOLD CO., 300 Pike St., Cincinnati, OH 45202
022 - WATSON-GUPTILL PUBLICATIONS, 1 Astor Plaza, New York, NY 10036
023 - JOHN WILEY & SONS, INC., 605 Third Ave., New York, NY 10016

Visual imaging simply means creating images (illustrations, symbols, visuals, etc.). For the non-artist, creating images could be a difficult task. This section on imaging has been included mainly for the individual with the desire to use or create images that communicate but lack the skills of an artist. Each imaging technique is here because of its uniqueness in providing or creating images for use in the preparation of visual media.

After the type of image has been decided, refer to the Imaging Selection Chart (page 11) for recommended imaging techniques. For example, images that require enlarging for final use, several unique techniques are recommended. Also included in this section are imaging templates (guides) for creating images. Examples of images created with these templates are illustrated here. Photosketching is an exciting technique for creating pen and ink images from original black and white photographs; it is features in this section.

Once the image has been created, several techniques for transferring the image to another surface are included here. Images can also be enhanced by adding color and other special effects (see Section 3), lettered on (see Section 4), mounted or laminated (see Section 5), put on display (see Section 6), and made into a transparency or slide (see Section 7).

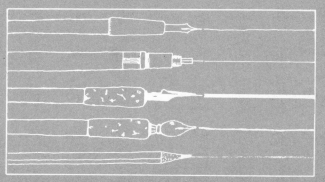

VISUAL IMAGING SELECTION CHART

This chart is designed to aid in the selection of appropriate imaging techniques and aids for solving visual imaging problems. The top left section of the chart lists assorted visual imaging problems. The selection symbols ● to the right indicate recommended imaging techniques and aids.

Visual Imaging Problems

#	Problem	Tracing Paper Transfer	Pencil Carbon Transfer	Carbon Paper Transfer	Pounce Pattern Transfer	Grid Pattern Imaging	Imaging by Direct Projection	Imaging by Reverse Projection	Pantograph Imaging	Photosketch Imaging	Thermocopy Imaging	Electronic Stencil Imaging	Image Paste-up	Clip Art	Cut-out Acetate Art	Dry Transfer Art	Symbol Templates	Stencil Duplicator Art	Compass	T square and Triangle	ModulArt
1	Reduce super-size visual (image) to small-size reproduction.					●		●	●												
2	Enlarge small-size visual to super-size reproduction.					●	●		●												
3	Make super-size circles																		●		
4	Create symbols and visuals.																●			●	●
5	Make pen-and-ink sketch with a photograph.									●											
6	Create images with T square and triangle.																			●	
7	Trace images from books and other sources.	●	●	●																	
8	Transfer images from one surface to another.	●	●	●	●						●	●									
9	Transfer images to another surface in *color*.				●																
10	Duplicate Stencil or spirit master paper copies of photographs or commercial clip art.										●	●		●	●	●		●			
11	Paste-up images for reproduction.												●	●	●	●		●			●
	Page	22	23	23	24	25	26	27	29	30	33	33	35	12	12	12	13	13	19	18	12

Imaging Techniques | Imaging Aids

Now, you don't have to be an artist to come up with professional-looking images (visuals, drawings, symbols, etc.) when preparing visual media. Here are several excellent commercial sources of direct use images of all types and sizes; modification for use is not necessary or required.

Clip Art

Clip art is ready-to-use, black and white line images (illustrations, visuals, symbols, and borders) covering every practical subject classification from A to Z. This art comes in books and sheets, with the art printed on one side only of a white sheet, and is designed to be clipped out and used directly. This art can also be traced, photocopied (Xerographic, thermocopy, etc.), or enlarged for use. The paste-up of clip art is discussed on page 35.

Cut-Out Acetate Art

Cut-out acetate art is graphic art (visuals, symbols, ornaments, borders, letters and numbers) printed on the underside of a microthin acetate film. The film is coated with a pressure-sensitive, repositionable adhesive. Art is cut out,

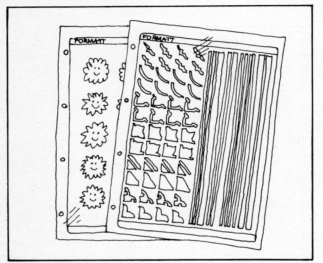

removed from the backing sheet, and positioned on the artwork. Artwork and drawings prepared with cut-out acetate art can be reproduced by any process, either photographic or direct, such as diazo (see page 140), thermocopy (see a page 137), or 3M Brand Color-key (see page 144).

ModulArt

ModulArt, by ARTYPE, is an exciting, direct use art designed to give maximum flexibility and creativity to the designer of visual media. While knowledge and skills in graphic art techniques are most helpful in using ModulArt, its use can also be extended to the non-artist.

ModulArt consists of a variety of specially designed illustrative figures, costumes, animals, backgrounds, vehicles, and accessories; all in modular form. These modular images are printed on the underside of sheets of

clear, matte-surfaced acetate in colors and in shades of gray. Each element is cut out separately and assembled on the drawing surface selected.

Dry Transfer Art

Here is black-image art printed on the underside of an acetate film (carrier sheet) and transferred to a working surface (paper, cardboard, glass, metal etc.) with the aid of a burnisher, pencil, or ball-point pen. This art is a member of the dry transfer letter family (see page 86). Dry transfer art is almost as quick and easy to use as rubber stamps. Currently, there is an endless variety of dry transfer art available (people, animals, vehicles, trees, buildings, etc.).

visual imaging

transparent plastic, are designed for direct imaging (tracing) on various surfaces (paper, cardboard, duplication stencils and masters, etc.) with pencil, pen or tracing stylus. The large assortment of symbol templates available include circles, squares, ellipses, people, maps, and so forth. For one use of symbol templates, see page 20.

Stencil Duplicator Art

Easy-to-trace art created by professional artists for stencil and spirit duplication. This art, available in book or single sheet form, is usually printed on one side of a white sheet that will permit enough light to pass through it for tracing on a viewing light box. Stencil duplicator art can also be used for any visual media requiring simple, sharp images. ◢

Images (visuals, drawings, symbols, etc.) need not originate with you, especially if you are not an artist. An unlimited number and variety of images can be obtained from newspapers, magazines, brochures, and other publications. These images can be traced, photocopied (Xerographic, thermocopy, etc), or modified for use in the preparation of visual media. Images obtained from any copyright source cannot be used in any published material, for this would be a violation of the copyright law. ▷▷

Symbol Templates

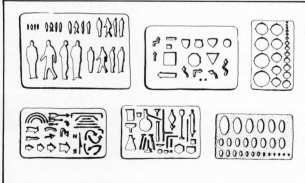

These semi-direct use imaging aids (symbol templates) can provide the non-artist with an aid for creating simple images and symbols. These symbol templates, made of

Filing for future use:

file folders

large envelopes

Collecting images for modification can be a fun experience. Magazines, newspapers, brochures, catalogs, etc., are excellent sources of images for modification. The YELLOW pages of the telephone directory, and an illustrated dictionary are two other good sources for images. Start an "Image Ideas" file, and in it place images and image ideas from the sources mentioned here. Collected images can be mounted on file cards, or filed in envelopes or file folders.

Once the images have been collected, and a decision has been made as to what modifications (enlarge, reduce, distort, etc) are required, appropriate solutions can be found in this section of the handbook.

Surface and base materials are, for most visual media, the foundation—the stage on which the elements of the media designer/producer's images are played. Excellence in the final production can be, in part, achieved by selecting the surface or base material whose physical and aesthetic qualities compliment the design elements.

Visual media demand, because of their physical characteristics and use, specific types of surface and base materials. Presented here are descriptions of the most commonly used surface and base materials and their application to the production of visual media. ◼

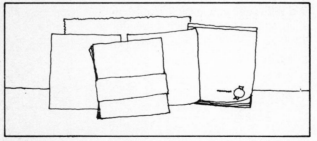

Papers

BUTCHER PAPER
A strong, bleached white Kraft paper. Usually comes in 36-inch-wide rolls. Uses include murals, posters, banners, signs, and projects which require a strong, heavy white paper.

CONSTRUCTION PAPER
A wood-pulp paper of sufficient body to accept crayon, chalk, paint, charcoal, or pencil. Its many uses include visual and letter cutouts and chart making. Available in assorted colors.

DRAWING PAPER
A great variety of papers ranging from coarse pulpy sheets to 100 percent selected rag papers, with almost as many different surface finishes. Each visual producer should experiment with different media on different qualities of paper to determine the best combinations for his of her individual purposes.

FLANNEL BOARD PAPER
Special paper with a black-flocked back that adheres to flannel (for flannel board). The front of each sheet has a pressure-sensitive adhesive. By adhering this paper to the back of visuals, they can be applied to and removed from flannel boards. Available in 8- by 10-inch sheets.

KRAFT PAPER
A heavyweight brown paper for murals, posters, and projects which require a strong, heavy paper.

NEWSPRINT PAPER
An inexpensive wood-pulp paper for making quick drawings and work not demanding permanence. Available in sheets, pads, and rolls.

SIGN AND POSTER PAPER
A 16-pound, smooth, white, multipurpose roll paper designed mainly for signs and posters. Available in 36- and 42-inch-wide rolls.

STENCIL PAPER
A semitransparent, oiled paper which retains sharp lines and is easy to cut out. Used as a letter or visual stencil on all surfaces.

TRACING PAPER
Papers that run from high transparency through various translucencies to opaque. The clear type is used for general purpose tracing and for overlays and even for transparent drawing paper.

VELOUR PAPER
Medium-weight colored paper with a velvety surface that imparts great depth to visuals, giving them a three-

dimensional quality. Ideal for preparing display materials, cutouts, and letters, and for use on the felt board. Available in colors.

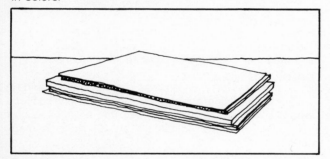

Boards

CHIPBOARD
A gray, uncoated heavy cardboard used for mounting, easels, construction models, etc. Usually comes on 30- and 40-inch width, with thicknesses from 1/16- to 3/16-inch.

CORRUGATED BOARD
An exciting material which has found a place in the production of visual media such as displays, bulletin boards, and visual and letter cutouts. This board is made up of two layers of thin, strong paper welded together. The base layer, as shown in the accompanying visual, is flat; the second layer consists of a series of corrugations glued to the surface of the base layer. Available in assorted colors and sizes.

FOAM-CORED BOARD (FOAM-CORE)
Foam-cored board with a smooth white surface (two sides). Combines strength with much lighter weight than an ordinary board. Resists moisture and remains rigid and strong during use because of its styrene foam-core center. Uses include displays, signs, wall art, models, and mounting. The surface accepts markers, poster colors, inks, etc. Cuts easily with a razor blade. Available in 3/16- and ½-inch thickness.

ILLUSTRATION BOARD
Made of fine drawing paper mounted on still backing boards. Surfaces range from very smooth to very rough. The surface will accept most drawing mediums: inks, airbrush, crayon, pencil, watercolors, etc.

MAT BOARD
Heavyweight cardboard with or without textured (pebbled) surfaces. Used for mat cutting, mounting, posters, displays, and visual media requiring a special-surfaced board. Ranges in thickness from 1/16- to 3/16-inch. Available in assorted colors and surfaces.

POSTER BOARD
A smooth-surfaced board especially suited for use with showcard colors to make posters, signs, and other visual media. Not intended for general drawing because its surface will not withstand repeated rubbing or erasing. Regular poster board is 14-ply (a little less than 1/16 inch thick). Lighter-weight boards, often called railroad boards, may be 4-, 6-, or 8-ply.

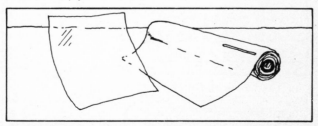

Acetates

CLEAR ACETATE
Transparent plastic used as a proctective cover, as a base to which films are adhered for color separation overlays, and in see-through maps, charts, etc. An excellent transparent drawing surface that will accept certain nylon-point pens and markers. Available in a variety of thicknesses and sizes—in roll and sheets.

COLORED ACETATE
Acetate sheets and rolls in vivid transparent colors. Can be used to add color background for overhead projection transparencies and other visual media requiring transparent color background.

MATTE (FROSTED) ACETATE
A noninflammable cellulose acetate with a frosted (matte) surface on one side. The frosted side permits the use of lead and colored pencils, inks, etc. The smooth (base) side permits the use of marking pens. Available in sheets, pads, and rolls.

PREPARED ACETATE
Clear plastic treated to take inks, paints and dyes without the necessity of adding anything to the medium. Use like paper. Both sides coated to accept the medium used. Corrections are made by washing off areas; does not affect working qualities of the surface. Usually available in one thickness (0.005). Available in sheets, pads, and rolls.

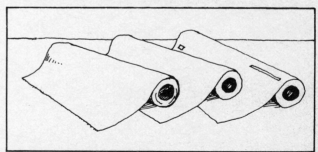

Special-Surfaced Materials

DRY BACKING CLOTH
A high-quality cotton fabric with a thermoplastic adhesive on one side. Ideal for mounting maps, charts, and other flat materials where a cloth backing is desired. Requires a dry mounting press or hand electric iron for mounting. Available in sheets and rolls.

SIGN CLOTH
A white, durable coated or treated cloth especially designed for outdoor signs and banners. Also an excellent surface material for charts, maps, and other visual media requiring a strong cloth-surfaced material. Available in widths of 50 and 54 inches.

VINYL PLASTIC BY CON-TACT
Vivid, solid-colored vinyl plastic by Con-Tact with a pressure-sensitive adhesive back. Comes in 18-inch-wide sheets. An excellent color medium for visual media requiring a strong paintlike color application. Ideal for cutout visuals and letters, wall and window supergraphics, etc. Vinyl plastic should only be applied on smooth, clean, flat, firm surfaces that are completely sealed, such as an enameled or oil-painted plaster, wood, glass, tile, metal, Formica.

The imaging aids selected for inclusion here include pencils, pens and markers, and drawing and cutting tools. Each has been selected because of its uniqueness in the creation of visual images of all types.

PENCILS
Here is a selected group of pencils, each having special imaging functions in producing visual media.

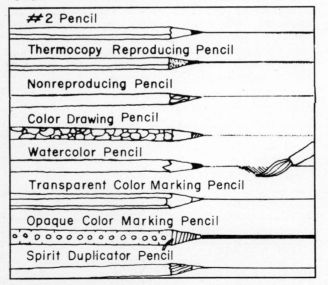

#2 LEAD PENCIL
The lead pencil recommended for drawing, writing and lettering on white paper for preparation of thermocopy transparencies

THERMOCOPY REPRODUCING PENCIL
Contains a special lead that can be reproduced in a thermocopy machine. Pencil lines give strong, clear copies. A soft lead pencil can also be used as a reproducing pencil.

NONREPRODUCING PENCIL
Produces a light shade of blue which is nonreproducing in line artwork. This special color pencil is also used to block in and mark key lines on sketches and line mechanicals.

COLOR DRAWING PENCIL
Special colored lead pencils used where a pencillike line in color is desired. Some pencils have leads that can easily be erased if desired; others have leads that will not smear or run under moisture. All pencils are available in many assorted colors.

WATERCOLOR PENCIL
Contains a water-soluble or special lead that has exceptional strength and brilliance. When colors are washed over with brush and water, the soluble colors blend into a watercolor wash.

TRANSPARENT COLOR MARKING PENCIL
A pencil that has been especially created for use with overhead projection equipment. Leads are smooth and strong and appear in deep transparent color when projected. Markings can be removed with a damp chamois or soft cloth.

OPAQUE COLOR MARKING PENCIL
Opaque color all-purpose marking pencil with a lead that writes in dense color on glass, plastic, acetate, cellophane, metal, etc. Marking pencils are also known as *grease* or China marking pencils. A damp cloth can be used to remove unwanted pencil marks from nonporous surfaces. Available in assorted colors.

SPIRIT DUPLICATOR PENCIL
An indelible copy pencil for use on spirit and hectographic duplicator masters. Writing, drawing, and lettering can be done directly on the master with this pencil.

PENS AND MARKERS

Hunt Bowl Pointed Pen (Model 512)

A bowl-pointed extra-fine pen recommended for lettering and drawing on prepared and matte (frosted) acetate.

Crow Quill Pen

A fine-line pen that has a flexible point with a tubular shaft that fits a special holder. Ideal for fine-line pen and ink drawing on opaque and transparent surfaces that will accept India ink lines.

Technical Fountain Pen (India or Drawing Ink)

A nonclogging fountain-type pen which uses India or regular drawing inks. Some models will accept acetate inks. Pen line widths range from 0.008 to 0.067 (pen size from 0000 to 6). This type pen is ideal for drawing directly on clear or matte acetate and for use with transparent irregular and ellipse guides (see page 19).

Speedball Lettering Pens

Metal lettering and drawing pens that fit into a metal, plastic, or wood pen holder. Ideal for lettering in poster making, for example. Special Pens are available for left-handed users.

Metal Brush Pens

A unique concept in lettering pens. The pens are made of flexible layers of steel and produce lines with a single stroke from 1/16-to 1-inch wide. Pens are ideal for making large posters and signs. Speed-ball steel brushes (pens) are available in four sizes. Coits pens are available in nine sizes.

Ruling Pen

A drafting instrument designed for drawing precision ink lines on opaque and transparent surfaces. Drawing inks of various colors can be used in this pen.

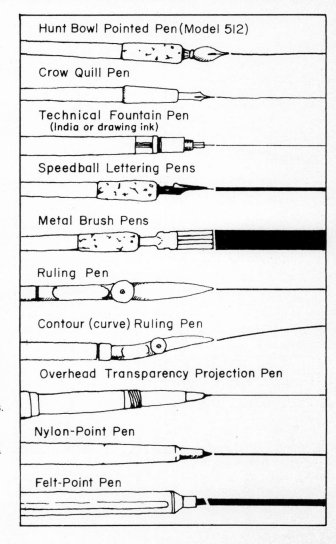

Hunt Bowl Pointed Pen (Model 512)

Crow Quill Pen

Technical Fountain Pen (India or drawing ink)

Speedball Lettering Pens

Metal Brush Pens

Ruling Pen

Contour (curve) Ruling Pen

Overhead Transparency Projection Pen

Nylon-Point Pen

Felt-Point Pen

Contour (Curve) Ruling Pen

A special ruling pen for drawing curves with the aid of irregular (French) curves and other similar drawing aids. The drawing blade turns easily and follows the smallest curve. The pen can also be converted into a regular pen.

Overhead Transparency Projection Pen

A nylon-pointed pen especially designed to produce vivid transparent color lines on overhead projection transparencies and other acetates. These pens are available in both permanent and removable colors. The removable (nonpermanent) pen lines can be removed with a dampened chamois cloth or soft paper tissue

Nylon-Point Pen

A fountain-type pen with a specially tapered point made of nylon or synthetic fiber which produces vivid colored lines on most surfaces. Assorted colors available.

Felt-Point Pen

A fountain-type pen with a special felt point designed for assorted-size and shape lines. Permanent and removable ink lines can be made with these pens. Ideal for layouts, drawing, coloring, overlays, and fine arts too. Assorted colors available.

DRAWING TOOLS

Here are several easy-to-use drawing tools that can be used by the non-artist to create and modify all types of images. Not only are they easy to use, they can be easily purchased from most art and drafting supply stores.

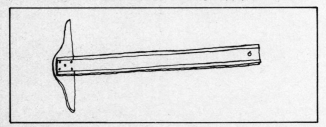

T Square

A T-shape metal, plastic or wood ruler for drawing parallel lines. Also used as a support for lettering and symbol templates, triangles, and other flat drawing aids. To use, hold the T square head against the left side of the drawing board for the top and bottom of the board may not be square. Line up the drawing surface with the top edge of the blade. While holding the T square firmly against the board, hold the pen or pencil vertically and draw horizontal lines. Move the T square downward for additional lines.

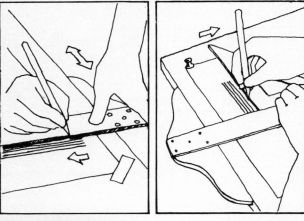

Plastic Triangle

A transparent plastic triangular drawing device for drawing vertical and angle lines. To use, hold the pen or pencil vertically and draw against the left edge as illustrated. Use the left hand to hold the triangle in place against the top edge of the T square. To raise the triangle off the working surface to prevent ink from smearing, tape small thin coins to the reverse side.

small coins

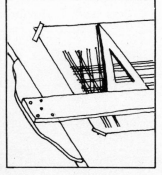

IMAGING WITH T SQUARE AND TRIANGLE

For an interesting, and different imaging technique, a T square and triangle can be used. Here is how it works:

1   DRAW LIGHT PENCIL GUIDELINE. Draw an accurate light pencil guideline (outline) of the image.

2   DECIDE ON PLACEMENT OF LINES. Decide on placement of horizontal and/or vertical lines within the image guidelines. Next, select the imaging tool (pencil, pen marker, etc.), and draw in the horizontal lines with the T square; vertical and slanted lines with the triangle. Various shading effects can be achieved by spacing the lines far apart or close together; practice this first on another sheet of paper. Different color lines can also be used to create different effects.

3   ERASE PENCIL GUIDELINE. After lines are dry, erase pencil guideline, and draw in remaining details.

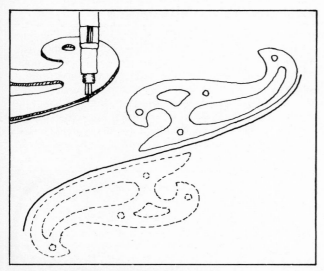

Irregular (French) Curves

Curves that cannot be made with a compass can be made with these assorted shape drawing aids. First, sketch the curve line in pencil, positioning the curve to get the desired line; then finish the line in the desired medium (ink, pencil, etc.). Ball-point, contour, reservoir, and technical fountain pens are recommended for use with irregular curves.

Adjustable (Flexible) Curve

A plastic or metal device that can easily be bent into any desired curve or shape. Once bent, the curve holds its shape without being held. The smooth edge of the curve permits drawing with a pen or pencil. This device is also useful for the preparation of visual layouts.

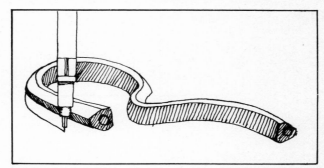

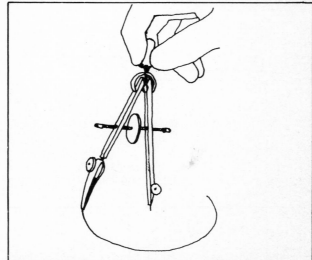

Ink Compass

Designed for making circles in ink. The compass is filled the same way a ruling pen is filled. To use, set the needle point of the compass at the center point of where the circle is to be drawn. Hold the pen vertically, and turn it clockwise by twisting thumb and index fingers as illustrated.

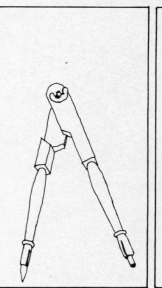
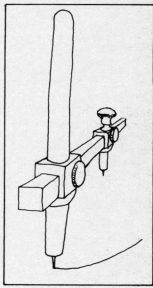

Chalkboard Compass

The chalkboard compass, made of wood, metal, or plastic, holds chalk, pencil or crayon in an adjustable holder on one leg. Useful for making large circles on the chalkboard, on cardboard, and on wood.

X-Acto Beam Compass

A metal compass tool for drawing and cutting circles from 1½ to 15 inches.

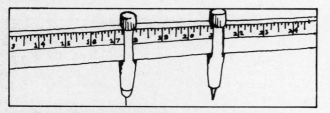

Yardstick Beam Compass

A beam compass consisting of two metal parts that fit a standard yardstick. Adjust to make and cut circles up to 66 inches in diameter. For cutting circles, the pencil holder should be replaced with a 24E blade or a No. 11 X-Acto knife blade.

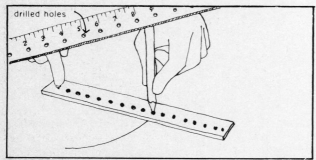

Handmade Beam Compass

A beam compass you can make. This compass can be made out of cardboard, wood, metal, or plastic. Also, a wood or metal yardstick will make a good beam compass. To make this compass, simply drill or punch ¼-inch holes about 1 inch apart as illustrated. To use the compass, place a pencil, nail or any other similar pointed instrument in the left-hand hole and a drawing or cutting tool in the hole desired (determined by the size circle desired), and move in a clockwise direction to complete the circle. ◼

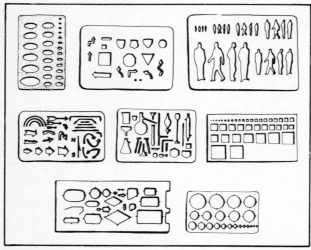

Almost any type of image can be created with symbol templates. These templates, made of transparent plastic, are designed for direct imaging on a variety of surfaces (paper, cardboard, etc.). The large assortment of symbol templates include circles, squares, triangles, ellipses, people, map and traffic symbols, etc. A trip to any art, drafting, or office supply store will reveal the popularity of these unique imaging aids.

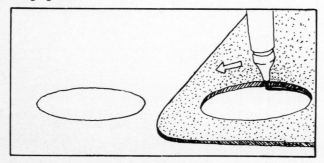

Imaging With Symbol Templates

Here are actual examples of images created with the aid of symbol templates; and they were created by non-artists. Try your hand at creating any of these images with symbol templates. First, analyze the image you wish to create to determine what forms or shapes it is made up of (circles, squares, ellipses, etc.). Next, pencil in, with the aid of the proper symbol template, details of the image. When the image desired is complete, go over the lines (with the proper template) in the imaging line of your choice (ink, crayon, etc.).

CUTTING TOOLS

Cutting straight, circular, and irregular lines in the imaging process requires cutting tools. Here are cutting tools that can solve all cutting requirements for visual media.

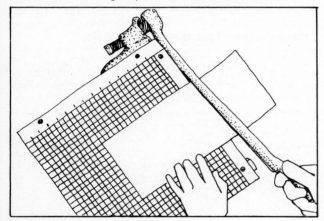

Paper Cutter

The most common precision tool for straight-line cutting is the blade-type cutter. The cutter illustrated here assures straight cuts when the material to be cut is lined up with the vertical and horizontal grid lines on the surface of the cutter.

Heavy Duty Razor Blade

Basic straight or irregular line cutting can be done with a single-edge heavy duty razor blade. There are a number of commercial blade holders designed especially for these blades. When the blade is used for an extended period of time without a holder, several windings of drafting tape around the index finger will help prevent soreness caused by the narrow top edge of the blade.

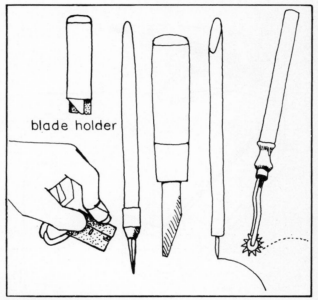

blade holder

Stencil (Frisket) Knife

The stencil knife is perhaps the most widely used cutting tool (X-ACTO No. 1-ST is one brand-name knife) for cutting straight, circular, and irregular lines. Most stencil knives will accept replacement blades. Blades can also be sharpened for continued use.

Mat Cutter

A heavy-duty cutting tool for cutting heavy-weight (thick) materials (cardboard, acetate, pliable plastic, etc.). Mat cutters are available with fixed or replaceable blades.

Cutting Needle

A unique cutting tool for cutting odd shapes from lightweight color or texture adhesive-backed sheets. This cutting tool is also used to cut out composition adhesive-type letters.

Pounce Wheel

A cutting tool with a small pounce wheel designed for cutting (perforating) small holes in paper, lightweight cardboard, and similar materials. Used mainly for image (pattern) transfer (see page 24).

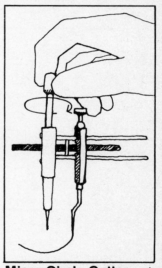 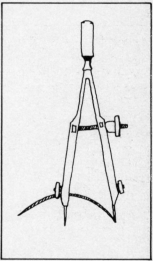

Micro Circle Cutter

A metal compass device for cutting perfect circles out of such materials as paper, acetate, and thin cardboard. It is used much like an ink or pencil compass. The model illustrated can be adjusted to cut circles from 1/16 to 3¾ inches in diameter.

Bow Divider

A drafting instrument that can substitute as a circle cutter. Used the same as a regular circle cutter.

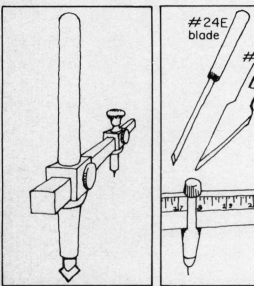

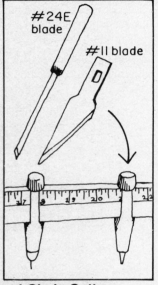

X-Acto Beam Compass and Circle Cutter

A metal compass device for drawing and cutting circles from 1½ to 15½ inches.

Yardstick Compass Cutter

A yardstick beam compass consisting of two metal parts that fit a standard-size yardstick. Adjust to make and cut circles up to 66 inches in diameter. For cutting circles, the pencil holder should be replaced with a 24E blade or a #11 X-Acto knife blade.

Corner Rounder

A metal cutting device for rounding corners of paper, cardboard, leather, acetate, etc. Cutting blades are interchangeable. The Lassco Model 20 illustrated is capable

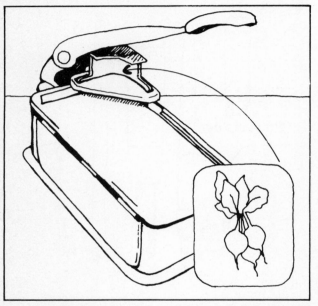

of cutting the corners shown in the diagram. The machine will cut fifty or more sheets of paper at a time.

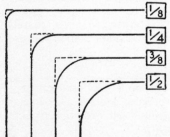

Exact-size and modified (enlarged, reduced, or distorted) images can be transferred from one surface to another by tracing paper, pencil carbon, transfer carbon paper, or pounce pattern techniques. These image transfer techniques are discussed on the pages to follow.

Tracing Paper Transfer

For images that cannot be directly transferred from the original source (book, magazine, etc.), the tracing paper transfer is a simple solution. First, lay a sheet of tracing paper or any translucent paper over the image to be

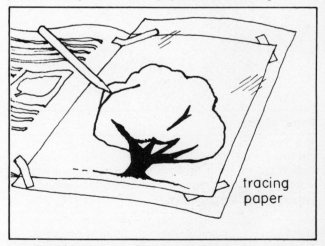

transferred and trace. After the image has been traced, remove the tracing from the original and refine (clean up). For aids in refining the traced lines see page 18 . To transfer the tracing to another surface, select one of the image transfer techniques included in this section.

Pencil Carbon Transfer

A simple technique for image transfer is pencil carbon. First, lay the original or traced image face down on a clean, smooth working surface and apply a heavy layer of soft pencil lead (No. 2 pencil works well) to the image lines.

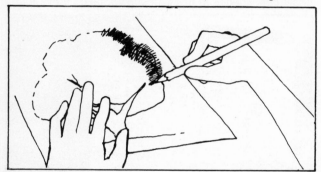

Next, rub the carboned lines with a tissue or old rag. This prevents pencil dust from smearing when transferred. Turn

image over, and tape to the surface on which the transfer is to be made. Using a stylus, pencil, or ball-point pen, carefully trace over the lines of the image. Be careful not to use too much pressure, as this will leave an indentation on the

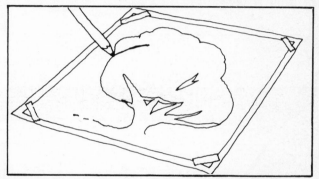

transfer. As the imaging tool traces over the image, the pencil carbon on the back will be transferred.

When all the lines have been traced, carefully lift one corner of the image to check the quality of the transfer. To ensure reregistration, if required (repeating lines not transferred as desired), simply lower the image back down on the surface. If the transfer is satisfactory, remove the original and complete the transferred image in whatever medium desired.

Carbon Paper Transfer

Another fine technique for image transfer, in color, is carbon paper transfer. The paper, coated with a special color carbon, is used like regular carbon paper. Image transferring with this special carbon paper (Saral is one brand name) can be done on any kind of paper, wood, glass, metal, or cloth. The imaging tool can be a pencil, stylus, ball-point pen, or pounce wheel (see page 24).

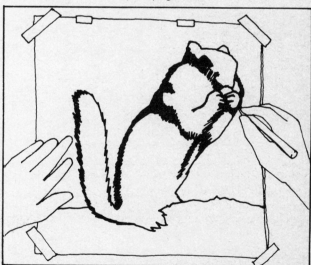

To use, insert the carbon paper (carbon side down) under the image to be transferred and tape both sheets (original and carbon paper) to the selected surface. Next, trace over the original image with the selected imaging tool. Make certain no lines are missed. When the tracing is completed,

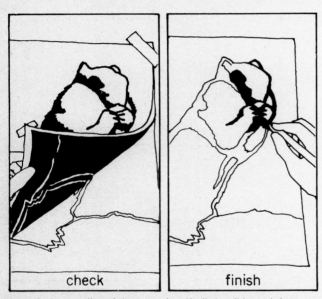

check

finish

check the quality of the transfer. If all detail is satisfactory, remove the carbon paper and the original image; a transferred image in color is the result . The carboned image can remain as is, or retraced with a selected imaging tool (pen, marker, etc.).

Pounce Pattern Transfer

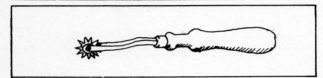

For transferring large and super-large images from one surface to another, pounce pattern could be the best technique. This technique involves the use of a pounce wheel for tracing the lines of the original image to create perforated lines(small holes).The perforated lines will permit powder or chalk dust to pass through and transfer the original image to the new surface.

INSTRUCTIONS

1 Place the original image on a piece of thick cardboard. The cardboard helps to protect the working surface and allows the pounce wheel to make good perforations.

2 With a firm, even pressure, trace the lines of the original with the pounce wheel. Make an early check of perforations to make certain complete holes are being cut.

3 To transfer the pounced image to another surface, hold the image firmly in place and pat (use short, firm motion) all perforated lines with powder or chalk dust. A powder puff or chalkboard eraser work well for the pouncing. When transferring the image to a light surface, a dark-colored chalk dust should be used. Check to make certain that a

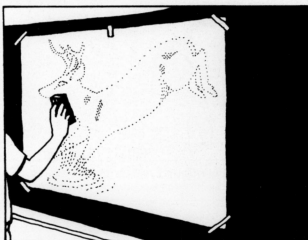

complete dot pattern has been transferred before removing the original image.

GRID PATTERN IMAGING

4 Complete the dot pattern image by tracing over the lines with pencil, pen, marker, or any other imaging tool of your choice.

Visual images (drawing, symbols, photographs, letters, etc.) that require exact enlargement, reduction, or even distortion can be reproduced with the grid pattern technique. In effect, the image (original) is subdivided through a grid pattern into smaller, less complex areas. This enables a person with little or no drawing skill to reproduce the small squared sections of the image one at a time, and upon its completion, have effectively reproduced a rather complex image larger and exact.

Instructions

1 Draw a penciled grid pattern (squares) over the image to be enlarged. The size of the squares will be determined by the complexity of the original image, as well as the experience of the "artist." A T square and triangle are recommended for drawing exact-size squares. Lettering or numbering the border squares may help in maintaining an orientation during the imaging process. If the original image is in a book or other source that will not permit drawing the grid pattern directly on it, trace the image on tracing paper or make a copy (thermocopy or Xerox) of it.

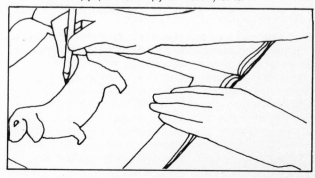

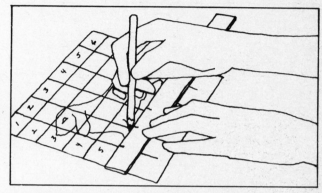

2 Decide on the size enlargement you wish (two, three, or four times larger). Next, on a larger surface, draw the same number of squares; only draw them two, three, or four times larger. Letter or number the squares the same as for the original smaller squares.

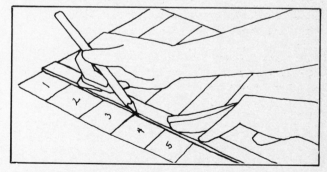

3 Carefully transpose lines from the original image square by square. Should any one square become difficult to work with, subdivide that square into additional squares both on the original and the enlarged grid. Now, transpose these smaller squares just as you did for the larger squares.

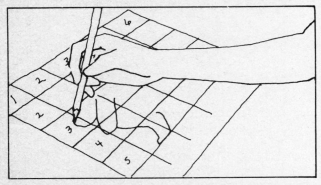

4 After the enlarged image is completed (inked or painted), erase all pencil marks. If image is to be transferred, see image transfer techniques starting on page 22 . ◼

add "motion" lines

Still projection machines, such as opaque, overhead, and slide projectors, can be used to make enlarged (super-size) and reduced reproductions of original images. Making super-size images by projection has been used for years to reproduce murals, billboard advertisements, signs, and supergraphics by projection.

Two methods for imaging by projection are included here: Imaging by Direct Projection for making image enlargements from small originals, and Imaging by Reverse Projection for making smaller images from super-size originals.

IMAGING BY DIRECT PROJECTION

Insert, project, and trace; it's just that simple to make super-size images from smaller originals. The original can be an illustration or map on a single sheet of paper or in a book, or it can be a three-dimensional object such as a spoon. The machine for enlarging the original onto another surface can be any one of the machines illustrated here.

INSTRUCTIONS

1 Attach large surface material (paper, cardboard, sign cloth, etc.), on which image is to be reproduced, to a flat, smooth surface (wall or chalkboard).

2 Position the projector so that it projects the desired size enlargement. It may be necessary to darken the room to project a bright, sharp image.

3 Simply trace the projected image with light pencil lines. These pencil lines will be retraced later with a finishing imaging tool (pen, crayon, etc.). Image distortion can be achieved, for visual impact, by moving the projector to extreme angles to the projection surface; it's fun—try it!

4 Remove the traced image from the working surface, and retrace with any of the imaging aids on page 18. To

refine straight or curve lines, try using the imaging tools on page 18 .

DIRECT PROJECTION MACHINES

Several simple projection machines are included here because of their uniqueness in the enlargement of small originals.

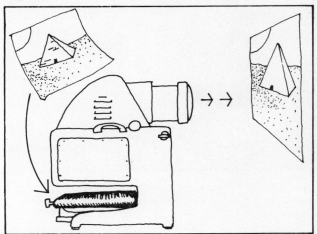

Opaque Projector

This projection machine is perhaps the easiest and most practical device for making image enlargements. It will accept originals of all descriptions; images in books, magazines, and newspapers; and real objects, such as rulers, precut letters, cardboard cut-outs. Because of the extreme heat generated by this projector, originals on acetate (transparencies) and originals on delicate surfaces (cloth and synthetics) should not be used.

Mini Opaque Projector

A mini-size opaque projector for enlarging flat and three-dimensional originals/objects (up to 6-by 6-inch) to super-

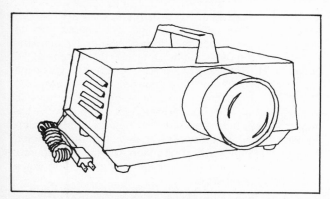

size enlargements. The light source is an ordinary incandescent light bulb.

Overhead Projector

Transparent originals (transparencies), or tracings on acetate (see page 125), are secured to the glass stage of the projector for image enlargement. Flat opaque objects can also be projected for image enlargement.

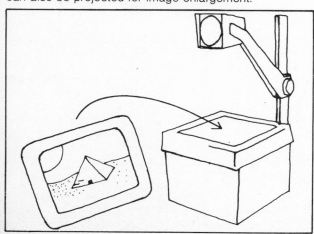

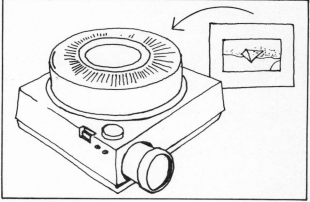

Slide Projector

Slide projectors can be used to enlarge images by projection. The original can be an appropriate size slide, or a tracing on acetate (see page 125).

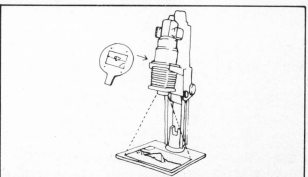

Photographic Enlarger

Any photographic enlarger can be used to enlarge images by projection. The original must be transparent (negative or positive), and a size acceptable by the enlarger. The original image is reflected down on the base attached to the

enlarger. Some enlarger heads can be adjusted to reflect the enlarged image on a wall. Tracing on acetate (see page 125), and cut-to-size transparencies (see Section 7) can be enlarged with the photographic enlarger.

IMAGING BY REVERSE PROJECTION

Large-size visuals, such as maps, charts, supergraphics, etc., can accurately be reduced to small visuals using the reverse projection technique. Required for the reverse projection technique are an overhead projector, light shield (for shielding out extraneous light), and a strong light source (photoflood lamp works best). Substitute light sources, such as table or floor lamps, or a sunlamp can be used. The

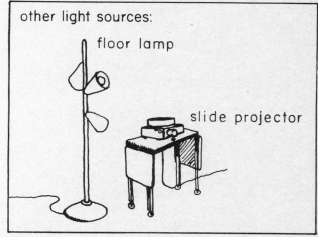

other light sources:

floor lamp

slide projector

overhead projector works much like a camera, with the lens of the projector reflecting the large visual onto the sheet attached to the stage of the projector; all you do is trace the reflected image on the sheet.

INSTRUCTIONS

1 Attach the large visual (upside down) to a flat vertical surface (wall, bulletin board, etc.).

2 Position the overhead projector so that the lens faces the large visual. Next, position the light shield on the stage of the projector as illustrated.

3 Position light source to evenly illuminate the visual.

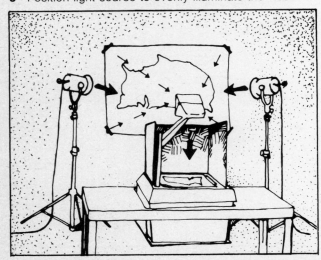

4 Tape a sheet of paper, or the surface on which the visual is to be reproduced, to the stage of the projector (DO NOT PLUG THE POWER CORD OF PROJECTOR INTO AN ELECTRICAL OUTLET).

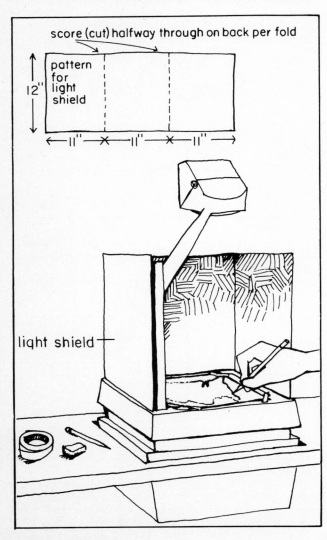

score (cut) halfway through on back per fold

pattern for light shield

12"

←11"→ × ←11"→ × ←11"→

light shield

5 Turn off room lights, or darken the room as much as possible. Turn on light source. The light reflection on the large visual will reflect back through the projector's lens system onto the paper surface attached to the stage of the projector. TO RAISE OR LOWER the reflected image on the paper, manipulate the lens housing up or down. TO ENLARGE the reflected image, move the projector towards the large visual. TO REDUCE the reflected image, move the projector away from the visual. TO FOCUS for a sharp image line, manipulate the focusing device of the projector. Adjustments may have to be made with the light source, such as moving the lights closer to the visual to get a brighter image reflection.

6 Now the easy step; simply stand at the rear of the projector and trace the lines of the projected image on the paper. Trace first with a pencil, then remove from the projector and refine traced lines with the desired imaging tool (pen, marker, etc.).

PANTOGRAPH IMAGING

The pantograph is a simple drawing instrument specially designed for proportionately reproducing enlarged or reduced images (drawings, maps, pictures, etc.). It is easy to use, and will reproduce images swiftly and accurately. This instrument is made of four wood, metal, or plastic bars containing a series of holes so calibrated that by connecting these bars together at predetermined points, approximately forty different ratios in enlargement or reduction can be achieved, depending on the particular model used.

Instructions

1   PREPARE THE WORKING SURFACE. When working with the pantograph, a sufficiently large, smooth working surface is essential. If a drawing board is being used, the pivot point of the device *(a)* should be mounted firmly at the lower left-hand corner. Some pantographs have a simple clamping device which clamps to the edge of the board, and others are fastened by thumbtacks or more permanently mounted with nails.

2   TO ENLARGE AN IMAGE. To enlarge an image, the tracer point is attached at *(b)*. At position *(c)* is located the pencil holder. How the device is operated depends upon the operator. Some people prefer to use the left hand to guide the tracing pin over the original drawing while the right hand guides the pencil. As illustrated, the tracing pin is guided by the right hand and the pencil is left free to make the enlarged drawing. In this case it is always wise to use a soft pencil lead to ensure a clean tracing. With some practice, a good reproduction can be made. It is important to guide the tracing pin smoothly to avoid exaggerated irregularities in the enlarged pencil drawing.

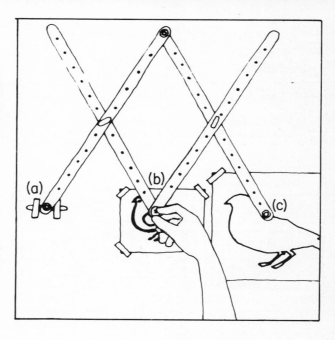

3   TO REDUCE AN IMAGE. To reduce an image, the position of the pencil and the tracing pin are reversed. The pencil will be at *(b)* and the tracing pin will be at point *(c)*. If an exact-size reproduction is desired, locate the pivot point at *(b)* and the tracing pin at *(a)* with the pencil at position *(c)*. When it is necessary to change the pantograph to different size ratios, the connection points at *(d)* and *(e)* are moved to the desired ratio points. ◼

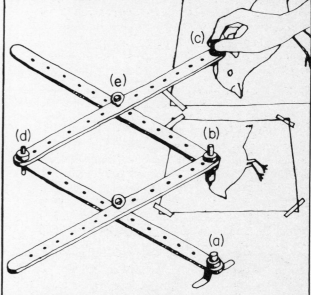

Here is a unique technique for producing a professional-looking pen and ink sketch from a black and white photograph; you have to try it to believe it. Photosketching is done by tracing (with waterproof India ink) all desired image lines directly on a black and white photograph. During the inking stage, details of the photograph can be omitted (leaving out telephone lines, people, etc.). Details of the photograph that were too light or too dark to be clearly seen can be corrected during the inking. Flaws and missing elements (broken windows, missing bricks, etc,) can also be taken care of during the inking. After the photograph has been inked, taking it through the remaining stages is where the fun is.

Image-Producing Instruments

Here are several instruments that can be used to produce image lines on the photograph. The pencil works best on matte-surfaced photographs because the rough surface will pick up the pencil carbon.

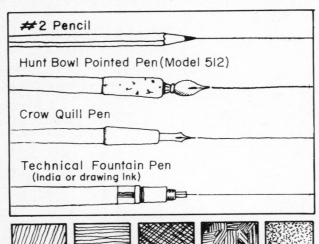

Shading and Texture Effects

To add shading or texture to the photograph during inking may be a bit difficult. However, a little practice with the imaging instrument should provide you with a start in adding some depth to the photograph.

INSTRUCTIONS

1 Using waterproof India ink, sketch directly on the surface of the photograph. Although photographs with a glossy surface may be used, the ink will adhere better to one having a matte surface. If possible, it is recommended that a light photographic print be used. Detail in dark areas of a photograph will be easier to see if placed on a light box. Generally, the light passing through the back of the print will reveal detail hard to see by reflected light. If the glossy surface of the print tends to resist ink, or if it has oily fingerprints on its surface, rub the surface throughly with baking soda. If

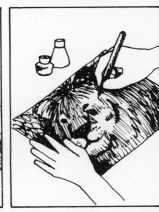

a mistake is made in the drawing, the ink may be removed immediately by wiping it off with damp cotton, or it may be dried and painted out later with white opaque.

2 Allow the ink to dry thoroughly. This may require at least thirty minutes. Often ink that appears to be dry may need more time. This is important since the image will be placed in liquid during the bleaching process.

3 Bleaching is the next step in the process. Regular iodine, procured from the local drugstore, may be used for

iodine solution

the bleach solution. This iodine, as purchased, may be diluted with 2 to 3 parts of water. Place the photosketch into a pan of iodine solution with the image side up. *Avoid touching the ink image during the entire bleaching process.* Be sure that the entire surface of the print is covered with iodine solution. Slight agitation helps speed up the process. The time the print remains in the bleach depends upon the characteristics of the photograph as well as the strength of the bleach solution.

4 When all traces of the dark photographic image have been replaced by one that is dark brownish orange, remove the photosketch from the iodine solution and rinse the excess iodine off in cool water.

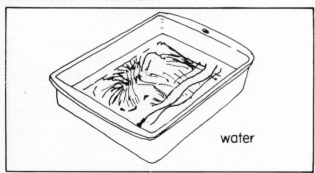
water

5 Place the print into a pan containing photographic fixing bath (hypo). This chemical can be obtained at any photographic supply store. The solution will bleach out the remaining iodine image, leaving a clean black and white drawing. Be sure that all traces of the yellow stain are removed before removing the print from the solution.

fixing bath

6 Place the photosketch in cool running water for about five minutes to remove the remaining chemicals.

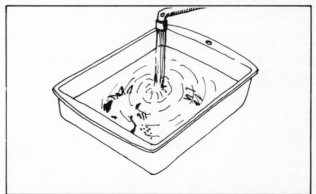

7 Although this print can be dried on a regular photographic dryer, it may also be air-dried by simply laying it out on a clean piece of paper for a period of time. If care is taken, excess water may be blotted off the sketch by using newsprint or some other absorbent material. Some curling of the sketch during drying can be discouraged by placing a heavy porous cloth on top to straighten and hold it in a flat position. ◼

You don't have to be an artist to produce professional looking images and lettering for stencil ("mimeo") or spirit ("ditto") duplication. Now there are imaging aids and equipment that will make you an "instant artist."

Here are imaging aids that can be used to create professional looking visuals for stencil and spirit duplication.

Stencil Duplicator Art

Easy-to-use drawings created by professional artisit for stencil and spirit duplication. Drawings are usually printed on one side of a white sheet that will permit enough light to pass through it for tracing on a viewing light box or a Mimeoscope. Stencil art books are also available for producing visuals. These books contain stencils of animals, space art, flowers, and numerous other subjects.

Clip Art

Clip art, in book or sheet form, can be traced for use on stencils and masters. Usually tracing will have to be made on tracing paper first and then retraced on the stencil (see page 22 for instructions). In any event, clip art provides an excellent source of art and art ideas. Check the Index for sources of additional information on clip art within this handbook.

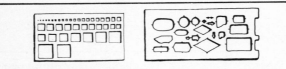

Symbol Templates

Transparent plastic outline symbol templates (guides) for use on stencils and masters. Almost any type of image can be created with these templates. The large assortment of symbol templates include circles, squares, triangles, ellipses, people, map and traffic symbols, etc. A trip to any art, drafting, or office supply store will reveal the popularity of these unique imaging aids. Instructions for the use of symbol templates, along with images created with these aids, can be found on page 20.

Plastic Shading Plates

A form of imaging is adding shading or texture directly to stencils and masters. There are two types of aids for creating shading or texture patterns directly on stencil and masters: plastic shading plates that contain raised texture patterns, and metal shading wheels. Instructions for shading plates will follow.

Companies like Columbia Ribbon-Carbon, Gestetner, Heyer, and Ditto, can provide you with current information related to the use of their stencil and spirit materials and equipment—just write them.

The instructions that follow will briefly suggest how to create images, lettering, and special effects on stencils and masters.

INSTRUCTIONS—DIRECT IMAGING ON STENCILS

1 TO DRAW, when stencil or clip art is used, insert the art under the writing plate and trace visual outlines with a tracing stylus. If a tracing unit is used, push the backing sheet of the stencil back out of the way for this operation.

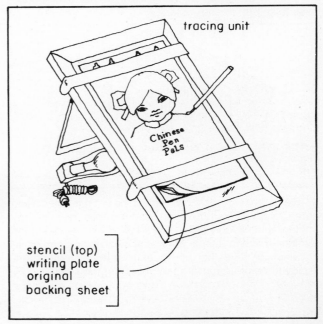

stencil (top)
writing plate
original
backing sheet

2 TO USE SYMBOL TEMPLATES, simply place the template in the desired location on TOP of the stencil and trace the symbol outlines with a ball-point stylus. Additional instructions for the use of symbol templates, along with examples of symbol images, can be found on page

3 TO ADD SHADING, place the shading plate directly under the image area to be shaded, holding the plate firmly in place. Rub over the desired area with a shading stylus in a circular fashion to produce the plate pattern.

INSTRUCTIONS—THERMOCOPY IMAGING

Here is a new method of transferring original copy to stencils and spirit masters by thermocopy means. Clip art, photographs, newspaper or magazine illustrations and printed matter, and typewritten materials can all be made into a stencil or master. These materials must be "faxable." The term "faxable" refers to an original that is capable of being copied with a thermocopy machine. A black on white original is best

To better prepare you for thermocopy imaging, read Thermocopy Transparencies on page 137. It contains more detailed information and instructions on thermocopying.

The instructions that follow are intended only to give you a general idea as to how thermocopy imaging of stencils

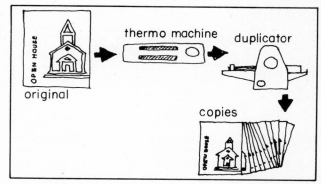

works. Specific instructions for each brand of thermocopy stencils are included with the stencils.

direct imaging

WE LISTEN TO YOU!

clip art

1 Prepare the original for thermocopy imaging (see instructions on page 137). Remember that all material (visuals, lettering, etc.) must be "faxable."

2 Set the recommended speed control of the copying machine (i.e., follow package directions for the type of thermocopy stencil used).

3 Follow the recommended instructions for assembling the original and thermocopy stencil unit. Most units are assembled as illustrated.

4 Insert folded edge of assembled unit into center of opening of machine; guide assembly through opening, stencil on top.

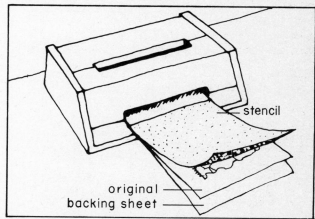

5 When assembly emerges from machine, remove original and attach stencil to duplicating machine just as you would a regular stencil.

INSTRUCTIONS—ELECTRONIC STENCIL IMAGING

Next to having a professional artist and printer produce high-quality printed matter (newsletters, brochures, posters, etc.) is the electronic stencil method. This remarkable machine, an electronic stencil maker, can produce stencils from anything written, typed, drawn, printed, clipped or photographed—or combined as a paste-up layout. Even transparencies for projection or display can be made with the electronic stencil maker (see page 142).

The instructions that follow are intended only to give you a general idea as to how electronic stencil imaging works. Specific instructions for each make of machine should be followed. To better prepare you for electronic stencil imaging, read Electronic Stencil Transparency on page 142. It contains more detailed information and instructions on this method of imaging.

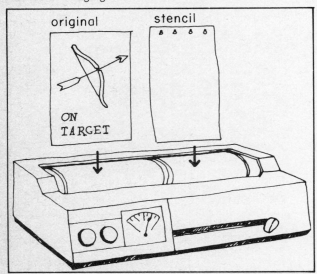

1   Place your original around one cylinder. Instructions for the machine being used will indicate which cylinder.

2   Set all controls as instructed. Now, simply push the "go" or start button. The rest is automatic. The machine will electronically "scan" the original and record (cut) a faithful, detailed reproduction (image) in the stencil for immediate run-off on your duplicator. Remember to use the electronic stencil designed for the duplicator you will be using.

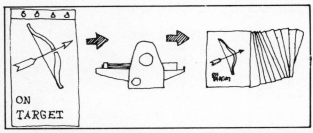

INSTRUCTIONS—DIRECT IMAGING ON SPIRIT MASTER

1   TO DRAW, when stencil or clip art is used, trace the art on a sheet of tracing paper. Next, pencil-carbon the back of the tracing and transfer to master (see page 23 for instructions). If you are using a master unit, such as the one illustrated, tape the tracing to the unit and retrace the image lines with a ball-point pen. The carbon from the carbon sheet will transfer to the underside of the master sheet. Remember to place the master unit on a firm, smooth surface for the imaging.

2   TO DRAW, when symbol templates are used, simply place the template in the desired location on the master and trace the symbol outlines with a ball-point pen or hard lead

pencil. For additional instructions and ideas, see page 20 .

3   TO ADD SHADING, place the desired shading plate directly under the area of the image to be shaded (carbon and master sheets on top of shading plate); hold the plate firmly in place, and rub the image area in a circular motion with a shading plate stylus. Carefully check to see if the pattern is transferring to the underside of the master sheet.

4   TO ADD COLOR, remove the original carbon (first color) sheet, insert second carbon sheet, and follow the instructions in item 1 or 2 for the second color; repeat for additional colors.

5   TO ADD LETTERING, check the Lettering Selection Chart on page 54 for lettering techniques recommended for spirit masters.

INSTRUCTIONS—THERMOCOPY IMAGING
Here is a new method of transferring original copy to spirit masters by thermocopy means. Clip art, photographs, newspaper or magazine illustrations and printed matter, and typewritten materials can all be made into a spirit

master. These materials must be "faxable." The term "faxable" refers to an original that is capable of being copied with a thermocopy machine. A black on white original is best.

To better prepare you for thermocopy imaging, read Thermocopy Transparencies on page 137. It contains more detailed information and instructions on thermocopy.

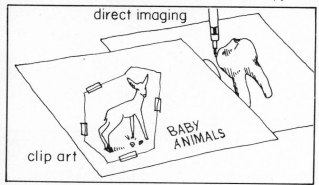

direct imaging

clip art

BABY ANIMALS

1 Prepare the original for thermocopy imaging (see instructions on page 137). Remember that all materials (visuals, lettering, etc.) must be "faxable."

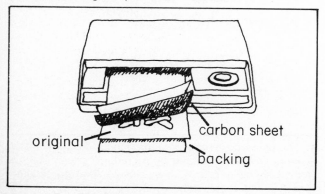

original

carbon sheet

backing

2 Set the recommended speed control of the copying machine (i.e., follow package directions for the type of thermocopy master used).

3 Follow the recommended instructions for assembling the original and thermocopy spirit master. Most units are assembled as illustrated. A special clear acetate carrier may be required.

4 Insert folded edge of assembled unit into center of opening of machine; guide assembly through opening.

5 When assembly emerges from machine, remove original, place assembly on flat surface with transfer sheet up, hold one corner of transfer sheet and peel it away from the master sheet keeping the transfer sheet at a low angle to prevent tearing. Attach master to spirit duplicator and make paper copies just as you would a regular master. ■

The term paste-up refers to art prepared in paste-up form specifically for any number of reproduction techniques (thermocopy, photocopy, electronic stencil copy, etc.). The true art of paste-up requires some professional knowhow. However, an attempt has been made here to simplify the techniques.

Hawaii: land of Aloha

"rough"

As a preliminary to the paste-up, it is a good idea to prepare a rough draft of what is intended to be the finished paste-up. This will help you visualize how the finished art will look and will serve as a guide in fitting all the art, lettering, shadowing, and so forth, together on the finished paste-up. The "rough" should be done on paper the size of the finished art.

Basic Tools and Materials

There are several basic tools and materials required for paste-up. They should include a drawing board, T square, triangle, cutting tools (such as scissors, razor blades, frisket knife), nonreproducing pencil, rubber cement, rubber cement eraser, and correction material (liquid or paper). The nonreproducing pencil is for drawing any guidelines or marks on the finished artwork which will not be sensitive to most reproducing techniques or methods. A light-blue color pencil can also be used.

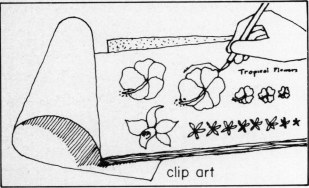

clip art

INSTRUCTIONS

1 Cut out the art (clip art is illustrated here) with one of the cutting tools. Note that protective cardboard is being used to prevent cutting the next sheet in the clip-art book.

2 Apply rubber cement to the reverse side of all paste-up art requiring adhesive. Next, apply cement to the areas on

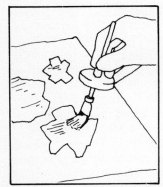 

the working surface (paper, cardboard) where the art is to go. Allow both cemented surfaces to dry. The rubber cement should be thinned, 4 parts rubber cement to 1 part rubber cement thinner (solvent). This will allow the cement to flow freely from the brush. Four other good mounting materials are pressure-sensitive rubber cement (page 95), spray-can adhesive (page 96), adhesive stick (page 99), and double-coated adhesive tape (page 99).

3 Attach the art to the working surface. Remove excessive cement from around the visual with a rubber cement eraser, or rub off with a clean finger. Opaque out the cut line around the visual with white correction liquid. See pages 48 to 50 for instructions on adding shadings.

white opaque

rubber cement eraser

4 The paste-up is ready for reproduction. Instructions for paste-up, related to a specific reproduction technique or method, should be followed very closely. What is presented here is intended only to be general instructions. ◗

SOURCES

Selected publications and audiovisual media have been annotated and sourced here to supplement the contents of this section. The figures in parentheses at the end of each entry (08) indicate the coded address source for the procurement of the reference. Complete addresses are listed under OUT-OF-TOWN sources at the end of this section.

Bockus, H. William: ADVERTISING GRAPHICS, MacMillan, 1974.
A workbook and reference for the advertising artist, and anyone involved in the design and preparation of visual media. It covers tools, design elements, and production processess as they relate to graphic media. (030)

Bowkes, Melvin K.: EASY BULLETIN BOARDS: NO. 2, Scarecrow Press, 1974.
Design suggestions on how-to-do-it form, using common materials. (034)

Callahan, Genevieve, and Lou Richardson: HOME ECONOMICS SHOW-HOW AND SHOWMANSHIP: WITH ACCENT ON VISUALS, Iowa State University Press, 1966.
An idea-packed book of ideas for preparing visual media related to home economics. (026)

Cardamone, Tom: ADVERTISING AGENCY & STUDIO SKILLS: A GUIDE TO THE PREPARATION OF ART AND MECHANICALS FOR REPRODUCTION, Watson-Guptill, 1968.
Treats the basic technical procedure of art studios and advertising art departments; paste-ups, mechanicals, printing processes, and specifications. (041)

Carlis, John: HOW TO MAKE YOUR OWN GREETING CARDS, Watson-Guptill, 1968.
Shows scores of simple ways to use inexpensive materials to make cards for every occasion. (041)

DeReyan, Rudy: CREATIVE PAINTING FROM PHOTOGRAPHS, Waston-Guptill, 1975.

Techniques and devices, such as opaque projector and pantograph, for creating original paintings from black and white color photographs. (041)

Freedman, Edward H.: HOW TO DRAW, Bantam, 1965.
Teaches how to make fine, recognizable drawings of buildings, furniture, cars, people, animals, and countless other things as easily as one can sign one's name. (07)

Lidstone, John: DESIGN ACTIVITIES FOR THE ELEMENTARY CLASSROON, Davis Publications, 1966.
An elementary art teaching guide which includes twenty-two creative things to do in the classroom. Activities include mural making, sculpture, and printing. (018)

Minor, Ed, and Harvey Frye: TECHNIQUES FOR PRODUCING VISUAL INSTRUCTIONAL MEDIA, McGraw-Hill, 1977.
The first four sections of this text deals with planning, designing, and creating visual media. (031)

Nelson, Leslie W.: INSTRUCTIONAL AIDS: HOW TO MAKE AND USE THEM, 4th ed., William C. Brown, 1970.
Includes a variety of instructional materials which can be prepared and used by the classroom teacher. (013)

CARDBOARD PRINTING, *35mm filmstrip, 43 frames, color, Society For Visual Education, 1965.*
Making posters, book covers, programs, greeting cards, and design duplication. (036)

CARDBOARD PRINTING, *35mm filmstrip, 43 frames, color, Society for Visual Education, 1965.*
Making posters, book covers, programs, greeting cards, and design duplication. (036)

DISCOVERING FORM IN ART, *16mm film, twenty-one minutes, sound, color, BFA, 1967.*
Shows the five basic forms in art: the sphere, cube, cone, cylinder, and pyramid. (09)

FELT PEN SKETCHING, *16mm film, eleven minutes, sound, b and w, McGraw-Hill Films, 1957.*
Demonstrates how the common felt-point marking pen can be used for sketching. (032)

HOW TO DO CARTOONS, *16mm film, twenty minutes, sound, b and w, Schulman, 1957.*
Artist Russell Patterson demonstrates a simple and direct approach to cartooning. (035)

HOW TO MAKE A MOVIE WITHOUT A CAMERA, *16mm film, five minutes, sound, Churchill Films, 1971.*
Shows limitless possibilities of filmmaking without photographic processing. (017)

HOW TO MAKE A STENCIL PRINT, *16mm film, twelve minutes, sound, color, BFA, 1961.*
Introduces simple ways to cut and print original stencils as an approach to creative design. (09)

INTRODUCTION TO GESTURE DRAWING, *16mm film, twelve minutes, sound, color, BFA, 1968.*
Shows and explains that gesture drawing is an exercise that describes motion. (09)

INTRODUCTION TO GRAPHIC DESIGN, *35mm filmstrips (2), 50 frames each, sound, color, BFA, 1967.*
A basic introduction to materials and techniques of the graphic artist. Included are materials, tools, layout, and paste-up. (09)

MAGIC OF THE FLANNEL BOARD, THE, *16mm film, nineteen minutes, sound, color, Instructo Corp., 1964.*
Shows ways creative visual cutouts may be used to stimulate learning. (025)

MIMEOGRAPH, THE, *35mm filmstrip, twenty-four minutes, sound, color, A. B. Dick.*
Shows choosing the right ink, inking the machine, and operating the mimeograph as well as shortcuts to color work. (019)

POSTER, *16mm film, sixteen minutes, sound, color, BFA, 1969.*
Explores the art of poster design in the works of three leading poster designers. (09)

POSTERS, *16mm film, fifteen minutes, sound, color, ACI Productions, 1968.*
Explains the basic concepts and methods of poster design. (01)

SIGNS, SYMBOLS, AND SIGNALS, *16mm film, sixteen minutes, sound, color, AIMS, 1969.*
Shows a kaleidoscope of basic visual communication depicting the signs, symbols, and signals that individuals and the community rely on. (02)

MIMEOGRAPHING TECHNIQUES, *16mm film, sixteen minutes, sound, color, BFA, 1958.*
Demonstrates the complete process of making a mimeograph stencil.

Most of the equipment and materials included in this section are available from local sources; such sources are indicated (L), and can be located in the *Yellow Pages* of the telephone directory. Items not readily available locally can be purchased directly, or purchase information obtained from the sources indicated (O).

ACETATES (L1, L4, O10, O12, O23)

BOARDS (L1, L4, O10, O12, O23)

CARBON PAPER (color carbon) (L1, L4, O10, O12)

CLIP ART (L1, O4, O38, O40)

CORNER ROUNDERS (L4, O15, O28)

CUT-OUT ACETATE ART (**FORMATT**) (L1, L4, O10, O12, O22)

CUTTING TOOLS (L1, L3, L4, L7, O3, O10, O12, O23)

DRAWING TOOLS (L1, L4, O3, O10, O12)

DRY TRANSFER ART (L1, L4, O4, O10, O12, O29)

ELECTRONIC STENCIL CUTTERS (L5, O19, O21, O33)

MINI OPAQUE PROJECTORS (L1, L4, L6, O10, O12, O27)

MODULART (L1, O6)

PANTOGRAPHS (L1, L4, O3, O10, O12, O14)

PAPERS (L1, L4, O10, O12, O23)

PENCILS (L1, L4, L7, O3, O10, O12, O23)

PENS AND MARKERS (L1, L4, L7, O3, O10, O12, O23)

PHOTOGRAPHIC ENLARGERS (L6, O11, O15)

PLASTIC SHADING PLATES (L5, O8, O19, O20, O21, O24, O33)

POUNCE WHEELS (L1, L4, L7, O10, O12)

PROJECTORS (opaque, overhead, and slide) (L2, L6, O10, O12, O37)

SIGN CLOTH (L1, L4, O10, O12)

STENCIL DUPLICATOR ART (L5, O8, O20, O21, O24)

SYMBOL TEMPLATES (L1, L4, L5, L7, O3, O10, O12, O14)

THERMOCOPY MACHINES (L2, L5, O19, O20, O21, O37)

THERMOCOPY SPIRIT MASTERS (L2, L5, O16, O19, O20, O21, O24, O37)

THERMOCOPY STENCIL UNITS (L2, O16, O19, O20, O21, O24, O37)

VINYL PLASTIC SHEETS (L3, J. C. Penney, Sears)

Addresses

LOCAL SOURCES (See Yellow Pages)

L1 - Artists' Materials and Supply Stores
L2 - Audio-Visual Equipment and Supply Stores
L3 - Building and Hardware Supply Stores
L4 - Drafting Equipment and Supply Stores
L5 - Duplicating Equipment and Supply Stores
L6 - Photographic Equipment and Supply Stores
L7 - Stationers' Stores

OUT-OF-TOWN SOURCES

O1 - ACI PRODUCTIONS, 35 W. 45th St., 11th Floor, New York, NY 10036

O2 - AIMS INSTRUCTIONAL MEDIA SERVICES, P. O. Box 1010, Hollywood, CA 90028

O3 - ALVIN & CO., P. O. Box 188, Windsor, CT 06095

O4 - A. A. ARCHBOLD PUBLISHERS, P. O. Box 57985, Los Angeles, CA 90057

O5 - ART DIRECTION BOOK CO., Advertising Trade Publishers, Inc., 19 W. 44th St., New York, NY 10036

O6 - ARTYPE, INC., 345 E. Terra Cotte Ave., Crystal Lake, IL 60014

O7 - BANTAM BOOKS, INC., 414 E. Golf Rd., Des Plaines, IL 60016

O8 - BECKLEY-CARDY CO., 1900 N. Narragansett, Chicago, IL 60639

O9 - BFA EDUCATIONAL MEDIA, 2211 Michigan Ave., Santa Monica, CA 90404

O10 - DICK BLICK, P. O. Box 1267, Galesburg, IL 61401

O11 - BOGEN PHOTO CORP., P. O. Box 448, Englewood, NJ 07631

O12 - ARTHUR BROWN & BROTHER, INC., 2 West 46th St., New York, NY 10036

O13 - WILLIAM C. BROWN BOOK CO., 135 S. Locust St., Dubuque, IA 52001

O14 - CHARLES BRUNNING CO., 1834 Walden Office Square, Schaumburg, IL 60172

O15 - BURKE & JAMES, 690 Portland Ave., Rochester, NY 14621

O16 - COLUMBIA RIBBON-CARBON MFG. CO., Herbhill Rd., Glen Cove, NY 11542

O17 - CHURCHILL FILMS, 662 N. Robertson Blvd., Los Angeles, CA 90069

O18 - DAVIS PUBLICATIONS, INC., 50 Portland St., Worcester, MA 01608

O19 - A. B. DICK CO., 5700 West Touhy Ave., Chicago, IL 60648

O20 - DITTO, INC., 6800 McCormick Rd., Chicago, IL 60645

O21 - GESTETNER CORP., Gestetner Park, Yonkers, NY 10703

O22 - GRAPHIC PRODUCTS CORP., 3601 Edison Pl., Rolling Meadows, IL 60008

O23 - HAWAIIAN GRAPHICS, 1312 Kaumualii St., Honolulu, HI 96817

O24 - HEYER, INC., 1850 S. Kostner Ave., Chicago, IL 60623

O25 - THE INSTRUCTO CORP., 1635 N. 55th St., Paoli, PA 19301

O26 - IOWA STATE UNIVERSITY PRESS, South State Ave., Ames, IA 50010

O27 - F. D. KEES MFG., CO., 700-800 Park St., Beatrice, NE 68301

O28 - LASSCO PRODUCTS, INC., 485 Hague St., Rochester, NY 14606

O29 - LETRASET USA, INC., 33 New Bridge Rd., Bergenfield, NJ 07621

O30 - MACMILLAN COMPANY, 866 Third Ave., New York, NY 10022

O31 - McGRAW-HILL BOOK CO., 1221 Avenue of the Americas, New York, NY 10020

O32 - McGRAW-HILL FILMS, 1221 Avenue of the Americas, New York, NY 10020

O33 - RONEO VICKERS, INC., One Alsan Way, Little Ferry, NJ 07643

O34 - SCARECROW PRESS, INC., Box 656, Metuchen, NJ 08840

O35 - SCHULMAN PRODUCTIONS, P. O. Box 1794, Trenton, NJ 08607

O36 - SOCIETY FOR VISUAL EDUCATION, INC., 1345 Diversey Parkway, Chicago, IL 60614

O37 - 3M COMPANY, Visual Products Div., 3M Center, St. Paul, MI 55101

O38 - VALDES ASSOCIATES, INC., P. O. Box 362, Westbury, Long Island, NY 11590

O39 - VAN NOSTRAND REINHOLD CO., 300 Pike St., Cincinnati, OH 45202

O40 - HARRY C. VOLK, JR., ART STUDIO, Box 72C, Pleasantville, NJ 08232

O41 - WATSON-GUPTILL PUBLICATIONS, 1 Astor Plaza, New York, NY 10036

Special effects, such as color, texture or shading, and "motion" add another exciting dimension to visual media. No attempt is made here to relate the psychological effect of color and other special effects upon the learning process, just their effectiveness in making visual media more exciting to look at.

Perhaps a good start at determining possible special effects that can be used for a particular material is to study the Special Effects Selection Chart on page 40.

Special Effects Selection Chart

Coloring Images

Pattern and Shading Films

Pattern and Shading Tapes

Polarized Transparencies

Sources

SPECIAL EFFECTS SELECTION CHART

This chart is designed to aid in the selection of appropriate special effects that can be added to the surface of visual media. The left section of the chart lists various surfaces to which special effects can be added. The selection symbols (see KEY) to the right indicate special effects recommended.

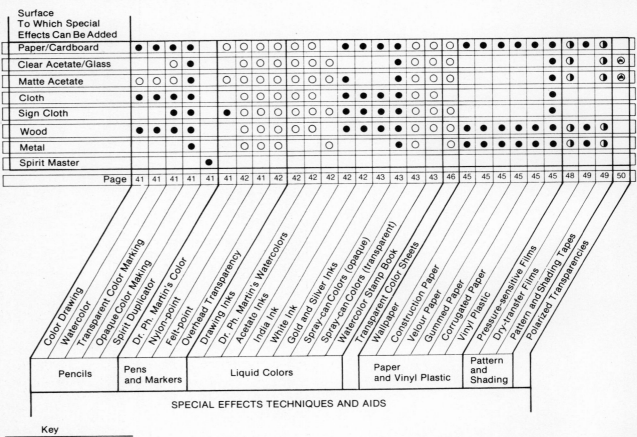

Surface To Which Special Effects Can Be Added	Color Drawing	Watercolor	Transparent Color Marking	Opaque Color Making	Spirit Duplicator	Dr. Ph. Martin's Color	Nylon-point	Felt-point	Overhead Transparency	Drawing Inks	Dr. Ph. Martin's Watercolors	Acetate Inks	India Ink	White Ink	Gold and Silver Inks	Spray-can Colors (opaque)	Spray-can Colors (transparent)	Watercolor Stamp Book	Transparent Color Sheets	Wallpaper	Construction Paper	Velour Paper	Gummed Paper	Corrugated Paper	Vinyl Plastic	Pressure-sensitive Films	Dry-transfer Films	Pattern and Shading Tapes	Polarized Transparencies
Paper/Cardboard	●	●	●	●		○	○	○	○		○	○		●	●	●	●	○	○	○	●	●	●	●	●	●	●	◐	●	◐	
Clear Acetate/Glass			○	●			○	○	○	○	○	○			●	○	○	○							●	◐		◐	⊛
Matte Acetate	○	○	○	●		○	○	○	○	○	○	●			●	○	○	○							●	◐		◐	⊛
Cloth	●	●	●	●			○	○	○	○	○		●	●	●	●	○								●				
Sign Cloth			●	●		●	○	○	○	○	○	○	●	●	●	○	○	○	○										
Wood	●	●	●	●			○	○	○	○	○		●	●	●	●	○	○		●	●	●	●	●	●	●	◐	●	◐	
Metal				●			○	○	○			○			●	○			○	●	●	●	●	●	●	◐	●	◐	
Spirit Master					●																								
Page	41	41	41	41	41	41	42	41	42	42	42	42	42	42	43	43	43	43	46	45	45	45	45	45	45	48	49	49	50

Pencils	Pens and Markers	Liquid Colors	Paper and Vinyl Plastic	Pattern and Shading	

SPECIAL EFFECTS TECHNIQUES AND AIDS

Key

○ Transparent

● Opaque

◐ Transparent or Opaque

⊛ "Motion" Effect

COLORING IMAGES   **COLOR WITH PENCILS, PENS, AND MARKERS**

From the many coloring materials and techniques for adding color to all types of visual media, those that offer quality color with minimal effort have been selected for inclusion here. Suggestions as to the selection of basic colors for visual media can be found on page 3. The Special Effect Selection Chart on page 40 recommends various coloring materials and techniques for visual media.

Color and special effects can be added to images with pencils, pens, and markers. Examples of these are on page 18 (Imaging with T-square and Triangle). Here are pencils, pens, and markers for adding color and special effects to images.

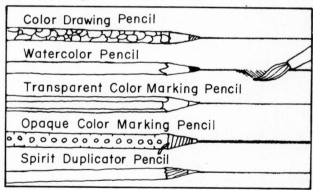

Color Drawing Pencil

Watercolor Pencil

Transparent Color Marking Pencil

Opaque Color Marking Pencil

Spirit Duplicator Pencil

Pencils

COLOR DRAWING PENCIL
Special colored lead pencils used where a pencillike line in color is desired. Some pencils have leads that can easily be erased if desired; others have leads that will not smear or run under moisture. All pencils are available in many assorted colors.

WATERCOLOR PENCIL
Contains a water-soluble or special lead that has exceptional strength and brilliance. When colors are washed over with brush and water, the soluble colors blend into a watercolor wash.

TRANSPARENT COLOR MARKING PENCIL
A pencil that has been especially created for use with overhead projection equipment. Leads are smooth and strong and appear in deep transparent color when projected. Markings can be removed with a damp chamois or soft cloth.

OPAQUE COLOR MARKING PENCIL
Opaque color all-purpose marking pencil with a lead that writes in dense color on glass, plastic, acetate, cellophane, metal, etc. Marking pencils are also known as *grease* or China marking pencils. A damp cloth can be used to remove unwanted pencil marks from nonporous surfaces. Available in assorted colors.

SPIRIT DUPLICATOR PENCIL
An indelible copy pencil for use on spirit and hectographic duplicator masters. Writing, drawing, and lettering can be done directly on the master with this pencil.

Pens and Markers

DR. PH. MARTIN'S COLOR PEN
A replaceable cartridge-type pen designed to use Dr. Martin's standard watercolors. The plastic pen tip will produce a broad variation of lines, depending on the pressure applied.

NYLON-POINT PEN
A fountain-type pen with a specially tapered point made of nylon or synthetic fiber which produces vivid colored lines on most surfaces. Assorted colors available.

FELT-POINT PEN
A fountain-type pen with a special felt point designed for assorted-size and- shape lines. Permanent and removable ink lines can be made with these pens. Ideal for layouts, drawing, coloring, overlays, and fine arts too. Assorted colors available.

COLOR WITH LIQUID COLORS

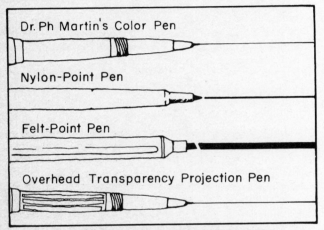

OVERHEAD TRANSPARENCY PROJECTION PEN

A nylon-point pen especially designed to produce vivid transparent color lines on overhead projection transparencies and other acetates. These pens are available in both permanent and removable colors. The removable (nonpermanent) pen lines can be removed with a dampened chamois cloth or soft paper tissue.

Coloring visual media with liquid colors is easy, and fun to do. These colors come in a variety of forms: brilliant color inks, pens and markers, spray can colors, poster paints, and dry color pages. The Special Effects Selection Chart on page 40 will suggest applications of liquid colors.

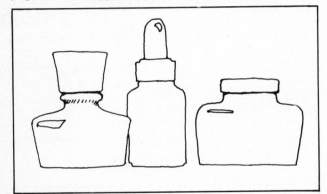

Drawing Inks

Transparent free-flowing color drawing inks. White is the only color that is not transparent. All colors are intermixable and work well in brushes, pens, and airbrushes.

Dr. Ph. Martin's (Aniline Dye) Watercolors

High-quality aniline dye watercolors available in two forms: synchromatic-transparent and radiant-concentrate. The synchromatic-transparent is recommended for photographic surfaces and for flat washes on illustration boards and papers. Radiant-concentrate colors are extremely concentrated to achieve the greatest possible brilliance and radiant tones in design and illustration on

paper surfaces. Over thrity-five colors available. Colors can be used in Dr. Ph. Martin's color pen.

Acetate Inks

Opaque or transparent inks designed for use on acetate or plastic surfaces. Some inks are permanent: others are removable. Inks can be applied with brush, pen, or airbrush. Transparent inks project in brilliant color. Special fountain-type pens are available for use with acetate inks.

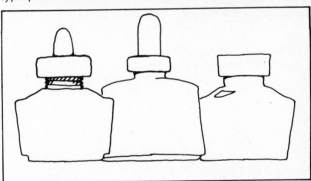

India Ink

Black drawing ink used in drawing and lettering and wherever a dense black image is required. Waterproof ink is ideal for use as a drawing or lettering ink for paper, cloth, and film.

White Ink

For dense white marking on practically all surfaces. Will work on x-ray films, photographic negatives, plastics, leather, cellophane, glass, and wood. Can be thinned for use in lettering pens. Ordinary food coloring added to ink can produce beautiful pastel shades.

special effects for images **3**

Gold and Silver Inks

Ready-to-use gold or silver ink for use with pen or brush.

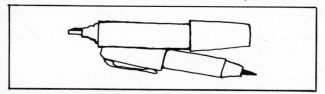

Liquid Color Pens and Markers

Fine, medium, and broad point pens and markers are ideal for adding to visual media. These pens contain brilliant liquid colors that can, depending on the type of ink contained, add color to opaque and transparent surfaces. For adding color to transparent surfaces (acetate or glass), special pens (see overhead transparency pen, page 42) should be used.

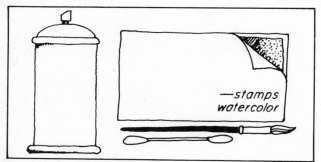

—stamps
watercolor

Spray-Can Colors

Opaque and transparent color in spray-can form (aerosol) provide an easy technique for adding color to all types of visual media. Even synthetic snowflakes in white and colors are available for special effects. The spray-can, with its fine spray, approximates the effect one can obtain with the airbrush. Instructions for use of spray-can colors are on page

TRANSPARENT spray-can colors are vivid transparent colors specially developed to apply high-quality color to a variety of surfaces including acetate, glass, metal, paper and wood. Surfaces sprayed with these transparent color dyes will not change, or its original surface texture be altered. "Spray Mark" is one brand name to remember when purchasing transparent spray-can colors.

Watercolor Stamp Book   (Peerless Transparent Water Colors)

Here is a unique form; a booklet containing water soluble pages (leaves) of transparent color. Color is removed from the page by touching it with a wet brush or by dissolving it in water. Colors are unexcelled for use in an airbrush. Colors are ideal for adding color to photographs, watercolor painting, and most other visual media requiring transparent color. Two book sizes are available; one with 10 assorted colors, and one with 15 assorted colors.

Spray-can (aerosol) colors come in coloring liquids of all descriptions: bright flourescent colors, enamels, plastics, metallic finishes, transparent dyes, and even synthetic snowflakes in white and colors.

Of the many spray-can colors on the market today, transparent spray dyes (SPRAY MARK is one brand name) have been selected for inclusion in this section. These transparent spray dyes come in a vibrant range of 13 standard art hues. Colors are permanent on porous surfaces and can be fixed on non-porous surfaces like acetate, glass, metal, etc. Colors can be mixed for different effects and can be used or reworked with watercolors, oils, charcoal, etc.

Instructions

1 Peel off the protective backing of the frisket paper and mount the paper on the artwork. Frisket paper is a liquid-resistant paper with a special rubber base adhesive backing. Substitutes for frisket paper are discussed here.

2 With a stencil knife, or similar cutting tool, cut out the area of the artwork to which color is to be applied. CUT ONLY THROUGH FRISKET PAPER. Peel cut paper from the artwork. Keep cut paper in tact as it may have to be used to cover its original area for the application of color to adjoining areas.

3 Spray color over the exposed area as recommended by the instructions on the spray-can.

FRISKET PAPER SUBSTITUTES

Here are two good frisket paper substitutes that can be used when frisket paper is not available, or is the best type of masking material for a particular job.

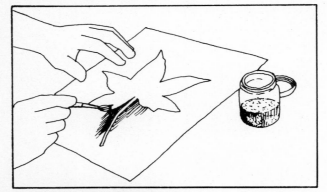

TINTED RUBBER CEMENT

Regular rubber cement thinned with rubber cement thinner to flow easily from a brush. To tint cement, add a small amount of mimeograph ink or oil stain. The tinted cement allows for instant recognition of areas covered on the artwork. Once the cement has been applied and dries, it works the same as stencil paper.

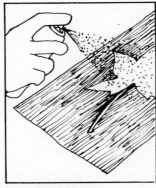

rub to peel off

LIQUID FRISKET

MISKIT and MASKOID are two trade name liquid frisket materials. These commercial preparations are similar to tinted rubber cement. Liquid frisket and tinted rubber cement may be applied to working surfaces with brush, pen, or ruling pen.

COLOR IMAGES WITH PAPER AND VINYL PLASTIC

Colored papers and vinyl plastic can be used to add exciting three-dimensional color to visual media.

    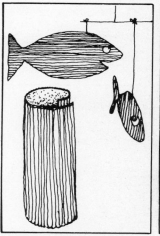 

CONSTRUCTION PAPER
Here is a low priced paper that comes in a wide range of colors and sizes (up to 24-by 36-inch). In addition to it being used as a coloring medium, its surface is suitable for crayon, charcoal, etc.

WALLPAPER
Wallpaper, with both raised and printed surfaces, can provide an easy-to-use coloring medium. In addition to purchasing wallpaper in rolls, wallpaper suppliers will often give you outdated sample books. These books contain large sheets of pattern and solid color paper. The instructions that follow later will suggest how wallpaper can be used to add color to images.

VELOUR PAPER
Medium-weight colored paper with a velvety surface that imparts great depth to visual images, giving them a three-dimensional quality. Ideal for preparing display materials, cutouts, and letters, and for use on felt boards.

GUMMED PAPER
An exciting coloring medium. This paper comes in bright colored gummed-back sheets. Bemiss-Jason's gummed paper comes in 9-by 12-inch sheets, and can be purchased from most stationers' and art supply stores.

CORRUGATED PAPER
An exciting material which has found a place in the preparation of visual media such as displays, bulletin boards, images, and letter cutouts. Corrugated paper (corrugated board) is made up of two layers of thin, strong paper welded together. The base layer is flat; the second layer consists of a series of corrugations glued to the surface of the base layer. Available in assorted colors and sizes.

VINYL PLASTIC
Vivid, solid-colored vinyl plastic (ConTact is one brand name) with a pressure-sensitive adhesive back. The ConTact vinyl plastic comes in 18-inch wide sheets. An excellent color medium for visual media requiring a strong paintlike color application. Ideal for cutout images and letters, wall and window supergraphics, etc. Vinyl plastic should only be applied on smooth, clean, flat firm surfaces that are completely sealed, such as enameled or oil-

painted plaster, wood, glass, tile, metal, formica. When applied to a cardboard surface, the surface should first be sprayed with a clear acrylic spray (Krylon).

Instructions—Applying Colored Paper or Vinyl Plastic

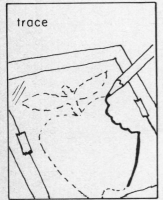

trace

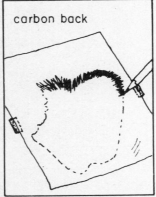

carbon back

1 Attach a sheet of tracing paper to the image to which color is to be added, and trace the exact outline of the area.

2 Turn the tracing over and apply a heavy layer of soft pencil lead (No . 2 pencil works well) to the image lines. If the coloring material is of a dark color, white chalk or crayon should be used in place of the pencil carbon. Next, rub the carboned or chalk layer with a tissue or old rag. This prevents the carbon dust from smearing when transferred.

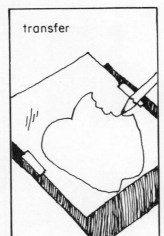

transfer

cut and apply

out to lunch

3 Turn tracing over and tape to selected paper or vinyl plastic. Carefully retrace the lines with a ball-point pen or hard lead pencil using a firm, even pressure. This tracing tool will leave an indented carbon line on the paper, making the cutting easier.

4 Place the paper or vinyl plastic on a piece of protective cardboard, and cut out with a stencil knife or similar cutting tool—even scissors if they work best for you. For large vinyl plastic cutouts, cut completely through the plastic and backing sheet. This will make later application easier.

5 To mount paper cutout color to image, use rubber cement (see page 95 for instructions). To mount large vinyl plastic cutouts, remove the top fourth of the backing sheet and position the plastic in the color area (exact placement is a must). Smooth down the top fourth in place. Next, use one hand to remove the remaining backing sheet, and the other hand to smooth down the plastic as the backing in being removed.

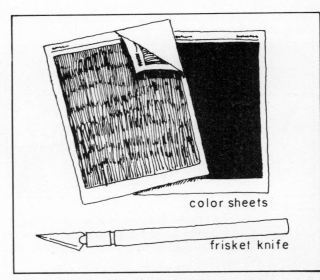

color sheets

frisket knife

Vivid colors can be added to either side of positive- or negative-image transparencies and to the surface of opaque paper-surfaced materials by applying transparent color adhesive-backed sheets and tapes. These coloring materials are made up of vivid transparent color printed on the underside of a thin film with a pressure-sensitive adhesive back. They come in assorted colors, and some sheets and tapes even contain a texture pattern to add still another effect to color.

Instructions—Color Sheets

1 With a cutting instrument (frisket knife, razor blade, etc.) score (cutting just through the color sheet) a section slightly larger than required for the area or image on which color is to go. Gently slide the point of the knife under the color sheet and peel off the cut section.

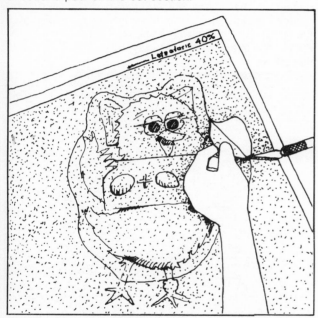

2 Position the cut section (adhesive side down) on the area or image. Care should be taken to position the color right the first time, since the adhesive of some color sheets will leave an adhesive residue when lifted and repositioned. It may be necessary to slightly burnish the color sheet in place to hold for cutting. For TRANSPARENCIES, if writing or marking is to be done on the surface during projection, apply the color to the REVERSE SIDE of the film. This will prevent the writing or marking from damaging the color.

3 With the cutting knife, trace (cutting just through the color sheet) around the image area. Peel away the unwanted color.

4 Smooth the color over the image area with the hand or finger so that it lies evenly. It is recommended that you use a clean sheet of white paper on top of the color during the smoothing; this will help protect the applied color from possible scratches and will also assist in assuring perfect adhesion. Should bubbles appear in the color, make a pinhole and smooth down once more.

Instructions—Color Tapes

The color tapes illustrated here (Letraset) come in plastic dispensers and have half-inch long grooves from the tape reels to the dispenser outlets. The grooves hold the tape steady and prevent any sideway movement as they are being laid down.

1 Draw tape steadily and firmly across the surface of the artwork using the dispenser to press the tape into contact. Cut the tape and lift the dispenser towards the cut to avoid more tape being pulled out.

2 To obtain a mitred corner, trim off the overlap and cut through both tapes from inside to outside corner.

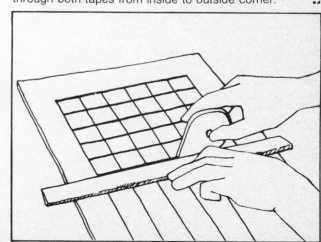

3 Remove both excess pieces of tape.

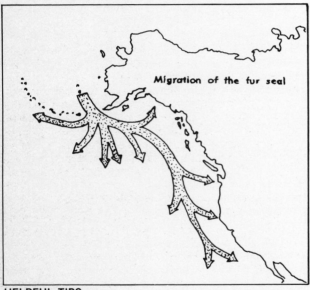

Migration of the fur seal

HELPFUL TIPS

For straight lines in color, use a ruler, T square, or triangle as a guide; for irregular lines, use an irregular curve or adjustable curve.

Two or more colors can be applied to the same area or image for different color effects.

For images requiring opaque color, opaque color sheets and tapes are available. ◗

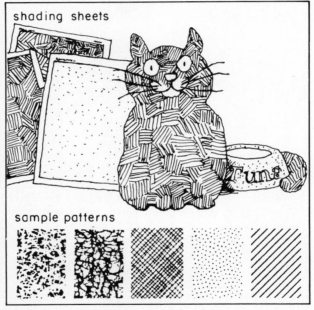

shading sheets

sample patterns

Pattern and shading films are excellent for adding an extra punch to visual media such as charts, graphs, maps, posters, and illustrations. For the non-artist, these films are "magic" for adding an exciting dimension to visual media. Pattern films are thin acetate sheets with over a 100 different patterns (bricks, sand, water, textile designs, etc.) printed on the underside of the film. Shading films are also thin acetate sheets with many different shading screens (dots, lines, etc.) printed the same as pattern films.

There are two types of pattern and shading film; one with a pressure-sensitive adhesive coating that requires the pattern or shading be cut out, and one that allows the pattern or shading to transfer to the artwork by rubbing over the surface of the film with a ball-point pen or similar tool. Pattern and shading films are easy to use, as the directions that follow will support.

Instructions—Pressure-Sensitive Film

1 Ink in solid lines and areas of the artwork. Next, select the appropriate pattern or shading film.

←ink in lines

2 Position the film, still on its backing sheet, over the area of the artwork to which the pattern is to be applied. Next carefully cut out a section slightly larger than the area to which the pattern is to be applied (you can see the artwork through the film). A stencil (frisket) knife works well for the cutting. Remove the cut section of film by inserting the point of the cutting tool under the film and peeling away from the backing sheet.

special effects for images

3   Position cut out pattern directly on the artwork. At this point, the film can be repositioned several times if necessary to ensure correct alignment. When finally

burnisher

positioned, smooth down lightly and trim off excess. Using the backing sheet for protection, burnish down firmly. A burnishing tool is recommended for this step.
INTERESTING EFFECTS can be achieved by overlaying different patterns and shading films.
PATTERNS AND SHADING IN COLOR are available for use where color is desired.

Companies like Artype, Chartpak, and Letraset have free literature that is most helpful in the use of pattern and shading films. Art supply stores will be more than happy to provide you with this literature, and even give you free samples.

Instructions—Dry Transfer Film

These unique dry transfer pattern and shading films (INSTANTEX by Letraset is one brand name), have printed patterns on the underside of a thin acetate film. Currently, 20 patterns are available.
1   Lay the printed side of the film on the artwork. Rub over the area required using the cap of a ball-point pen or similar stylus.

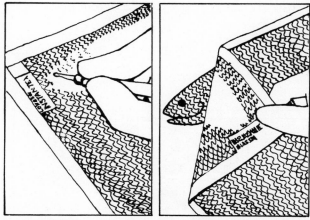

2   Lift the film, and the transfer is complete. Unwanted pattern can be removed from the artwork by rubbing with adhesive tape.

Pattern and shading tapes are strips of acetate film with many different patterns, symbols, and shading screens printed on the underside of the film. Some tapes have a pressure-sensitive adhesive coating to allow for easy application; others (Letraset's Letratape) are the dry-transfer variety, and work the same as dry transfer letters. Pattern and shading tapes are ideal for making charts, graphs, layouts, floor plans, and similar graphic media requiring repetitive patterns and shading in strip form. These tapes usually range in width from 1/32 to 1-inch. Many tapes come in colors.

Instructions—Pressure-Sensitive Tapes

1   Ink in solid lines and areas of the artwork. There are solid line tapes and solid color sheets that can also be used for this.

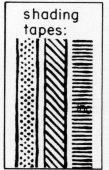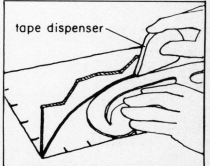

shading tapes:

tape dispenser

2   Place end of tape at the desired starting point on the artwork and unroll until it is approximately one inch beyond the cut-off point. To cut the tape, place a cutting tool (knife or razor blade) at the desired cutting point. Holding tape with thumb and forefinger, pull tape up against edge of knife with a diagonal movement while applying slight downward pressure with knife. If you wish to correct or revise the positioning of the tape, simply lift and reposition. ◣

A new dimension can be added to overhead projection and display transparencies with the use of polarizing (Polarmotion) materials. Almost any existing or new original overhead transparency can be made into an exciting instructional medium. Polarizing is an invaluable technique in conveying concepts of sequence, flow, and cause and effect. Even subject matter that is considered static in content can be made more interesting and exciting with the application of polarized material applied directly to the surface of the transparency. In addition to the application of the polarized material, all that is needed is a manual- or motor-driven polarized spinner and an electric light source (projector, lightbox, etc.); the result is a transparency with "motion."

Instructions

1 Place the finsihed transparency, less the polarizing material, on a viewing light box (light table or tracing board) or on the stage of the overhead projector. This will provide a light source for analyzing the transparency for polarizing and for the actual placement of the material.

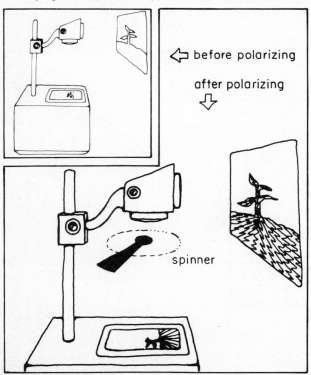

⇐ before polarizing

after polarizing
⇩

spinner

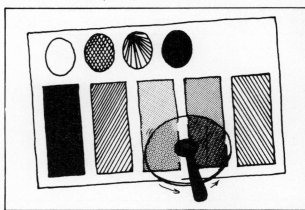

2 Select the desired polarizing (Polarmotion) material with the aid of a manual spinner. This can be done by placing the sample sheet (Polarmotion demonstration plate) on the stage of the projector or by holding it up to a light source and rotating spinner.

3 Place the desired motion material over the area to which motion is to be added; and while holding it firmly in place, take a pencil and trace an outline in the desired shape. Use

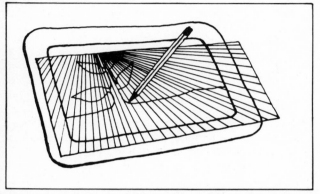

a straightedge where straight cuts are desired. Press hard enough with the pencil to make a clear outline for final cutting.

4 Cut out the motion material with a pair of sharp scissors. Before removing the backing sheet, place the material on the transparency area to be animated to check the fit.

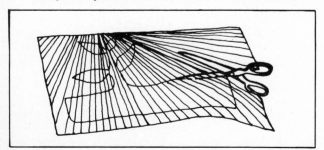

5 Remove the backing sheet, and with the point of the cutting knife wrapped with a piece of pressure-sensitive tape

(sticky side out), pick up the motion material (knife tip on top) and position on the transparency as desired. Press material firmly in place; it will bond on contact.

HELPFUL HINTS

1 Reversal film (Kodalith or negative transparencies) usually makes the best polarized transparencies.

2 Design transparencies with "motion" in mind.

3 The larger the motion area, the easier it is to work with and it is more effective.

4 Keep the design as simple as possible.

5 Use sharp cutting instruments. If possible, work under a magnifying glass. It will make cutting much easier.

6 Use bold, vivid colors that have brilliance. Diluted colors tend to wash out, and dark colors tend to mask out the motion action.

7 Use a polarizing spinner or sunglasses when working. It will help to see the motion design while laying out and cutting the motion material.

Detailed instructions, information, and samples can be obtained from manufacturers and distributors of polarizing equipment and materials. ◗

SOURCES

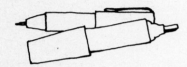

Most of the equipment and materials included in this section are available from local sources; such sources are indicated (L), and can be located in the *Yellow Pages* of the telephone directory. Items not readily available locally can be purchased directly, or purchase information obtained from the sources indicated (O).

ACETATE INKS (L1, L3, 04, 05, 09, 010, 019)

CORRUGATED PAPER (L1, L6, 09)

DRY TRANSFER PATTERN AND SHADING FILMS (L1, L3, 01, 06, 014, 018)

FIRSKET PAPERS AND LIQUIDS (L1, 04, 05, 010, 019)

GUMMED PAPER (L1, L6, 04)

LIQUID COLORS (drawing, India, white, gold, and silver inks; and watercolors) (L1, L3, L6, 04, 05, 010, 018, 019)

PATTERN AND SHADING FILMS AND TAPES (L1, L3, 01, 06, 014, 018)

PENCILS (color drawing, watercolor, and opaque color marking) (L1, L3, L6, 04, 05, 09, 010, 018)

PENCILS (spirit duplicator) (L4, 07, 08, 012)

PENS (overhead transparency marking) (L1, L2, 04, 010, 013, 017, 019)

PENS AND MARKERS (nylon- and felt-point) (L1, L6, 04, 05, 018)

POLARIZING EQUIPMENT AND MATERIALS (L2, 02, 03, 016, 017)

TRANSPARENT COLOR SHEETS AND TAPES (L1, L3, 01, 06, 014, 018)

TRANSPARENT SPRAY-CAN COLORS (L1, 04, 05, 010, 018)

VELOUR PAPER (L1, 04, 05, 013)

VINYL PLASTIC SHEETS (L1, SEARS, J. C. PENNEY, 06, 011)

WATERCOLOR STAMP BOOK (L1, 010, 015, 019)

Addresses

LOCAL SOURCES (See Yellow Pages)

L1 - Artists' Materials and Supply Stores
L2 - Audio-Visual Equipment and Supply Stores
L3 - Drafting Equipment and Supply Stores
L4 - Duplicating Machines and Supply Stores
L5 - Hobby/Crafts Supply Stores
L6 - Stationers' Stores

OUT-OF-TOWN SOURCES

O1 - ARTYPE, INC., 345 E. Terra Cotta Ave., Crystal Lake, IL 60014

O2 - AMERICAN POLARIZERS, INC., 141 S. 7th St., Reading, PA 19603

O3 - AUDIO VISUAL SUPPLY CO., Rome St., Farmingdale, NY 11735

O4 - DICK BLICK, P. O. Box 1267, Galesburg, IL 61401

O5 - ARTHUR BROWN & BROTHER, INC., 2 West 46th St., New York, NY 10036

O6 - CHARTPAK, One River Rd., Leeds, MA 01053

O7 - A. B. DICK CO., 5700 West Touhy Ave., Chicago, IL 60648

O8 - DITTO, INC., 6800 McCormick Rd., Chicago, IL 60645

O9 - SAM FLAX, 25 E. 28th St., New York, NY 10016

O10 - A. I. FRIEDMAN, INC., 25 W. 45th St., New York, NY 10036

O11 - GRAPHICA INTERNATIONAL, 1936 Euclid Ave., Cleveland, OH 44115

O12 - HEYER, INC., 1850 S. Kostner Ave., Chicago, IL 60623

O13 - THE INSTRUCTO CORP., 1635 N. 55th St., Paoli, PA 19301

O14 - LETRASET USA, INC., 33 New Bridge Rd., Bergenfield, NJ 07621

O15 - PEERLESS COLOR LABORATORIES, 11 Diamond Pl., Rochester, NY 14609

O16 - SCOTT GRAPHICS, INC., 195 Appleton St., Holyoke, MA 01040

O17 - STAREX, INC., 655 Schuyler Ave., Kearny, NJ 07032

O18 - TAYLOR'S ART CENTER, 2601 J. St., Sacramento, CA 95814

O19 - VISUAL PLANNING DIVISION, MPC, North Main St., Champlain, NY 12919

With few exceptions, practically every kind of visual medium (charts, graphs, transparencies, etc.) requires lettering or printing of one type or another. In view of the importance of lettering to the production of visual media, this section of the handbook illustrates and discusses what is believed to be a rather comprehensive assortment of lettering and printing techniques.

Available on the market today is an unlimited variety of letters, lettering guides, mechanical tracing lettering systems, printing machines, tape and plastic embossers, phototype composing machines, paste-up types, and so forth. Such a multitude of techniques and aids might frustrate the novice producer of visual media. However, a quick glance at the "Lettering Selection Chart" on page 54 is a suggested starting point for the selection of lettering techniques and aids designed for a particular lettering problem. To assist with creating attractive lettering layouts and designs, one can refer to page 55. With problems of letters and word spacing and alignment, a look at page 57 should be helpful.

This section, while written mainly for the non-artist, should also be helpful to the professional visual media producer seeking solutions to media involving lettering.

Finally, it should be kept in mind that there are no hard-and-fast rules governing the selection of lettering or printing techniques. The selection should be made only after an analysis of lettering requirements of the visual media being produced. The choice may depend upon what is available or the ability of one to use a particular technique. In any event, it is hoped that from among the techniques included in this section an answer can be found for the lettering problem at hand.

LETTERING SELECTION CHART

This chart is designed to aid in the selection of appropriate letters and lettering techniques for preparing visual media. The top left section of the chart lists surfaces to which letters and lettering techniques may be directly applied. The bottom left half, Special Lettering, lists several special applications of lettering. Page references for each letter or technique are also listed. The selection symbols ● indicate the lettering recommended for use. Symbols with superior numbers are specific pages in the handbook which should be referred to for instructions.

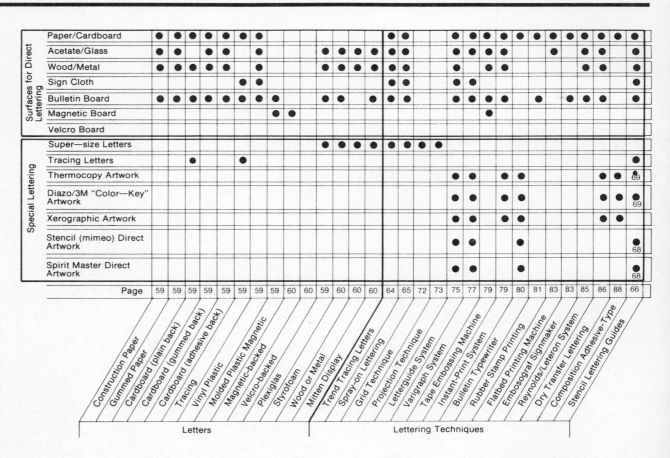

LETTERING IDEAS: SOURCES AND EXAMPLES

effective and interesting letter arrangement (design); others may suggest ideas for color of letters or backgrounds on which lettering appears.

The lettering ideas on this page have been taken from some of the sources mentioned here. The "Letter Sheet" (see page 74) contains several letter sets that can be traced or enlarged for use.

Ideas for good and exciting lettering are all around you; in newspaper and magazine ads, posters, bus and car cards, telephone YELLOW PAGES, and brochures. A trip up the aisles of the supermarket looking at the many packages will reveal the variety of ways that letters are used to attract attention. Notice the style, size, and color of letters and how they reflect the feeling of the product. It's a good idea to keep a note pad or piece of paper handy to jot down lettering ideas.

Start a "Lettering Ideas" file, and in it place ideas taken from the sources just mentioned. Some ideas may only suggest

Whatever technique or lettering or imaging is to be used, the preparation is most important and should be given careful attention. Here are a few tips for preparing the working surface (paper, cardboard, acetate, etc.) for use.

A good drawing board, T square, and perhaps a triangle are the basic tools required for preparing the working surface. A Cam-lock drawing board or a board to which a Cam-lock channel is attached and a Cam-lock T square are highly recommended in that the T square can be locked into working position.

Aligning and Securing the Working Surface

1 Place the T square head against the left side of the drawing board and move to position (A) as illustrated.

2 Line up the working surface with top edge of the T square blade. Secure the surface to the board with pressure-sensitive tape, double-coated adhesive tape, or pushpins (see instructions ➡).

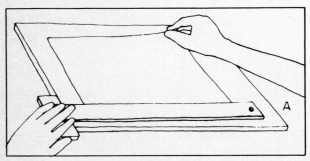

3 Move the T square to the desired working position (B). The selected lettering instrument (guide, template, etc.) can be placed on the top edge of the T square blade.

AIDS FOR SECURING LETTERING SURFACE TO THE BOARD

There are several good aids for securing the lettering surface to the drawing board; here are three:

Pressure-Sensitive Tape

While any pressure-sensitive tape can be used to attach the working surface to secure it to the drawing board, drafting tape works best as it has an adhesive side that sticks to most surfaces with slight hand pressure, yet removes easily when work is completed. Roll 1-inch pieces (2 or 4) of tape, "sticky" side out, the thickness of a small pencil, and stick one to each corner contact point under the surface material. A slight pressure at corner contact points will fasten the lettering surface to the board.

Double-coated Tape

Attach strips of small pieces of this tape to the drawing board surface at points where contact is desired. Attach the working surface face to the board as instructed in steps 1, 2, and 3. If the working surface is paper or cardboard, spray with clear plastic spray; this will prevent damage to the back of the working surface when it is removed from the board.

Pushpins

Metal or glass pushpins can be inserted at corner contact points of the surface material. ◀

LETTER AND WORD SPACING, ALIGNMENT, AND SPECIAL EFFECTS

One of the most difficult aspects of lettering is that of letter and word spacing. Letters are not equidistant from each other, due to differences in width and shape.

Letter Spacing

Good letter spacing is the arrangement of letters in a line so that they will appear to have equal or uniform distances between them. To achieve this effect, it is often necessary to position the letters at varying distances from one another, depending on the style, size, and combination of letters involved. One way of assuring correct letter spacing is to envisage the areas between letters as being irregular containers of liquid, the objective being to space the letters so that no matter how irregular the shape of the these "liquid containers," they will each hold the same amount of liquid. This technique of spacing is also known as optical spacing. Note that although the letters in (A) are equally spaced, the "containers" between them are unequal. Part (B) illustrates the results of spacing letters so that the "containers" are nearly equal.

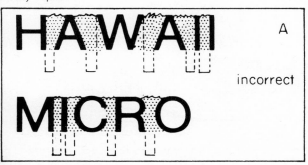

incorrect

A

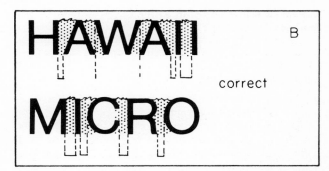

correct

B

Another good rule to follow for letter spacing is to space round letters (B, C, D, G, O, P, Q, R, and S) a bit closer to each other and to any straight letter (E, H, I, M, N, and U) next to their rounded side. Irregular formed letters (A, F, J, K, L, T, V, W, X, Y, and Z) also fit closer together according to their shape. Three letters, I, M, and W, are generally considered as problem letters. For the I, do not position too close to adjoining letters; for the M and W, do not squeeze as these are actually wider than other letters.

Word Spacing

In arranging captions, a good rule to follow is to keep the space between words about the same, even though spaces between individual letters may vary. Should one word end

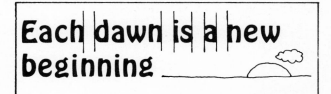

and another begin with narrow letters (I or T), position them a bit closer than words which end and begin with round or open letters.

Letter Alignment

The arrangement and form given to letters contribute a great deal to the preparation of visual media where lettering is involved. Basic to lettering is alignment. Here are two suggested approaches to the alignment of letters and words.

FOR PRECUT, VINYL PLASTIC, PREFORMED, RUBBER STAMP, STENCIL, DRY TRANSFER, AND COMPOSITION ADHESIVE – TYPE LETTERS

1 Write down the words intended for one line of lettering.

2 Count up the letters and spaces between the words. Mark the center letter.

3 Assume that the line of lettering is to be centered on the working surface, make a light pencil mark at the center point as illustrated.

4 Make a light pencil guideline on the working surface for letters that require such a line.

5 Position the middle letter at the center point on the working surface. First, work to the left of the middle letter, and then work to the right of the middle letter until all letters are in place.

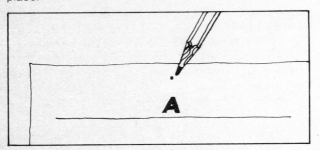

FOR MECHANICAL TRACING AND STENCIL TRACING LETTERS

1 Letter the intended line of letters, with the lettering device selected for the job, on a scrap sheet of paper. Make a mark at the center letter. Make certain to count all letters and spaces when picking out the center letter.

2 If the lettering is to be centered on the working surface, make a light pencil mark at the center point. Match up the center mark on the scrap sheet of paper with the mark on the working surface. Repeat the lettering on the working surface, using the scrap sheet as a guide for letter and word spacing. If the line of lettering is not to be centered, position the scrap sheet containing the first lettering where desired and repeat the lettering on the working surface. ◼

Special Effects

A variety of art aids and assorted-shape objects can be used to create special effects in lettering; the adjustable curve can be bent into any desired curve or shape to act as a guide for alignment of letters and words. Irregular (French) curves are useful for arranging small letters into special effects. Audio records are excellent for arranging letters in a circular design. Other round objects, such as dishes and container tops, provide adequate guides for letter arrangement. See page 55 for special effect ideas.

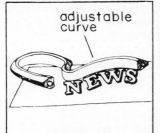

PRECUT AND PREFORMED LETTERS

See page 61 for mounting aids. See page 57 for "Letter and Word Spacing, Alignment, and Special Effects."

Precut and preformed letters add an exciting dimension to visual media. Perhaps the greatest advantage of these letters is that they are in ready-to-use form and need only be mounted or attached to the desired surface. Precut and preformed letters come in a large assortment of styles, sizes, and materials. Included here are several tested and approved precut and preformed letters.

Construction Paper Letters

Die-cut from colorful construction paper. Ideal for posters, charts, signs, displays, bulletin boards, etc. They can be pinned, pasted, stapled, or suspended with string.

Gummed Paper Letters

Die-cut paper letters with a gummed-back adhesive. A pair of tweezers, a straightedge (ruler), a moist sponge, and a blotter are the only tools necessary to produce professional-looking lettering. See page 62 for mounting gummed paper letters.

Cardboard Letters (Plain Back)

Die-cut from heavy cardboard. Available in colored or uncolored stock and in a wide range of sizes and styles. Ideal for displays, signs, etc. Letters can be used for tracing and spray-on lettering (see page 65).

Cardboard Letters (Gummed Back)

Cardboard letters with a gummed back, easily applied like a postage stamp to special guide strips and then attached to the desired mounting surface. Letters range in height from ¾ to 2 inches.

Cardboard Letters (Adhesive Back)

Pressure-sensitive adhesive-backed cardboard letters. Ideal for displays, signs, posters, etc. Letters range in size from ¾ to 2 inches.

Tracing Letters

Cardboard letters designed for tracing (see page 64 for instructions). Ideal for visual media requiring large, attractive letters. Letters range in height from 1 to 6 inches.

Vinyl Plastic Letters

Die-cut plastic letters with a pressure-sensitive adhesive back that will stick to most surfaces. Height of letters ranges from ½ to 6 inches. See page 63 for instructions.

Molded Plastic Magnetic Letters

A semiflexible molded plastic letter with permanent magnetism built in. Letters will stick to any steel or magnetic-treated surface. Letters range in height from ½ to 2 inches and come in several colors.

Plexiglas Letters

Translucent color letters made of Plexiglas. Designed for display and outdoor use. Range in height is from 5 to 24 inches.

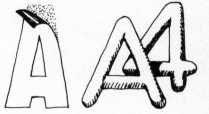

Wood or Metal Letters

Precision-cut wood or metal letters available in heights up to 30 inches. Designed mainly for sign and display use.

Velcro-Backed Letters

Dimensional plastic letters backed with Velcro ("hook") tape. Designed for use on Velcro (Hook-n-Loop) surfaces and boards.

Magnetic-Backed Letters

Molded plastic letters with small metal or rubber magnets attached to the back. For use on magnetic boards or steel surfaces.

Styrofoam Letters

Molded styrofoam letters that have the appearance of expensive metal letters. At this printing, only 12-inch high letters are available.

Mitten Display Letters

Made of precision-molded plastic ceramic or tile composition. Available in over 130 sizes and styles. Illustrated are four types of Mitten display letters.

PINBAK

Pin-on letters are thumbtack-simple to apply and ideal for quick lettering changes. Pins easily into all soft surfaces: cork, Upsonboard, Homasote or Mitten Display Panels.

SA'NBAK

Glue-on letters for hard surfaces such as wood, tile, metal, glass, plastic or heavy cardboard. Recommended for indoor use with Mitten-Stay Indoor Cement or Mitten Mighty Mount pressure sensitive tape. For outdoors use Mitten Greenwood Cement or other strong waterproof adhesive.

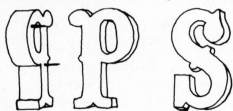

TRAKK

Standing letters which can be used either in an upright position or at an angle. The permenant lug-base on each letter is custom-fitted for easy insertion into Mitten's ready-made wooden tracks.

STANDEES

Extra depth letters that stand upright completely unaided. Reusable and rearrangable in just seconds. ◾

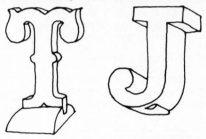

AIDS FOR MOUNTING LETTERS

Most manufacturers of precut and preformed letters recommend certain mounting aids for mounting or attaching their letters. While not specifically designed for mounting letters, there are several good mounting aids recommended here for mounting and attaching precut and preformed letters.

RUBBER CEMENT

Ideal for mounting most lightweight precut letters on porous surfaces. See page 95 for rubber cement mounting.

PRESSURE-SENSITIVE ADHESIVE (AEROSOL CAN)

Pressure-sensitive adhesive spray-can form. For mounting precut letters on most surfaces.

LIQUID PLASTIC ADHESIVE

A fast-setting white or transparent all-purpose adhesive that holds on wood, paper, cardboard, glass, and all porous and semi-porous letters.

ADHESIVE STICK

One of the newer forms of mounting adhesives. Comes in lipstick-like form and can be used for mounting precut paper and lightweight cardboard letters on most surfaces.

WAX ADHESIVE STICK

A colorless, odorless wax adhesive in stick form. For mounting and attaching most of the lightweight precut letters.

EPOXY CEMENT

An extra-strong, clear, waterproof cement for metal, glass, plastic, and other nonporous precut and preformed letters. Consists of two tubes (one resin and one hardner) which are mixed together in the quantity required just before use.

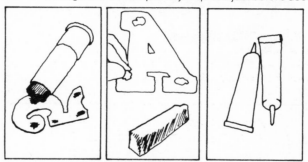

DOUBLE-COATED ADHESIVE TAPE

A double-coated pressure-sensitive tape for attaching paper and lightweight cardboard to most surfaces. Some tapes have a carrier strip that must be peeled away from the adhesive tape to permit mounting.

FOAM TAPE

Double-coated foam tape. Has pressure-sensitive adhesive on both sides. For mounting most precut and preformed letters on most surfaces. 3M brand tape is packaged as "Mounting Squares."

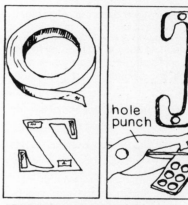

ADHESIVE-BACKED PAPER TAB

A special mounting paper tab for mounting paper and cardboard letters on most surfaces. The tab has pressure-sensitive adhesive on both sides.

DISPLAY PINS

Steel straight pins designed for mounting and attaching display materials. Ideal for mounting paper and cardboard letters. Regular straight pins can also be used.

MOUNTING GUMMED PAPER LETTERS

See page 57 for "Letter and Word Spacing, Alignment, and Special Effects."

Gummed paper letters require no special skill for making attractive media requiring precision-cut paste-up letters. Here are five easy steps for mounting gummed paper letters:

1 Use a guideline—either draw a light pencil line or use the edge of a blotter, heavy paper, or card.

2 Pick up the letter with tweezers, or between the fingers and a knife blade.

3 Moisten the letter slightly, keeping it firmly attached to the tweezers, and at the same time move the letter slightly so that it will not stick to the lifting tool.

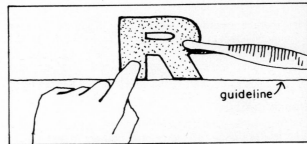

4 Use the forefinger of the left hand to press the letter lightly while removing the tweezers.

5 When the line of letters is complete, use a blotter or a sheet of paper; press over all, and the lettering is finished.

VINYL PLASTIC LETTERS

Vinyl plastic pressure-sensitive letters are weatherproof, washable, permanent, and can be used indoors or outdoors. These letters are ideal for posters, charts, graphs, signs, etc. See "Lettering Selection Chart" on page 54 for other suggested uses. "Super Stick" letters by E-Z Letter Quik Stik Company come in sizes from ¼ to 6 inch, and in eight brilliant colors.

INSTRUCTIONS

See page 56 for "Preparation of Working Surface for Lettering."

See page 57 for "Letter and Word Spacing, Alignment, and Special Effects."

1 Peel off the surplus vinyl plastic material from the protective backing sheet before you start to use the letters. Remove only the material around each letter or number.

This makes it possible for each character to remain securely attached to the sheet itself and ready for instant use.

2 Before removing letters from the protective backing, position with ruler and pencil two parallel guidelines to insure straight placement of letters or numbers. For example, if you are using a 2-inch letter, draw two parallel lines 2-inches apart.

3 Use the point of a knife or single edge razor blade to peel the desired letter off the backing sheet. Centers of letters such as A, B, and D will remain on the backing sheet.

guidelines

4 Letters can be applied directly to the lettering surface. Remember, once you stick the letters down, they can't be removed, so be extra careful to properly lay out the space to be used (see page 57). Typesetting aids for straight or circular positioning of letters can be made out of thin plastic sheeting or metal (see page 89). ◗

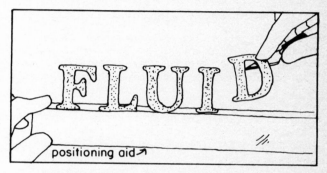

positioning aid➚

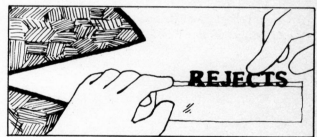

REJECTS

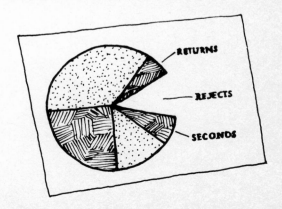

RETURNS

REJECTS

SECONDS

Trend Enterprises has manufactured a die-cut letter designed just for tracing (decorative borders and corners too). These letters are particularly well-suited for use on bulletin boards, signs, posters, banners, displays, etc. In addition to being an excellent tracing aid, these letter sets are effective flash cards or manipulative instructional materials for young children in learning to recognize letters and numbers, and in learning to spell. Trend letters come in assorted styles and range in height from 2 to 6 inches. Kenworth Educational Services manufactures "Trace or Paste" letters that range in size from 1 to 6 inches.

Here are suggested uses for the tracing letters:

For Tracing Only

See page 56 for "Preparation of Working Surfaces for Lettering." See pages 57 to 58 for "Letter and Word Spacing, Alignment, and Special Effects."

1 Use a pencil; ball-, nylon-, felt-point pen; crayon; or chalk to trace the letter form.

2 Color with felt-point pen or any other coloring technique desired (see Section 3 for coloring techniques).

For Tracing and Cutout

Interesting, unique letters, numbers or borders can be achieved by cutting them from a variety of commonly available materials such as construction, craft, gift-wrap foil, or corrugated paper, wallpaper, carpeting, burlap, cork. linoleum, etc. Exciting effects can be added to cutout letters by cutting letters out of durable paper or thin cardboard, then gluing cotton, tissue paper twists, small seeds, or glitter over the surface of each form.

1 Trace letters with pencil or ball-point pen. A ball-point pen line provides a grooved guideline for cutting.

2 Cut out letters.

3 Mount letters (see page 61 for mounting aids). ∎

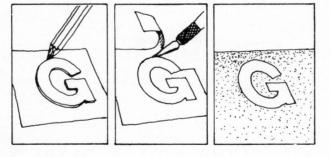

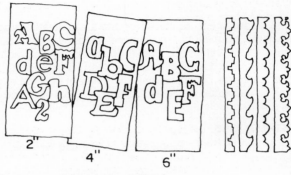

letters and borders available

suggestions:

SPRAY-ON LETTERING

Attractive signs and posters can be made quickly with precut and special spray-on letters. Commercial spray-on letters are the best type for this technique in that they are usually made of die-cut thick sponge rubber and will not shift or move when sprayed. American Jet Spray Industries and The Holes Manufacturing Company sell spray sign kits. Letters range in height from ¾ to 12 inches. A variety of aerosol spray-can paints provide excellent colors for this technique.

INSTRUCTIONS FOR A TWO-COLOR SIGN POSTER

1 Place the surface upon which the lettering is to be done on a flat protected surface. Use a piece of cardboard or thick paper to cover one section of the lettering surface.

2 Select the letters and numbers desired, and arrange them on the lettering surface. A T square or straightedge can be used to align the letters.

3 Select the color or colors, and spray lightly over and around the letters, holding the spray can about 12 inches away at right angles. The resulting letter will be sharp and clearly defined. If a three-dimensional effect is desired, hold

the spray can at about a 45° angle and spray as instructed. Various angles at which spraying is done will result in a variety of effects. Allow the paint to dry; this usually takes

about ten minutes, depending on the type of paint used. Carefully remove the letters from the surface.

4 Cover the sprayed section of the surface with a piece of cardboard or thick paper, and position the cutout forms, letters, symbols as desired and repeat Step 3.

5 To avoid possible clogging of the spray can, turn it up-side down and spray short jets of air to clear the air passage.

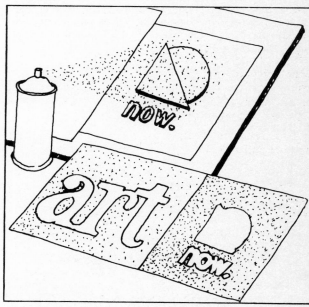

Cardboard, metal, and plastic stencil lettering guides provide a fast, economical way for lettering on opaque and transparent surfaces. Some guides even have features for assuring perfect spacing. Stencil lettering guides come in three basic forms: individual letter, card-type, and plastic tracing guides, with the latter two having a number of letters on a single card or plastic sheet. Today, a number of exciting letter styles and sizes are available, ranging in height from ½ to 8 inches.

Individual Cardboard Letter Guides

Sharp, clean die-cut individual letter guides made of yellow oil board. See page 67 for instructions.

Individual Metal Letter Guides

Heavy metal letter guides that do not interlock. Used the same as cardboard guides. The guides illustrated, available from Lewis Artist Supply, range in height from 5 to 40 mm.

Metal Interlocking Letter Guides

Individual metal letter guides that interlock to form a complete word that can be traced, sprayed with paint or ink, or printed with a stencil brush and ink. Vertical and horizontal guides are available.

Plastic Interlocking Letter Guides

Individual polyester plastic letter guides that interlock with brass fasteners to form a complete word that can be traced, sprayed with paint or ink, or printed with a stencil brush or brayer and ink. Guides come in sets of full Gothic capitals and number fonts, and heights range from ½ to 6 inches.

INSTRUCTIONS FOR USE OF INDIVIDUAL LETTER GUIDES

Individual letter guides are unique in that they can be arranged to form complete words for tracing, spraying, brush, or brayer and ink application.

1 To align letters, use a straightedge. For best results, overlap the stencils slightly. Spacing may be varied by changing the amount of overlap.

2 Fasten letters together with pressure-sensitive tape along the top and bottom edges of the stencils.

3 Tape assembled letters to the area to be stenciled. If required, use protective paper to mask the area around the stencils. Spray with ink or paint, or apply ink with a stencil brush or brayer.

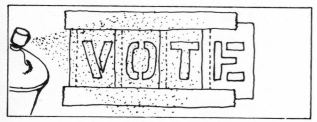

Stencil Letter Cutting Machine

A hand-operated stencil-cutting machine for cutting stencil letters out of stencil oil board. Models available for cutting letters range from ¼- to 1-inch in height.

Card-Type Stencil Lettering Guides

Stencil board or plastic card-type stencil guides with outlines of letters, numbers, and symbols that can be traced or filled in with any marking medium from pencil to paint. Gothic- and Roman-style letters are the more widely used. Old English, Western, and "Hoot-Nany" are three other styles now available. Letters range in height from ½ to 12 inches.

plastic stencil

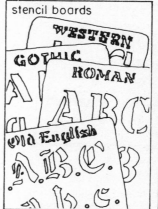

stencil boards

guideline

INSTRUCTIONS

If using new guides, first, push out all the letters, figures, and guide holes.

1 Draw a light pencil guideline on the lettering surface above which letters are to be traced. If guide holes are at the bottom of the stencil letter, draw the guideline below where the letters are to be traced.

2 Position for the first letter and trace the outline with the selected imaging tool (pencil, pen, etc.). The traced letter can be filled in with any marking medium (pencil, crayon, ink, etc.). Before moving the guide to the next letter, make a pencil dot in the guide hole at the lower right of the letter just completed.

3 Position the next letter so that the dot just made shows through the guide hole at the lower left of the letter to be outlined next. Trace the letter, and repeat the foregoing steps until the word has been completed. Erase the pencil guideline.

Lettering Guides for Stencil and Spirit Duplication

Lettering guides for stencil and spirit duplication are made of plastic and have openings in the shape of letters and numerals. There are usually two guides for each letter set, one for capital letters and one for lowercase letters.

Stencil lettering guides work equally well for both stencils (mimeograph) and spirit masters. The use of a plastic writing plate (sheet) is recommended when using lettering guides.

INSTRUCTIONS—STENCIL

1 Where possible, a glass surface with a light source behind it should be used when lettering on a stencil. Place the plastic sheet directly behind the stencil as illustrated. Position and secure the T square in place.

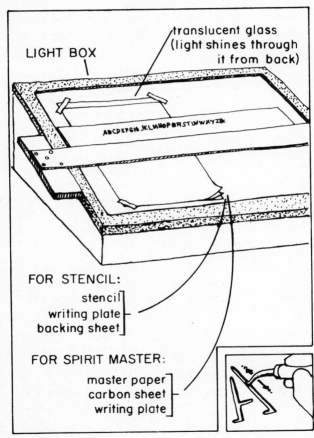

LIGHT BOX

translucent glass
(light shines through
it from back)

FOR STENCIL:
stencil
writing plate
backing sheet

FOR SPIRIT MASTER:
master paper
carbon sheet
writing plate

2 Choose the lettering guide and the correct stylus. The proper stylus to use is usually indicated on the lettering guide. First make a very light line in the letter selected. Then go back and forth over the line just drawn several times until sufficient stencil coating is pushed aside from the base tissue to make a clear white line (see insert).

3 Always draw toward a point formed by the junction of two lines. For example, when drawing the letter F, draw the long line first; then start at the outer points of the two short lines and draw toward the long line—never away from it.

Spacing is achieved by estimating the proper distance between each letter with the eye (see pages 57 to 58 for helpful instructions on letter and word spacing).

INSTRUCTIONS --SPIRIT MASTER
Lettering on spirit masters with stencil lettering guides is much the same as lettering on stencils.

1 Place a plastic writing plate under the spirit master as illustrated, or, if a writing plate is not available, place the master on a hard, smooth surface. Remove the interleaf sheet so that the carbon sheet is next to the master.

2 Choose the lettering guide and correct stylus. Some ballpoint pens with a fine point will sometimes work just as well as a stylus. Trace the letter with a firm, steady pressure. Check the master to make certain the carbon is transferring a solid-line letter.

3 To change the color of the letter, change the carbon sheet for another color carbon. Corrections can be made by carefully scraping carbon transfer off the master and erasing with a correction pencil. Tear off a small section of the carbon sheet, position it under the correction, and retrace the letter.

WRICO SIGN-MAKER SYSTEM

The Wrico Sign-Maker system consists of transparent plastic lettering guides, a metal guide holder, and a brush or felt-point pen. Letters range in height from ⅜ to 4 inches. There are a number of letter styles to choose from, including modern mathematics symbols. The Sign-Maker is an ideal lettering system for preparing posters, signs, charts, graphs, maps, television, filmstrip, motion-picture, and slide titles, and flash cards.

INSTRUCTIONS

1 To fill the pen, press the plunger down and insert only the brush portion of the pen in ink, and, without raising the pen, release the plunger slowly. The pen is now ready for use. To adjust the pen properly for use, twist the adjustment nut until the end of the brush is even with the end of the tip of the pen. If the brush is not out far enough, turn the nut to the right. If the brush is out too far, turn the nut to the left. Finally, turn the adjustment nut a quarter of the way to the left so that the brush is recessed slightly; this will permit the ink to flow freely under the brush and allow for well-inked lines.

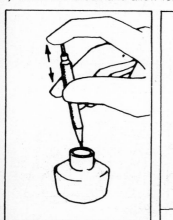
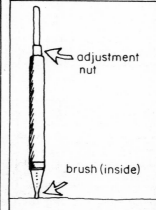

adjustment nut

brush (inside)

2 Place the metal guide holder on the surface to be lettered so that the rubber strips on the bottom of the holder set firmly upon the surface. Then rest the lettering guide in the channel of the guide holder. This permits the guide to be moved smoothly to the right or left without touching the surface to be lettered, thus preventing ink smudges. The guide holder stays securely in position wherever it is placed. This eliminates the necessity for straightedges, weights, thumbtacks, or tape.

3 Move the lettering guide so as to position the first letter where desired on the lettering surface. Insert the pen in the first letter. Hold the pen vertically, and glide it through the letter form. Best results are obtained with very light pressure on the point. Many of the characters, both letters and numbers, are made complete with a single opening. Some require two openings. For example, when making the letter B, use any Vertical line and then move the guide until the curved portion of the B is in position to complete the letter.

4 Slide the guide to the next letter and repeat the process. The lowercase letters c, f, i, j, l, m, n, o, r, s, t, u, v, x, y, and z are made by simply following the proper openings. The other letters require two openings. Part of the letter is made with one opening and completed with the other. The openings used for these letters are also indicated.

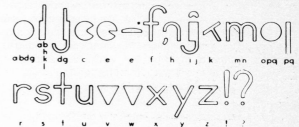

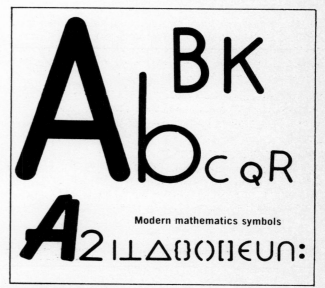

Modern mathematics symbols

Sample Letter Styles

Here is a simple, but unique technique for producing large-size display letters with the aid of a stencil pattern known as a Unistencil. The Unistencil illustrated here can be enlarged by the grid technique (see page 72) or by projection (see page 73), and cut from a manila file folder, cardboard, metal, wood, or plastic sheeting. The stencil can be used to produce all letters of the alphabet. While the basic letter produced with the stencil is rather formal, various modifications can be made to create special effects.

INSTRUCTIONS

1 Draw a base guideline on which the Unistencil can be aligned.

2 Trace the basic letter form from the stencil (refer to illustrated "Stencil Positioning for Letters").

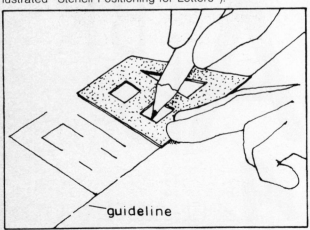

guideline

3 Draw in the necessary (remaining) lines to complete the letter. Modifications can be made with round objects, irregular curves, etc.

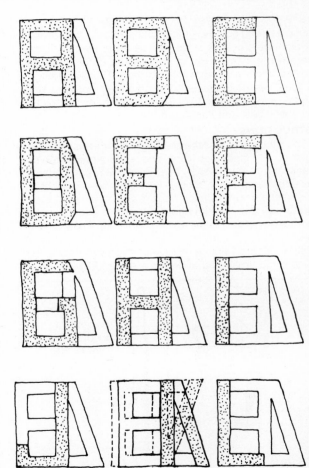

DELO

See page 57 for "Letter and Word Spacing, Alignment, and Special Effects."

Stencil Positioning for Letters

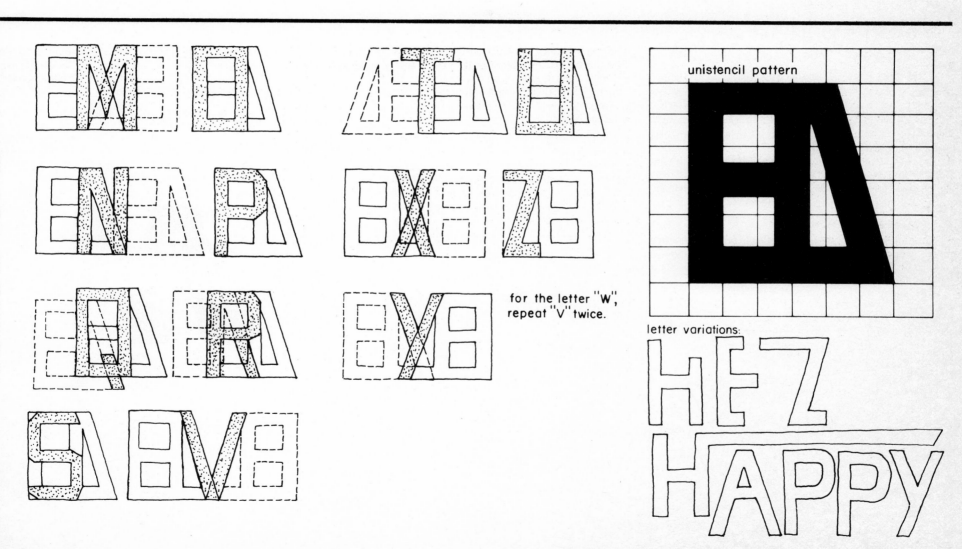

for the letter "W",
repeat "V" twice.

unistencil pattern

letter variations:

Grid Technique

Small-size letters can be made into super-size letters with the grid technique. Other techniques for producing super-size letters are by projection (see page 73) and the pantograph (see page 29). The grid technique is an easy way to enlarge letters so that all parts remain in proportion to the original letter.

INSTRUCTIONS

1 Accurately trace, or mount the letter to be enlarged on a sheet of paper. For traced letters, tracing paper is recommended. Letters from the "Letter Sheet" (page 74) are available for your use.

2 With light pencil lines, mark off the traced or mounted letter with squares (a T square and triangle are

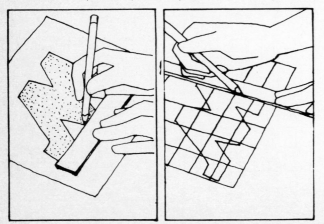

recommended for drawing accurate squares). The size of the squares will be determined by the size and complexity of the letter. One-quarter inch squares are recommended for letters 1 inch high or wide. Number the border squares as illustrated; this will keep you oriented when reproducing the enlarged letter.

3 For the enlargement, mark off the second sheet of paper with the same number of enlarged squares. Size of squares is determined by the degree of enlargement. For example, if the enlarged letter is to be five times as large as the original letter, the enlarged squares should be FIVE TIMES AS LARGE. Number the enlarged squares the same as for the smaller squares.

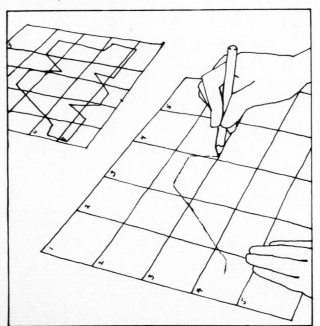

4 Carefully draw in the outline of the original letter in the corresponding larger squares with a pencil. DRAW IN ONE SQUARE AT A TIME. For straight lines of the letter, a ruler, triangle, or T square is recommended.

5 Refine the pencil outline of the completed letter and transfer (pencil carbon, page 23 ; carbon paper, page 23 ; or pounce pattern, page 24) to the desired surface.

Projection Technique

Where large display-type letters are desired, one of a variety of projection devices can be used very effectively. With any one of these devices, it is possible to produce large letters of any size on a variety of materials. The letter to be reproduced is inserted in the device used and projected onto the drawing surface. Precut letters are ideal for this technique. However, any printed letter that can be inserted in the projection device can be used. Letters from the "Letter Sheet" (page 74) are available for your use. Here are general instructions for producing letters by projections. For each of the projection devices, additional instructions may be given.

INSTRUCTIONS

1 Insert the letter in the projection device. It may be necessary to anchor the letter to a sheet of paper or clear acetate to prevent movement while reproducing larger letters.

2 Fasten the surface on which the letter is to be reproduced to the wall or floor or to wherever a projected image would normally appear.

3 Position or adjust the projection device to give the letter size desired.

4 Trace the outline of the projected letter with a pencil. For straight lines of the letter, use a ruler or yardstick as a tracing guide. Remove the finished work, and ink or complete as desired.

Opaque Projector

Insert the precut or printed letter in the projector as illustrated. It may be necessary to attach the letter to a sheet of contrasting paper or cardboard to hold the letter in place and to increase the visibility of the letter for tracing. It may be necessary to turn off the room lights while tracing the enlarged letters. Follow steps 2, 3, and 4.

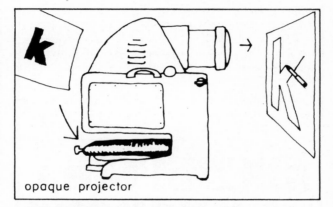

opaque projector

Photographic Enlarger

Only a precut paper or thin cardboard letter can be used, and it must be a size that can fit into the negative carrier. If the carrier is glass, simply sandwich the letter between the two pieces of glass and insert in the enlarger. If the carrier is glassless, cut two pieces of clear acetate to fit the carrier and sandwich the letter between them and fit into the carrier. Insert in the enlarger. Follow steps 2, 3, and 4.

Overhead Projector

Place a precut letter on the stage of the projector. It may be necessary to place a sheet of glass or clear acetate on top of the letter to hold it in place. Follow steps 2, 3, and 4.

Slide Projector

Insert the precut letter between two pieces of slide cover glass or two pieces of clear acetate and insert in a reusable mount (see page 160 for mount description). Insert the mounted letter in the projector. Follow steps 3 and 4.

Art Aid Projector

The Projector illustrated is a miniature opaque projector designed for use as an art aid (for enlarging visuals). Insert the lettering to be enlarged under the projector or in the position indicated. Follow steps 2, 3, and 4.

photographic enlarger

overhead projector

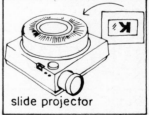

slide projector

art aid projector

LETTER SHEET FOR TRACING / PROJECTION

ABCDEF
GHIJKL
MNOPQ
RSTUV
WXYZ
?!TAHB

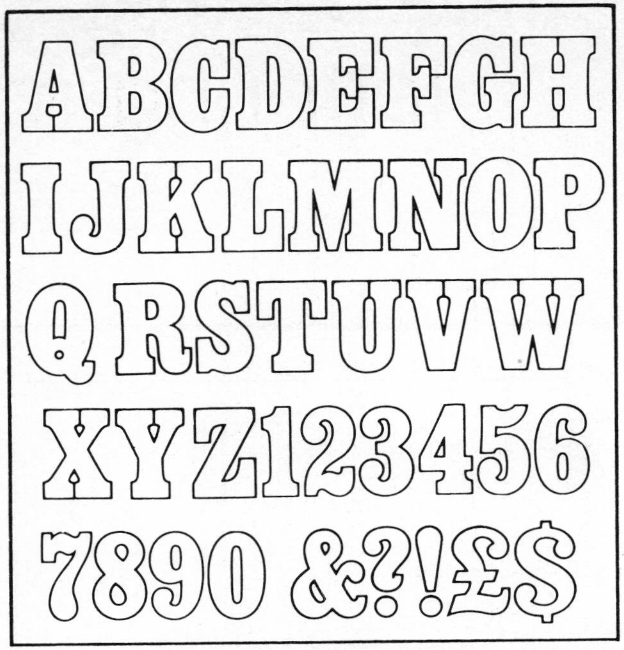

ABCDEFGH
IJKLMNOP
QRSTUVW
XYZ123456
7890 &?!£$

ABCDEFGHIJK
LMNOPQRST
UVWXYZÆ
abcdefghijkl
mnopqrstuv
wxyzæø 1234
567890&?!

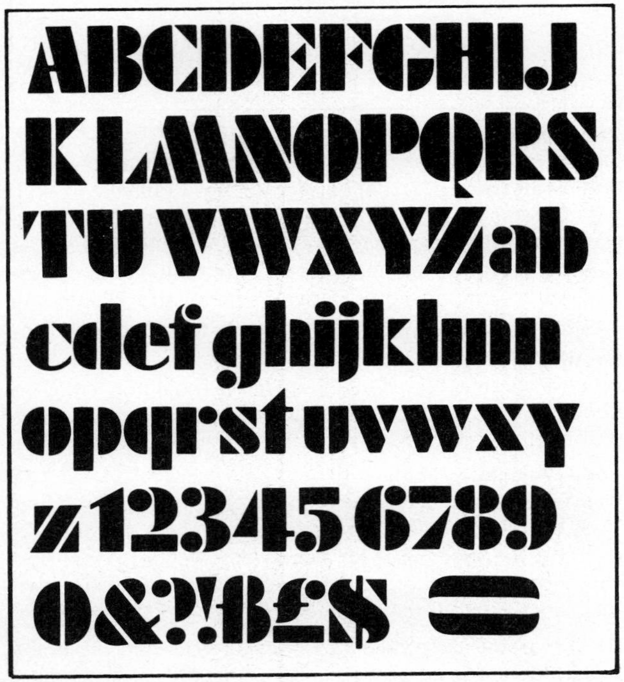

ABCDEFGHIJ
KLMNOPQRS
TUVWXYZab
cdefghijklmn
opqrstuvwxy
z123456789
0&?!B£$

ABCDEFGHIJK
LMNOPQRSTU
VWXYZ12345
67890&?!£$

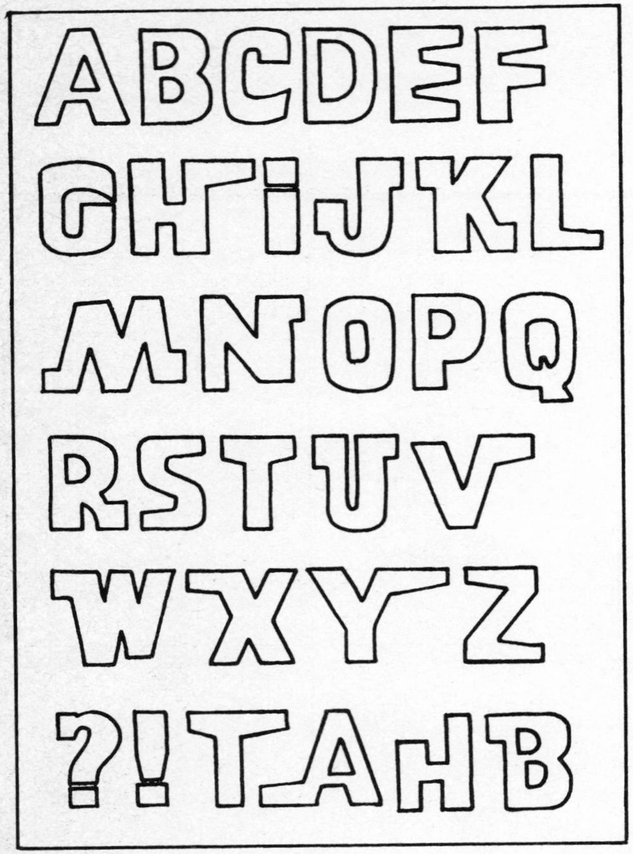

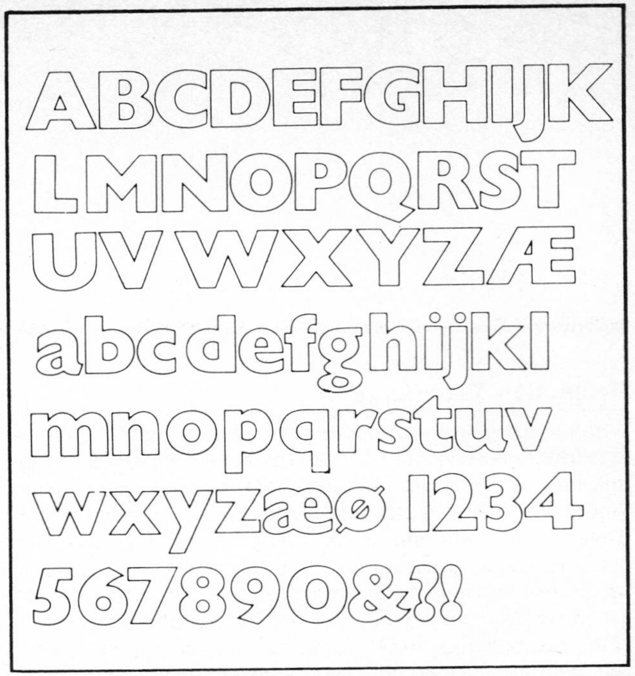

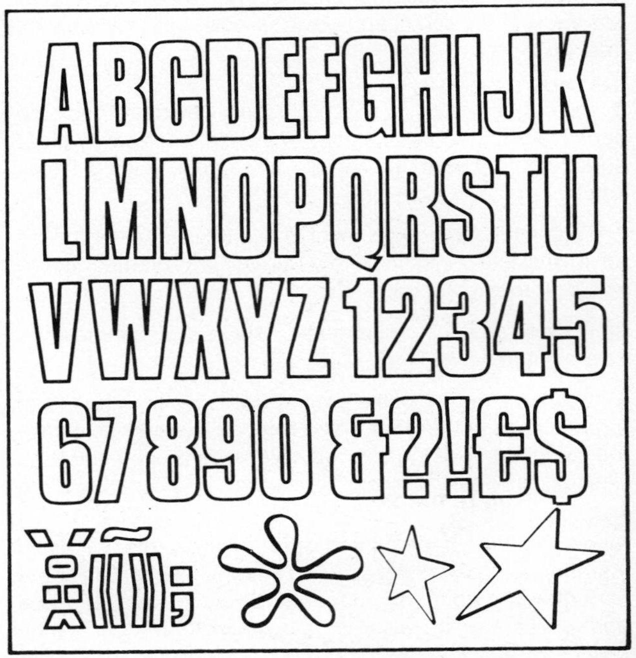

Here are five sets of letters and symbols for use in making super-size letters by the grid or projection technique. The letters may be traced, projected, or photocopied directly from the sheet. Xerox or similar photocopy method may be used to make duplicate copies of letters for preparing art or originals for transparencies, charts, and other visual media requiring paste-up letters.

LETTERGUIDE LETTERING SYSTEM

The Letterguide system consists of a precision-engineered mechanical lettering scriber, lettering templates with typographical faces and alphabets engraved in plastic, and a variety of lettering accessories. Over 500 different templates are available in a variety of type faces. Sizes range from 3/16 up to 3/4 inch in most styles and up to 2 full inches in several styles. The scriber is calibrated so that with a single adjustment letters can be enlarged (height), reduced, and slanted from just one template. The templates are designed to align horizontally with a T square or straightedge.

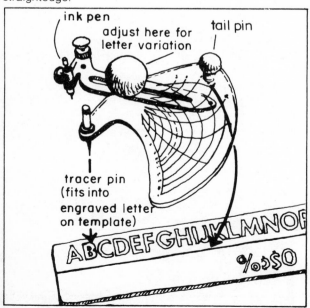

ink pen

adjust here for letter variation

tail pin

tracer pin (fits into engraved letter on template)

ABCDEFGHIJKLMNOP
%¢$0

Accessories

INK PEN

For ink lettering on paper, cardboard, acetate, etc.

RESERVOIR PEN

A fountain-type pen holding a large supply of ink which will last for weeks. Pen is also used for fill-in work.

BALL POINT PEN-STYLUS

For lettering on paper, cardboard, stencil units, and spirit masters.

LEAD CLUTCH

For pencil lettering and direct lettering on paper offset masters when equipped with reproducing lead.

SILK SCREEN KNIFE

For cutting silk screen direct from outline templates (open letters).

SWIVEL KNIFE

Cuts all types of silk screen film, color and texture adhesive sheets, and thin stencil papers from outline templates.

Instructions

See page 56 for "Preparation of Working Surface for Lettering." See page 57 for "Letter and Word Spacing, Alignment, and Special Effects."

1 Position the template on the lettering surface and next to the T square. A Cam-lock T square is illustrated here.

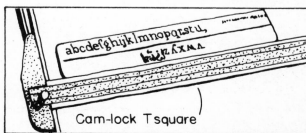

abcdefghijklmnopqrstu,
wxyz ÁXMA

Cam-lock T square

2 Insert the desired imaging accessories in the scriber, and adjust the scriber for letter size and degree of slant (if slant is desired). If the ink pen is used, fill pen with India ink

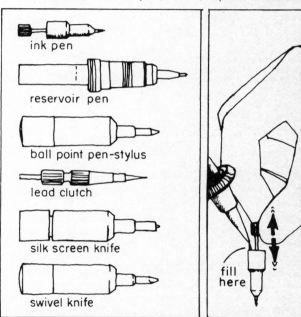

ink pen

reservoir pen

ball point pen-stylus

lead clutch

silk screen knife

swivel knife

fill here

as illustrated. To start the ink flowing, gently work the cleaning pen up and down.

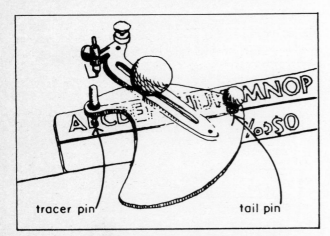

tracer pin   tail pin

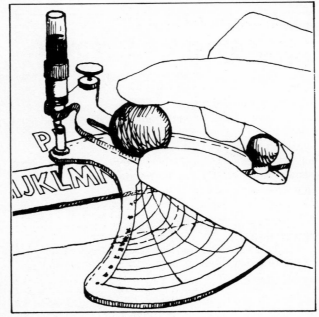

3 To letter, set the tail pin of the scriber in the center black groove of the template; set the tracer pin in far left point of the first letter and move both template and scriber along the T square to position for start of lettering. It is suggested that the scriber be tilted back from the lettering surface while moving from one letter to another. For the first letter, hold the template in place with the left hand and trace the letter with the right hand. Left-handers can experiment with inverting both the template and scriber under the lower edge of the T square and operate the scriber with the left hand. For the next and remaining letters, slightly raise the scriber (leaving the tail pin in the black center groove), slide the template to position the next letter, and repeat the instructions for the first letter.

Send for the free Letterguide catalog; it's full of ideas for using the Letterguide system.

TRY IT UNDER
SHADOW
VERTICAL
FAST
ION
VOGUE
STYLE
reverse
EASY

special effects
with Letterguide

VARIGRAPH LETTERING SYSTEM

The Varigraph lettering system was developed primarily for the production of display typography for photographic reproduction processes such as offset printing and letter press. However, because of its versatility and increased popularity, it is now used for many additional applications such as silk-screen printing; chart, graph , map, and diagram work; posters overhead projection transparencies; television, motion picture, filmstrip, and slide titles; certificates; diplomas and related engrossing work; displays; and exhibits.

The Varigraph system is made up of a compact, precision-built, mechanical typesetting instrument (7 by 7 by 1½ inches), a metal matrix (lettering template), and a pen (standard or reservoir), or pencil attachment .

Two models of instruments are available; one which produces vertical letters and another which produces back-slant or italic letters (italic model) from a standard Varigraph matrix. There are over 200 matrixes which make possible hundreds of sizes and shapes of type from 14 to 72 points. Here are a few of the many letter styles.

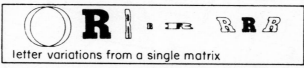

A Single Alphabet *SLANTS* THEM ALL BIG SMALL SQUAT TALL Many Type *STYLES*

R letter variations from a single matrix

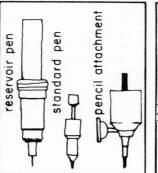

reservoir pen   standard pen   pencil attachment

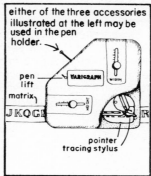

either of the three accessories illustrated at the left may be used in the pen holder.

pen lift
matrix
pointer tracing stylus

Instructions

A good T square or straightedge is most essential in that the Varigraph instrument has to move from letter to letter; it is also used for achieving parallel lines of lettering. The Boardlock T square has been designed especially for the Varigraph instrument and similar lettering systems.

1 For right-hand operation (tracing stylus in lower right corner), slide the matrix under the instrument from the left side, being certain that it goes between the supporting feet which receive the matrix, and retain it with the instrument.

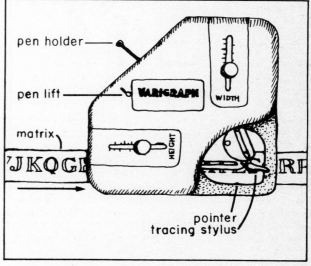

pen holder
pen lift
matrix
VARIGRAPH
WIDTH
HEIGHT
pointer tracing stylus

For left-hand operation (tracing stylus in lower left corner), slide the matrix in the instrument the same as for right hand operation.

While holding the instrument stationary with the left hand, slide the matrix with the right hand to position the desired letter in front of the pointer on the base of the instrument. With the right hand, position the tracing stylus in the groove at a point in the extreme left side of the letter. Apply only a

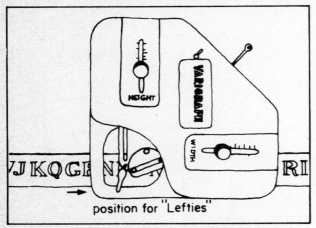

position for "Lefties"

very slight pressure on the tracing stylus, but do not allow it to come out of the letter groove before completing all the remaining instructions.

the movements of the pen are controlled by the tracing stylus

2 Observe the position of the pen, and slide the instrument with the left hand until the pen hovers over the point at which the left side of the letter is to begin. The tracing stylus must be held lightly in the groove so that the matrix will move along with the instrument and the desired letter will remain in the proper tracing position.

3 With the index finger of the left hand, push the pen lift fully forward to lower the pen. Begin tracing immediately after the pen touches the paper. Trace around the letter just once. If the pen does not write, retract the pen and raise the cleaning pin slightly up and down once or twice to start the ink flowing. Retrace the letter according to the foregoing instructions. Repeat these steps for each of the remaining letters.

TAPE EMBOSSING MACHINE

INSTANT-PRINT LETTERING SYSTEM

A letter-printing machine for producing letters, numbers, and symbols on pressure-sensitive plastic, metal or 3M Brand magnetic tape. Assorted letter styles, sizes and colors are available. Tape widths range from ½- to 1- inch. Standard or optimum spacing, vertical or horizontal, reverse, and special-character embossing wheels are available for some makes and models of embossing machines. Uses include name tags, signs, equipment labeling, exhibit and display lettering, and other visual media requiring embossed-type lettering.

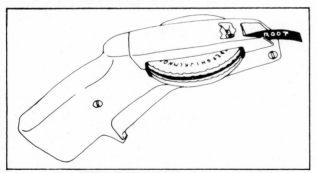

Sample Letter Styles

The Instant-Print Lettering System represents a unique departure from conventional methods of hand, dry transfer, mechanical tracing and cold typesetting for many applications. This lettering system produces instant dry carbon letters in color (black, white, red or blue) on a polyester-based tape. No chemical or processing is required. The tape has a matte finish on one side and is pressure-sensitive. The 3M Brand Promat system prints both positive and negative image letters simultaneously. Tapes are available in translucent, opaque white, and opaque black (for reverses). Currently, numerous style letters

MICROGRAMMA
FUTURA MED. HELVETICA
SCHOOLBOOK MICROFONT
UNIVERS LIGHT COND. *FLASH*
GOTHIC EXTRA COND. GOTHIC
UNIVERS MED. COND.

are available in sizes ranging from 8 to 36 points. Uses include overhead transparencies and masters (originals), labels, name plates, charts, graphs, maps, etc. Printed tapes are applied directly to the selected surface.

Instructions

See page 56 for "Preparation Of Working Surface for Lettering." See the "Lettering Selection Chart" on page 54 for instant-print lettering applications.

pressure-sensitive tape with letters

paper backing

1 With the desired letter font locked into the machine, letters are made at the touch of a button. Letter spacing and word alignment are automatic.

2 The printed tape is then removed from the machine, the backing peeled away, and the lettered tape adhered to most any surface.

The Bulletin typewriter, or Primary typewriter as it is sometimes called, is a "natural" for providing large-size type (letters) for the preparation of overhead projection transparencies, slide titles, scripts for public speakers and exhibits and display captions, and can be used wherever large typewriter type can be the answer. This typewriter produces letters, in a variety of type faces, up to ¼ inch high.

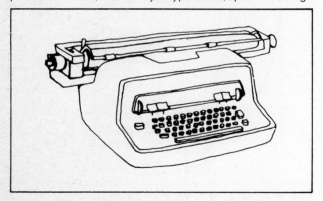

Carbon ribbons produce the best type impressions, especially for the preparation of original for thermocopy or diazo reproduction. The type faces shown here are available from Royal Typewriter Company and SCM Corporation. The IBM Selectric typewriter system has several type faces suitable for large-type uses. ◗

stencil unit

spirit master

UNITED WE STAND

CAT FAMILY

GRAPHIC SYMBOLS

MATH GAMES

slide / filmstrip art

thermocopy originals

CARTOON TYPE
ROYAL TYPE NO.104

**BULLETIN TYPE
ROYAL TYPE NO.102**

LARGE VOGUE
Royal Type #120

Basic Writing
Basic Writing No.67

RUBBER STAMP PRINTING

Rubber stamp printing provides a neat, inexpensive method for printing such things as charts, graphs, maps, flash cards, nameplates, posters and signs. Basic to rubber stamp printing is the rubber stamp itself. A rubber type

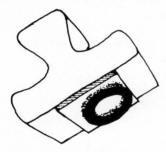

(letter) is securely cemented to an indexed wooden molding made to rigid specifications. A complete printing set, such as the one illustrated, includes rubber stamp type,

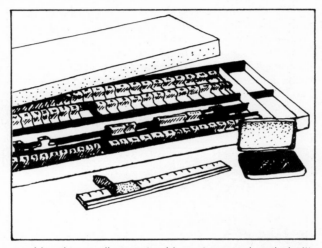

a guide ruler, an alignment guide, a stamp pad, and a bottle of black ink and applicator. Some typical type faces are illustrated.

Sample Letter Styles

Picture language rubber stamps add another exciting dimension to this printing method.

available from Summit Industries

available from Universal Four

Instructions

See page 56 for "Preparation of Working Surface for Lettering." See page 57 for "Letter and Word Spacing, Alignment, and Special Effects."

1 Position the guide ruler and aligning guide against a T square or straightedge as illustrated. For special effects in printing, refer to the special effects illustrated here and to the pages indicated above.

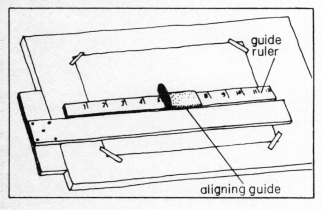

guide ruler

aligning guide

2 Ink the first letter stamp on the stamp pad, and position the bottom portion next to the guide ruler and against the metal aligning guide; this will assure a straight letter impression. Make certain the **dot** on the stamp is at the lower right of the letter. Move the stamp and aligning guide along the ruler to the place on the surface where the impression is to be made. Make certain the stamp is tilted away from the surface to prevent the letter from making an impression before it is properly located. Hold the ruler and aligning guide in place with the left hand.

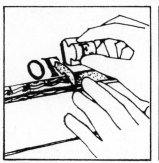

3 Press the stamp on the surface with a "rocking" motion. This will ensure a complete letter impression.

4 Print the second letter and remaining letters by moving the selected stamp and aligning guide to the next letter position and repeating steps 2 and 3.

HELPFUL TIPS

1 Keep type clean with a mild detergent and warm water.

2 To add color, simply select another color ink pad.

special effects suggestions:

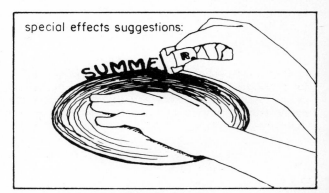

SUMMER

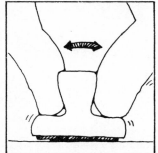

VICTORY

irregular curve

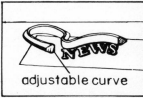

NEWS

adjustable curve

82

FLATBED PRINTING MACHINE

EMBOSOGRAF SIGNMAKER

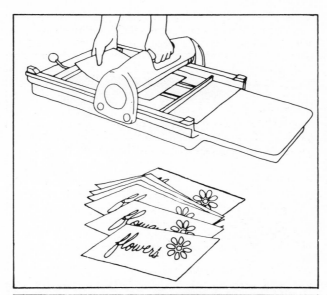

For producing just one or hundreds-of-a-kind posters, signs, etc., this flatbed printing machine offers a combination of speed, simplicity, versatility and economy. The machine offers complete freedom of layout, color and type selection. Printing can be done with metal or wood plates as well as type with equal agility on paper, cardboard, acetate, Scotchlite, magnetic sheeting or practically any surface up to ¼ inch thick. Two or more colors can be printed at the same time.

There are models available for producing printed materials up to 30-by 44-inches. Letters up to 4 inches high in assorted styles add to the versatility of this printing method.

The Embosograf Signmaker will produce embossed and die-cut letters for signs and other visual media on plastic, aluminum, and cardboard. Signs and other visual media can range in height from 4 to 12 inches and lengths up to 8 feet long.

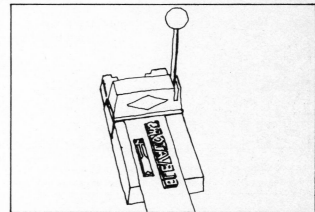

Embossed-Type Lettering

The Embosograf Signmaker will produce embossed-type letters on plastic, aluminum, and cardboard. Here is how the Signmaker works:

1 Select and set the metal type on the setup plate of the machine.

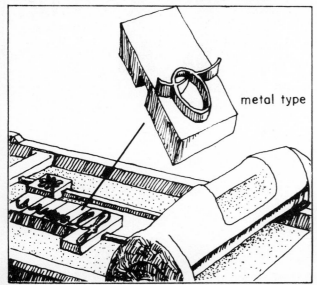

metal type

Barclay **B**
DELPHIA **PUEBLO BOLD**
AMERICANA *Brush*
B Flair
B **BALLOON** ❁

Sample Letter Styles

2 Place the color "top paper" over the type with the color side down. This is a special paper for producing letters in color.

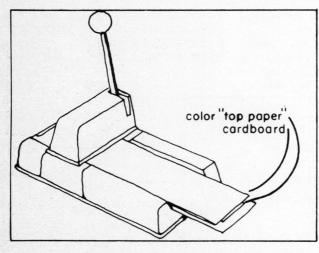

3 Lay the sign cardboard face down over the type and top paper, and push the setup plate under the pressure area. Pull down the side lever causing the type to emboss the top paper into the cardboard.

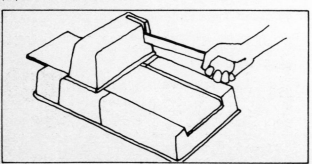

4 Pull the setup plate out, and pick up the cardboard. Remove any excess top paper. Repeat steps 2, 3, and 4 for duplicate signs.

Die-Cut Letters

The Signmaker will produce die-cut letters from Embosograf magnetic sheeting material (15 to 20 mils thick) and from Embosograf polyethylene foam material. The magnetic material may be painted any color and is for use on magnetic boards or other suitable surfaces. The foam material comes in color with a pressure-sensitive adhesive backing for easy application to most surfaces.

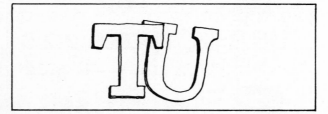

SPECIAL CREATIVE SERVICE
Embosograf will help you create your own effective signs and other similar media—there is no charge unless extensive artwork is required—just write them.

Sample Letter Styles

REYNOLDS/LETERON AUTOMATIC LETTER-ING SYSTEM

Here is a new and exciting lettering system from Reynolds/Leteron Company that produces pressure-sensitive-backed letters, words, and sentences **in sequence** for both indoor and outdoor lettering. The system

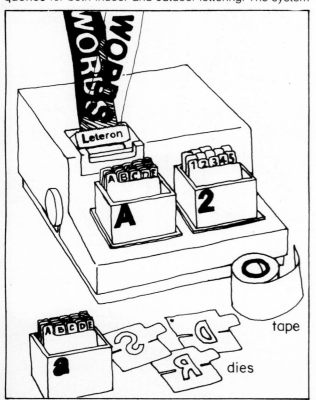

tape

dies

includes a manual or electric die-cutting machine, cutting dies, and Letertape (0.003-inch acrylic material).

At present, letters are available in a wide choice of styles and sizes. Letter range in height from 5/16 to 1 1/2 inches (22 to 108 points). The tapes from which letters are cut come in eight colors.

Here is how Leteron works:

1 Drop the Letertype die in the slot. Press the actuator for each letter or character.

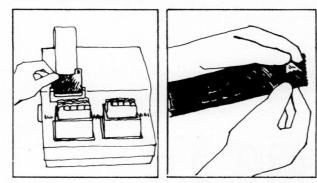

2 Remove the tape from the machine.

3 Separate the transparent carrier (letters attached) from the tape.

4 Position the letters on the surface intended.

5 Remove the carrier from the mounted letters.

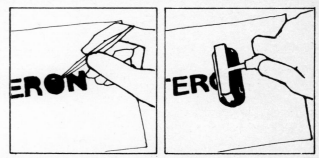

6 Remove the "centers" with tweezers or the tip of a cutting knife.

7 Roll the letters down for complete adhesion.

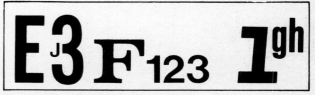

Sample Letter Styles

Refer to page 54, "Lettering Selection Chart" for recommended uses.

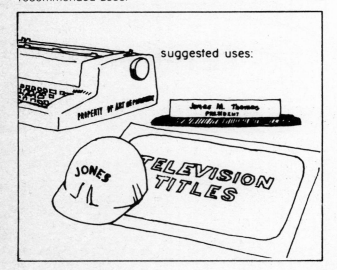

suggested uses:

Dry transfer lettering, known also as PRESS-ON, RUB-ON, and TRANSFER TYPE, is considered to be one of the most modern lettering techniques available today. The letters, made up of carbon and wax, are printed on a plastic, acetate, or polyethelene carrier sheet. Letters transfer to virtually any dry surface such as paper, wood, metal, or glass by rubbing over the letter with a dull pencil, ball-point pen or a special burnisher designed for dry transfer lettering. Dry transfer letters are available in black, white, and a variety of colors. They are also available in transparent colors for use on acetate surfaces. For artwork intended for heat-producing reproduction equipemnt, heat-resistant dry transfer letters are recommended. For recommended applications of dry transfer letters, refer to the LETTERING SELECTION CHART on page 54 .

Sample Letter Styles

Lettering on Opaque Surfaces

When lettering on opaque surfaces (paper, cardboard, metal, etc.), here are basic instructions:

1 Draw a light pencil line on the surface to which lettering is to be transferred. Remove the protective backing sheet and position the desired letter, using the alignment marks located under the letter or at the beginning and end of each row.

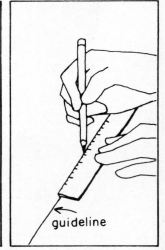

2 Rub lightly over the first letter with a dull pencil, ball point pen or burnisher. Do not use more pressure than is necessary to transfer the letter. Hold the carrier sheet firmly in position during burnishing to avoid cracking the letter. A broad ended burnisher should be used for large letters.

3 Carefully lift away the carrier sheet, making certain the entire letter has been transferred to the receiving surface. Repeat until your word or phrase is complete. For letter and word spacing, alignment, and special effects, see page 57.

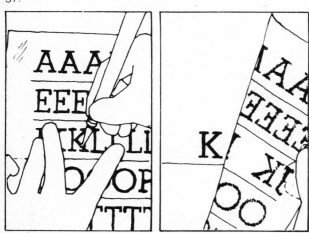

4 To ensure permanence and secure placement, place the protective backing sheet over the transferred letters, hold in position and burnish firmly the entire area with a blunt instrument such as the flat end of a burnisher. To remove the guideline, place a sheet of paper over the letters and erase the guideline with a soft pencil eraser.

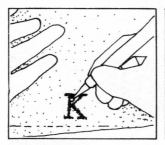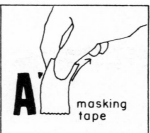

CORRECTIONS

To remove letters from paper or other soft surfaces, lay a piece of adhesive tape over the letter, rub very lightly, then peel off. On hard surfaces such as glass, acetate or metal, adhesive tape can be used. When removing one letter that is in close proximity to another, mask off the rest of the letters by cutting a hole in the backing sheet and laying this hole over the faulty letter before applying the tape. Large-size letters can easily be removed by applying a light coat of rubber cement thinner to the letter prior to removing with tape. CORRECTIONS SHOULD BE MADE BEFORE FINAL BACKING SHEET BURNISHING.

PROTECTION

Under normal handling and copying conditions, lettering needs no further protection if instructions are followed. Letters that are exposed to outside conditions such as signs, posters, etc., should be sprayed with several coats of clear acrylic or plastic spray. Spray lightly at first and let dry. Avoid applying a heavy coat of spray.

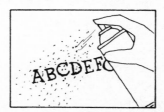

Lettering on Acetate Surfaces

When lettering on acetate surfaces (clear or matte acetates), transparent color letters are recommended as they are designed for application to these surfaces, when projected, bold, vivid colors result. Transparent dry transfer letters are transferred like regular dry transfer letters. Guidelines can either be drawn directly on the acetate with marking pencil or removable ink nylon point pen, or the acetate can be positioned over a separate sheet of paper that has been guidelined. Grid paper can also be used under the acetate. Instructions for transferring transparent color letters are the same as for regular dry transfer letters.

Composition adhesive-type is another form of paste-up letter consisting of multiple alphabets printed on a thin acetate sheet with a pressure-sensitive adhesive or wax backing. The printing is usually on the adhesive side. Each letter is carefully cut with a razor blade or similar cutting tool, aligned on the artwork, and then burnished down to form the word desired. The printed lines between and underneath individual letters provide for ease of alignment and standard letter spacing of copy. Guidelines are removed when word composition is completed. For diazo or other heat-generating copying systems, the adhesive-backed rather than the wax-backed type should be used in that the wax-backed type will melt at high temperatures. A heat-resistant type is available from a number of manufacturers.

In addition to alphabets in a wide variety of sizes and styles, common phrases, borders, symbols, etc., are also available. For applications of Composition Adhesive Type, see LETTERING SELECTION CHART on page 54 .

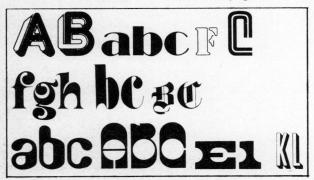

Instructions for Standard Typesetting

Important to good lettering is the preparation of the working surface for lettering, see page   56 . For letter and word spacing, alignment, and special effects see page 57 .

1 Draw a light-blue guideline (nonreproducing or light-blue pencil) on the lettering surface with a T square or straightedge. The guideline distance is determined by the printed guideline on the letter sheet. If the lettering is to be done on acetate, draw the guideline with a marking pencil directly on the acetate.

2 Cut lightly (not cutting through the backing sheet) around the desired letter, including the printed guideline below it, with a cutting knife, sharp stylus, or razor blade. Insert the point of the cutting tool under the letter, press the letter lightly against the point of the tool, and lift it away from the backing sheet.

3 Position the letter with the printed guideline in register with the guideline on the artwork, and press into place. Burnish lightly with a burnisher so that changes can be made before final burnishing. Repeat this step for each letter until the assembly is complete. Letter or words can be carefully lifted and repositioned as desired. See also instructions for using type-setting aids for straight and circular setting.

4 When the assembly is completed and corrections have been made, burnish firmly the upper portion of the letters. Cut away the guidelines and complete burnishing. Erase the pencil guideline. The finished assembly is now ready for sharp clear reproduction.

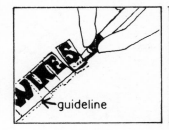

←guideline

Instructions for Typesetting Aids

For straight-line type setting, a typesetting aid can be made out of a 6- by 2½-inch piece of thin cardboard or plastic. FORMATT has a HEADLINE-SETTER (usually free) designed for straight-line setting. Simply draw a guideline on the card as illustrated. Here is how this aid is used:

1 Position the guideline underneath the letter and over the line which is along the edge of the type-setting aid.

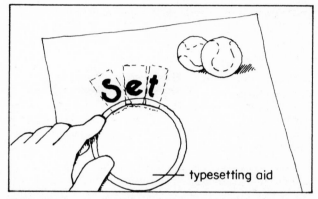

typesetting aid

2 Move the complete word or headline (after setting) into the proper position on surface to which lettering is to be placed. Follow the instructions covered by Step 4 of the instructions for standard type setting. For circular type set-

typesetting aid

ting, make a circular cut-out of thin cardboard and with a compass, draw s guideline close to the edge as illustrated. Follow the instructions for using the straight-line typesetting aid. ◼

Selected publications and audiovisual media have been annotated and sourced here to supplement the contents of this section. The figures in parentheses at the end of each entry (O8) indicate the coded address source for the procurement of the reference. Complete addresses are listed under *OUT-OF-TOWN* sources at the end of this section.

Biegeleisen, J. J. : DESIGN AND PRINT YOUR OWN POSTERS, Watson-Guptill.
Covers layout, hand lettering techniques, sample alphabets, equipment, color, and printing. (O59)

Cataldo, John W.: LETTERING: A GUIDE FOR TEACHERS, Davis Publications, 1974.
Treats the evolution of letter forms and symbols with basic strokes clearly explained and illustrated. (O10)

Gates, David: LETTERING FOR REPRODUCTION, Watson-Guptill, 1969.
Contains step-by-step techniques covering proportions, letter spacing, laying out and inking all styles of lettering, and useful production tricks. (O59)

Leach, Mortimer: LETTERING FOR ADVERTISING, Van Nostrand Reinhold, 1975.
A modern treatment of lettering techniques and aids for advertising. (O57)

LETTERING TECHNIQUES, University of Texas at Austin, 1965.
A booklet covering lettering techniques and aids for the preparation of visual media. (O52)

McDonald, Byron J.: THE ART OF LETTERING: THE BROAD PEN, Pentalic, 1966.
A how-to-do-it book on lettering with the broad pen. (O39)

Mann, William: LETTERING AND LETTER DISPLAY, Van Nostrand Reinhold, 1974.
Graphic treatment of lettering as applied to displays. (O57)

Minor, Ed, and Harvey Frye: TECHNIQUES FOR PRODUCING VISUAL INSTRUCTIONAL MEDIA, McGraw-Hill, 1977.
Contains a comprehensive section on 30 lettering techniques and aids. (O33)

LETTERING, *35mm filmstrip, sound, color, Doubleday Multimedia, 1970.*
Discusses the various types of lettering and describes some of the common errors of the beginning mechanical artist. Depicts the correct size, shape, and proportion of lettering. (O12)

LETTERING INSTRUCTIONAL MATERIALS, *16mm film, twenty minutes, sound, b and w or color, Indiana University, 1955.*
Easy-to-use lettering equipment for lettering on signs, posters, bulletin boards, displays, and materials for projection. (O25)

LETTERING: SKILL DEVELOPMENT, *35mm filmstrip, 52 frames, sound, color, Educational Media, 1967.*
Explains simple lettering techniques. Explores the use of stencils spray paints, lettering fonts, lettering standards, and other lettering devices. (O14)

LETTERING: WIRE BRUSH LETTERING EQUIPMENT, *35mm filmstrip, 38 frames, sound, color, Educational Media, 1967.*
Exhibits applications for and use of pen and guide lettering sets. Details such as pen and guide sizes and styles, felt-pen sets, and step-by-step processes of use are explained. (O14)

Most of the equipment and materials included in this section are available from local sources; such sources are indicated (L), and can be located in the *Yellow Pages* of the telephone directory.

Items not readily available locally can be purchased directly, or purchase information obtained from the sources indicated (O)

CARDBOARD LETTERS (adhesive back) (L1, O22, O36)
CARDBOARD LETTERS (gummed back) (L1, O5, O22, O50)
CARDBOARD LETTERS (plain back) (L1, L7, O5, O50)
BULLETIN TYPEWRITERS (L5, O38, O42, O44)
CARD-TYPE STENCIL LETTER GUIDES (L1, L4, L7, O1, O4, O5, O16, O54)
COMPOSITION ADHESIVE-TYPE LETTERS (L1, L4, O3, O19, O61)
CONSTRUCTION PAPER LETTERS (L1, L7, O4, O23, O36, O50)
DRY TRANSFER LETTERS (L1, L4, L7, O3, O28, O61)
EMBOSOGRAF LETTERING SYSTEM (O15)
FLATBED PRINTING MACHINES (L1, O35, O46, O47)
GUMMED PAPER LETTERS (L1, L7, O50, O51)
INDIVIDUAL CARDBOARD LETTER GUIDES (L1, L3, L7, O1, O5)
INDIVIDUAL METAL LETTER GUIDES (L1, L3, O30)
INSTANT-PRINT LETTERING SYSTEMS (L2, O6, O27, O40, O53)
LETTERGUIDE LETTERING SYSTEM (L1, L4, O29)
MAGNETIC-BACKED LETTERS (L2, O9)
METAL INTERLOCKING LETTER GUIDES (L1, L3, O5, O43)
MITTEN DISPLAY LETTERS (L1, L6, L7, O34)
PICTURE RUBBER STAMPS (O7, O48, O56)
PLASTIC INTERLOCKING LETTER GUIDES (L1, L3, O16)
PLEXIGLAS LETTERS (L3, O5)
REYNOLDS/LETERON LETTERING SYSTEM L1, O41)
RUBBER STAMP PRINTING SETS (L7, O4, O23, O43)
SPRAY-ON LETTERS (L1, L3, O2, O5, O11, O22, O49)
STENCIL AND SPIRIT DUPLICATION LETTER GUIDES (L1, L5, L7, O4, O17, O23)
STENCIL LETTER CUTTING MACHINES (O32, O43)
STYROFOAM LETTERS (L1, L3, O5)
TRACING LETTERS (O26, O55)
VELCRO-BACKED LETTERS (L2, O21, O37)
VINYL PLASTIC LETTERS (L1, L7, O16, O18, O45)
WOOD AND METAL LETTERS (L1, L3, L7, O5)
WRICO SIGN-MAKER LETTERING SYSTEM (L1, L4, O60)

Addresses

LOCAL SOURCES (See Yellow Pages)

L1 - Artists' Materials and Supply Stores
L2 - Audio-Visual Equipment and Supply Stores
L3 - Building and Hardware Supply Stores
L4 - Drafting Equipment and Supply Stores
L5 - Duplicating Equipment and Supply Stores
L6 - Photographic Equipment and Supply Stores
L7 - Stationers' Stores

OUT-OF-TOWN SOURCES

O1 - ALVIN & CO., P. O. Box 188, Windsor, CT 06095

O2 - AMERICAN JET SPRAY INDUSTRIES, INC., P. O. Box 14006, Denver, CO 80214

O3 - ARTYPE, INC., 345 Terra Cotta Ave., Crystal Lake, IL 60014

O4 - BECKLEY-CARDY CO., 1900 N. Narragansett, Chicago, IL 60639

O5 - DICK BLICK, P. O. Box 1267, Galesburg, IL 61401

O6 - W. H. BRADY CO., P. O. Box 571, Milwaukee, WI 53201

O7 - CENTER ENTERPRISES, P. O. Box 1361, Hartford, CT 06101

O8 - CHARTPAK, One River Rd., Leeds, MA 01053

O9 - CLARIDGE PRODUCTS AND EQUIPMENT, INC., Harrison, AR 72601

O10 - DAVIS PUBLICATIONS, 50 Portland St., Worcester, MA 01608

O11 - DEWEY-CARTER CO., P. O. Box 822, Doylestown, PA 18901

O12 - DOUBLEDAY MULTIMEDIA, P. O. Box C-19518, Santa Ana, CA 92705

O13 - EBERHARD FABER, Crestwood Rd. 3, Wilkes-Barre, PA 18703

O14 - EDUCATIONAL MEDIA LABS, 4101 S. Congress Ave., Austin, TX 78745

O15 - EMBOSOGRAF CORP. OF AMERICA, 38 W. 21st st., New York, NY 10010

O16 - E-Z LETTER-QUIK STIK CO., P. O. Box 829, Westminster, MD 21157

O17 - GESTETNER CORP., Gestetner Park, Yonkers, NY 10703

O18 - GRAPHICA INTERNATIONAL, 1936 Euclid Ave., Cleveland, OH 44115

O19 - GRAPHIC PRODUCTS CORP., 3601 Edison Pl., Rolling Meadows, IL 60008

O20 - HEYER, INC., 1850 S. Kostner Ave., Chicago, IL 60623

O21 - THE HIGHSMITH CO., INC., Box 25, Fort Atkinson, WI 53538

O22 - THE HOLES-WEBWAY CO., Webway Park, St. Cloud, MN 56301

O23 - HORDER'S STATIONERY STORES, INC., 321 S. Jefferson St., Chicago, IL 60606

O24 - HOWARD HUNT PEN CO., Advertising Dept., 7th and State St., Camden, NJ 08101

O25 - INDIANA UNIVERSITY, Audio-Visual Center, Bloomington, IN 47401

O26 - KENWORTHY EDUCATIONAL SERVICES, INC., P.O. Box 3031, Buffalo, NY 14205

O27 - KROY INDUSTRIES, INC., Graphic Systems Div., P. O. Box 269, Stillwater, MN 55082

O28 - LETRASET USA, INC., 33 New Bridge Rd., Bergenfield, NJ 07621

O29 - LETTERGUIDE CO., INC., P. O. Box 30203, Lincoln, NE 68503

O30 - LEWIS ARTIST SUPPLY CO., 6408 Woodward Ave., Detroit, MI 48202

O31 - MAGNA VISUAL, INC., 1200 North Rock Hill Rd., St. Louis, MO 63124

O32 - MARSH STENCIL, 707 E. B St., Belleville, IL 62222

O33 - McGRAW-HILL BOOK CO., 1221 Avenue of the Americas, New York, NY 10020

O34 - MITTEN DESIGNER LETTERS, Mitten Bldg., Redlands, CA 92373

O35 - THE MORGAN SIGN MACHINE CO., 4510 N. Ravenswood Ave., Chicago, IL 60640

O36 - MUTUAL EDUCATION AIDS, 1924 Hillhurst Ave., Los Angeles, CA 90027

O37 - OHIO FLOCK-COTE CO., INC., 13229 Shaw Ave., East Cleveland, OH 44112

O38 - OLIVETTI CORP. OF AMERICA, 500 Park Ave., New York, NY 10022

O39 - PENTALIC CORP., 132 W. 22nd St., New York, NY 10011

O40 - PIERCE DIVISION, 6238 Oasis Ave., North Stillwater, MN 55082

O41 - REYNOLDS/LETERON CO., 9830 San Fernando Rd., Pacoima, CA 91331

O42 - ROYAL TYPEWRITER CO., INC., 850 Third Ave., New York, NY 10001

O43 - SALT LAKE STAMP CO., 380 West 2nd South, Salt Lake City, UT 84101

O44 - SCM CORP., 299 Park Ave., New York, NY 10017

O45 - SETON NAME PLATE CORP., 592 Blvd., New Haven, CT 06505

O46 - SHOWCARD MACHINE CO., 320 West Ohio St., Chicago, IL 60610

O47 - THE SIGNPRESS CO., P. O. Box 1267, Galesburg, IL 61401

O48 - SOUTHPORT GRADING STAMPS, P. O. Box 512, Southport, CT 06490

O49 - SPRAYWAY, INC., 484 Visto Ave., Addison, IL 60101

O50 - STIK-A-LETTER CO., 1787 S. Iris Lane, Escondido, CA 92026

O51 - TABLET & TICKET CO., 1021 W. Adams St., Chicago, IL 60607

O52 - THE UNIVERSITY OF TEXAS at Austin, Instructional Media Center, Drawer W., University Station, Austin, TX 78712

O53 - 3M COMPANY, Promat Project, 3M Center, St. Paul, MI 55101

O54 - TIME SAVINGS SPECIALTIES, 2922 Bryant Ave., South Minneapolis, MN 55408

O55 - TREND ENTERPRISES, INC., P. O. Box 3073, St. Paul MN 55165

O56 - UNIVERSAL FOUR, INC., 430 North Scoville Ave., Oak Park, IL 60302

O57 - VAN NOSTRAND REINHOLD CO., 300 Pike St., Cincinnati, OH 45202

O58 - VARIGRAPH, INC., P. O. Box 690, Madison, WI 53701

O59 - WATSON-GUPTILL PUBLICATIONS, 1 Astor Plaza, New York, NY 10036

O60 - WOOD-REGAN INSTRUMENT CO., INC., 184 Franklin Ave., Nutley, NJ 07110

O61 - ZIPATONE, INC., 150 Fencl Lane, Hillside, IL 60162

mounting and laminating images

Most visual media, at one stage or another, require some form of mounting or laminating. Mounting could simply involve attaching one surface to another, such as mounting paper on cardboard. More complicated mounting could involve mounting paper on cloth or metal. Mounting adhesives come in an interesting assortment of forms; liquids, solids, sprays, and tissues. Laminating, as used in this section, makes use of cold and heat laminating acetates.

This section includes illustrated instructions for some of the most modern mounting and laminating techniques and aids available today. The Mounting and Laminating Selection Chart on page 94 has been designed to make the problem of technique or aid selection easy.

Sources for print and nonprint materials, and for equipment and materials are listed at the end of this section.

 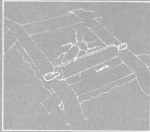

MOUNTING AND LAMINATING SELECTION CHART

This chart is designed to aid in the selection of appropriate mounting and laminating techniques and aids for visual media. The left portion of the chart lists surfaces that can be mounted or laminated together. The selection symbols ● indicate mounting or laminating recommended. Page references for mounting and laminating techniques are also listed.

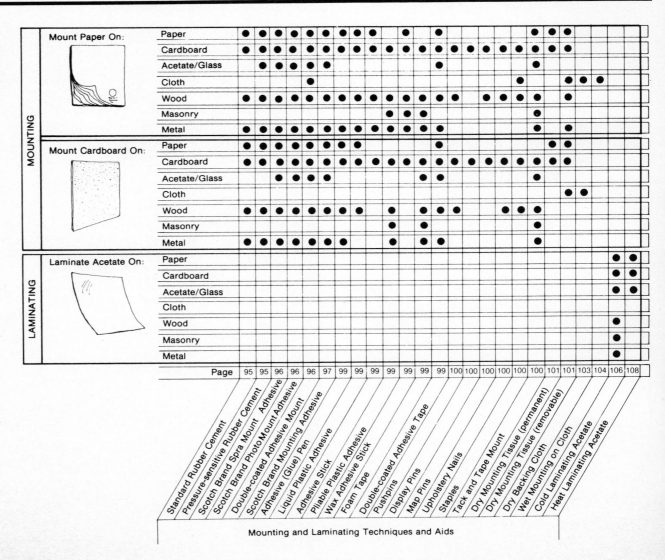

MOUNTING

Mount Paper On: Paper, Cardboard, Acetate/Glass, Cloth, Wood, Masonry, Metal

Mount Cardboard On: Paper, Cardboard, Acetate/Glass, Cloth, Wood, Masonry, Metal

LAMINATING

Laminate Acetate On: Paper, Cardboard, Acetate/Glass, Cloth, Wood, Masonry, Metal

Page: 95 95 96 96 96 97 99 99 99 99 99 99 99 99 100 100 100 100 100 100 101 101 103 104 106 108

Mounting and Laminating Techniques and Aids:
Standard Rubber Cement · Pressure-sensitive Rubber Cement · Scotch Brand Spra Mount Adhesive · Scotch Brand PhotoMount Adhesive · Double-coated Adhesive Mount · Scotch Brand Mounting Adhesive · Adhesive (Glue) Pen · Liquid Plastic Adhesive · Adhesive Stick · Pliable Plastic Adhesive · Wax Adhesive Stick · Foam Tape · Double-coated Adhesive Tape · Pushpins · Display Pins · Map Pins · Upholstery Nails · Staples · Tack and Tape Mount · Dry Mounting Tissue (permanent) · Dry Mounting Tissue (removable) · Dry Backing Cloth · Wet Mounting on Cloth · Cold Laminating Acetate · Heat Laminating Acetate

94

mounting and laminating images

RUBBER CEMENT MOUNTING

Here is a mounting technique that is quick, easy, and clean. It is ideal for mounting many flat visual media such as photographs, prints, display pieces, and certain precut letters. Standard (regular), pressure-sensitive, and Scotch brand spray-can cement are discussed here.

Standard Rubber Cement

This is still the most popular type of rubber cement used today. To assure good adhesive quality, the cement should be stored in brown bottles and kept away from high temperatures. It should be thinned with rubber cement thinner (solvent) if the cement does not flow freely from the brush used to apply it. Special plastic or glass dispensers with a built-in brush are available. Here are instructions for permanent mounting with rubber cement.

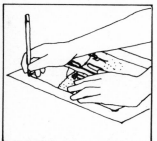 

Before starting the mounting, trim the visual to the desired size. The trimmed visual is then positioned on the mounting board, and a small, light pencil guideline is placed at each corner. A thin, even coat of rubber cement is applied to the back of the visual. This should be done with smooth, even brush strokes, making sure the entire surface is covered. Going back over rubber cement which is not thoroughly dry will cause scuffing and produce a rough surface; the result will be an imperfect mounting.

Apply a coat of rubber cement to the mounting board, extending it slightly beyond the guide marks. Better adhesion will be assured if the brush strokes are at a 90° angle to those used on the back of the visual. Allow the rubber cement to dry. Place two sheets of household wax paper on the cemented surface of the mounting board so they slightly overlap at the center.

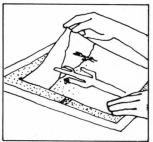 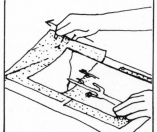

The wax surface prevents the visual from adhering to the mounting board during positioning. Place the visual on the wax paper with corners registered on the guide marks. Firmly hold the lower half of the picture in place as the top sheet of wax paper is withdrawn.

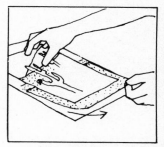 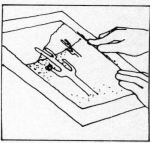

This permits the two rubber-cemented surfaces to come into direct contact with each other. Next, remove the bottom wax sheet.

Finally, smooth down the surface of the visual, starting in the center and working in an outward direction. It is advisable to use a protective sheet of clean paper over the visual to prevent damage to the surface. Often a small rubber roller is used for this purpose. When the visual is firmly mounted, remove excess rubber cement by gently rubbing with a finger along the edges of the visual. A rubber cement eraser can also be used to remove excess cement. Erase the guide marks, and the mounting is completed.

The technique of mounting just described is often referred to as a permanent method. It is not truly a permanent mounting, however. The quality of the rubber cement used, the mounting technique used, and the storage conditions will determine to a great extent how long the mount will last.

Pressure-Sensitive Rubber Cement

Pressure-sensitive rubber cement is a clear, transparent adhesive that requires only one coat to the material to be mounted. It remains "tacky" indefinitely; thus allowing the mounted material to be removed and remounted without applying additional adhesive. Apply a coat of cement to the

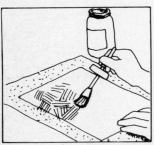

back of the material to be mounted. Let dry for 2 or 3 minutes. Next, press adhesived materials firmly into position; may be removed and remounted without applying additional adhesive. Use recommended thinner for reducing or thinning.

Scotch Brand Spra Mount Adhesive

This is a clear aerosol adhesive that bonds a variety of lightweight materials, yet allows them to be repositioned or removed. Spray one surface for quick, easy mounting. Additional instructions are on the can.

Scotch Brand Photo Mount Adhesive

A strong high-grade adhesive designed for mounting black and white or color photographic prints, including resin-coated papers. Just spray adhesive on the back of material, let dry until "tacky" and press into position. The result is a permanent bond. ■

A quick, easy way to mount drawings, prints, photographs, etc., without heat or liquid adhesives. Indispensable where heat or wet mounting would damage the material to be mounted. This mounting technique involves the use of an

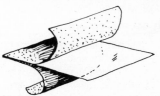

acetate or special sheet with pressure-sensitive adhesive on both sides which bonds on contact with the material to be mounted.

The instructions that follow are for using Falcon Perma/Mount. However, the same basic instructions can be used with other similar products.

1 Peel back the release paper from one side of the card (about halfway), and fold it against the card.

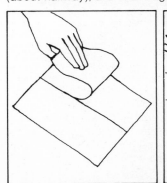

mounting and laminating images

2 Perma/Mount cards are supplied slightly oversize to allow ease in positioning. Leaving a small margin at the top and sides, gently apply the visual to the bare adhesive. Then peel the remainder of the release paper from under the visual and allow the visual to smoothly come in contact with the rest of the card.

3 Press down firmly over the surface of the visual, applying pressure from the center out to the edges.

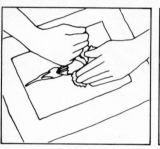

4 Trim the visual to final size using a paper cutter, mat knife, or scissors.

5 Turn the visual over, and remove the release paper from the reverse side of the visual. Try not to touch the exposed adhesive.

6 You are now ready for mounting. Gently place the print on the surface to which the visual is to be mounted in the position desired.

7 *Do not apply any finger pressure to the surface of the visual at this time.* First make sure the visual is accurately positioned on the mount. The position of the visual can still be shifted if necessary by just tapping against the edge of the visual to slide it to the correct position.

8 Now press down firmly over the entire surface of the visual. The card thickness eliminates the problem of air bubbles. Mounting is now complete, and the mounted visual can be handled normally. ▪

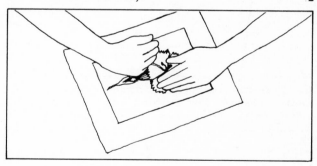

A unique cold mounting adhesive developed by the 3M Company. This permanent adhesive comes in 8-by 10-inch sheets, and is available at most photographic (camera) supply stores. The adhesive unit is made up of two sheets; an adhesive-coated sheet, and a single side, silicone-coated Kraft paper release sheet. Recommended for mounting photographs, posters, signs, paste-ups, etc.

Instructions

1 Place the mounting sheet on a hard, clean working surface. Make certain the release paper (dull surface) is down.

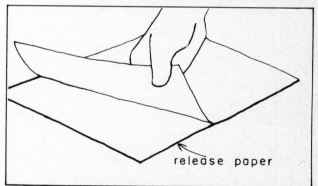

release paper

2 Peel adhesive coated sheet from release paper by scratching up at corner and pulling back. ⋮

3 Place item for mounting face down on release paper and position adhesive coated sheet against item. Unitl pressure is applied, the adhesive coated sheet can be moved for proper alignment.

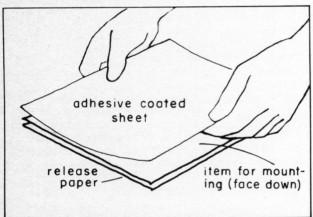

4 Apply firm pressure with roller or squeegee to back of the adhesive coated sheet, being certain to apply pressure over the entire area of the item to be mounted.

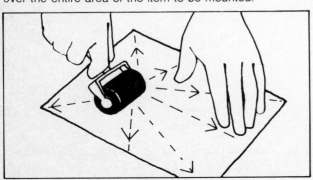

5 Slowly peel the item to be mounted away from the adhesive coated sheet.

6 Place the now adhesive coated item against the desired mounting surface. Item can be moved on mounting surface until desired position is achieved.

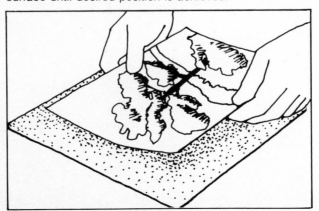

7 When desired position is achieved, firmly apply pressure with roller or squeegee over entire surface of item being mounted. Use the release paper as a protective sheet if desired.

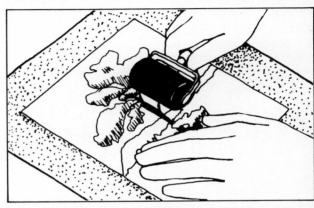

Helpful hints for mounting items small or larger than the mounting adhesive are included with purchased sheets.

mounting and laminating images

MOUNTING AIDS

A number of good-quality and unusual mounting aids are available to help simplify mounting problems. Illustrated and briefly discussed are several recommended mounting aids.

Adhesive (Glue) Pen

A pen-type refillable liquid-adhesive dispensing device using a ball-point principle to dispense dots of adhesive for mounting purposes. Most pens, when filled, will dispense several thousand adhesive dots.

Liquid Plastic Adhesive

A fast-setting white or transparent all-purpose adhesive that holds on wood, paper, cloth, and all porous and semi-porous materials. Can be used in an adhesive pen.

Adhesive Stick

One of the newer forms of mounting adhesive. Comes in lipsticklike form, and is designed for gluing paper, card-board, and styrofoam materials.

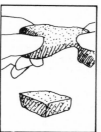  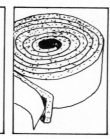 

Pliable Plastic Adhesive

A reusable pliable plastic adhesive for attaching materials such as papers, maps, charts, and photographs to most dry surfaces. To use, pull like candy taffy until warm. Tear off a small piece, and attach to the back of the material to be mounted.

Wax Adhesive Stick

A colorless, odorless wax adhesive in stick form. For mounting paper and lightweight cardboard.

Foam Tape

Double-coated foam tape. Has pressure-sensitive adhesive on both sides. For mounting on all types of walls, tile, plaster, wood, and any surface that is clean, dry, and smooth. Not recommended for use on wallpaper. 3M brand tape is packaged as "Mounting Squares."

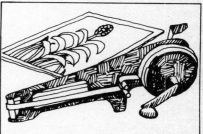

Double-Coated Adhesive Tape

A double-coated pressure-sensitive transparent tape for mounting everything from thin paper tissue to cardboard where tape mounting is desired. Some tapes have a carrier strip that must be peeled away from the adhesive tape to permit mounting.

Tape Edger

Applies, folds, and cuts pressure-sensitive adhesive edging tape as it is needed. For mounting a tape border on papers, maps, charts, and thin cardboards.

BULLETIN BOARD MOUNTING

How flat visual materials (photographs, illustrations, posters, etc.) and three-dimensional materials mounted on a bulletin or message board will add or detract from its overall general appearance. The Mounting and Laminating Selection Chart on page 94 is a good starting point for solving bulletin board mounting problems. For mounting precut and preformed letters, see page 61 for mounting suggestions.

Here are several good mounting aids and methods for attractively mounting materials on the bulletin board.

Mounting Aids

PUSH-PINS
Attractive steel point pins with metal or plastic heads. These pins are ideal for mounting flat or three-dimensional materials. To use, simply grasp the pin between thumb and forefinger and insert with a twist of the wrist. They are removed in the same manner.

DISPLAY PINS
Extra long steel straight pins specially designed for mounting and attaching display materials. Regular straight pins can also be used.

MAP PINS (TACKS)
Spherical head pins that come in assorted colors. These pins are specially designed for map use, but also make attractive mounting aids for thin materials.

UPHOLSTERY NAILS
These decorative-head nails make excellent supports for heavyweight visual or three-dimensional materials mounted on bulletin boards. Upholstery nails come in

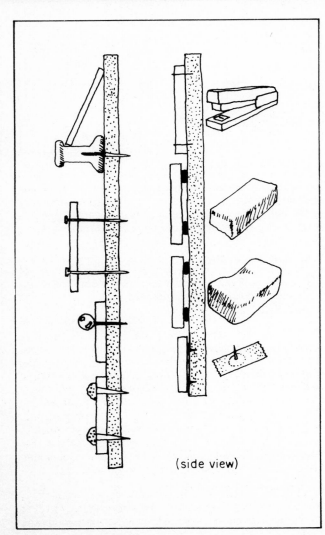

(side view)

assorted design and color heads, and are available at most stationers' stores and stores selling "notions."

STAPLES
Staple guns and staplers that can be adjusted for open stapling, make excellent tools for mounting lightweight materials.

WAX ADHESIVE STICK
Wax adhesive, similar to paraffin, used to mount from light to fairly heavy materials to most surfaces. To use, pinch off a piece of the wax and roll into a small ball. Next, place wax at several contact points of material to be mounted; turn over and press firmly into position.

PLIABLE PLASTIC ADHESIVE
A reusable plastic adhesive for attaching materials such as papers, maps, charts, and photographs to most dry surfaces. To use, pull like candy taffy until warm. Tear off a small piece, and attach to the back of material to be mounted.

TACK AND TAPE MOUNT
A handmade hidden mounting aid for attaching lightweight materials to the bulletin board. TO MAKE, mount a 1-inch strip of adhesive tape (sticky side down) down and over an upright thumb tack as illustrated. Make as many of these mounts as may be required to support the material being attached to the board. Longer and wider strips of tape may be required for supporting very large and heavier materials. Next, position mounts at desired contact points on back of

mounting and laminating images 5

material (tack point up, and sticky side of tape down). Press tape firmly into place at both sides of tape. TO MOUNT material, turn it over and position as desired on the bulletin board. Press into place at all tack and tape contact points. ◗

Mounting with dry mounting tissue has long been recognized as perhaps one of the best techniques for mounting. A heat-sealing adhesive-coated tissue is placed between the two materials to be bonded. Under the heat and pressure of a dry mounting press (or electric hand iron) the adhesive in the tissue is activated, forming an exceptionally strong bond between the two materials.

Two types of mounting tissue have been selected for inclusion here; Seal MT5 permanent tissue, and Seal Fotoflat removable tissue.

Permanent Tissue (MT5)

A fine grade of thin amber color paper that contains a specially formulated coating of heat-sealing adhesive on both sides. The adhesive bonds while hot and is permanent. This tissue is ideally suited for bonding smooth papers, regular photographs, newspaper clippings, construction paper, lithographs, posters, etc., onto mounting boards, foam-cored, masonite, plywood, aluminum. Cut sheets come in sizes 5-by 7-inch to 40-inch by 50-yards.

Removable Tissue (Fotoflat)

A pure white paper that contains a specially formulated coating of low temperature heat-sealing adhesive on both

sides. Bond occurs during cooling cycle, and is removable while heated. Low temperature makes this tissue excellent for mounting delicate materials such as water colors, opaque oriental silks and color prints which are heat sensitive. The thick adhesive is also suited for textured materials, cloths, leaves, butterflies, flannels, etc. Fine also for general mounting of temporary displays where removal is important.

INSTRUCTIONS
1 WARM UP PRESS. The recommended temperature for general PERMANENT tissue mounting is 225°F; for REMOVABLE tissue, 180°F. Set temperature on the press and allow the unit to stabilize at that heat.

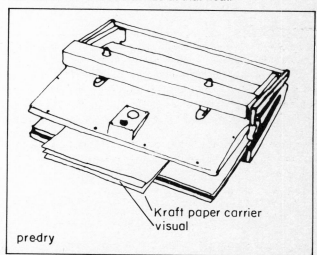

Kraft paper carrier

visual

predry

2 REDUCE MOISTURE. All prints and boards should be pre-dried in the heated press to reduce moisture levels. Position the work in a carrier of Kraft, or other smooth porous paper, and place in the heated press for 45 seconds.

Open press momentarily and repeat cycle for 30 additional seconds. Both steps should be completed with the mount board also.

3 TACK TISSUE TO VISUAL. Place visual face down and cover back with a sheet of tissue. Tack one edge of tissue to one edge of visual in a 3-inch continuous line through Seal

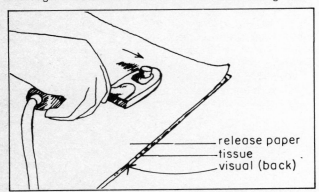

— release paper
— tissue
— visual (back)

Release Paper. Trim tissue to size if necessary. For mounting visuals that are larger than the press platen, eliminate tacking procedure totally. Also, begin mounting larger visuals in the center first, working to outside edges in successive "bites." To avoid wrinkling, slide work through the press when changing position. DO NOT LIFT!

4 TACK WORK TO MOUNT BOARD. Position work on mounting board. Lift visual edge opposite that which is tacked from Step 3 above, and fasten tissue to mount board in a continuous line through the release paper.

release paper
tissue
board

5 BOND VISUAL TO MOUNT BOARD. Insert work into a protective carrier line release paper or Kraft paper, and place in press. Lock press closed for 30 to 45 seconds for 8-

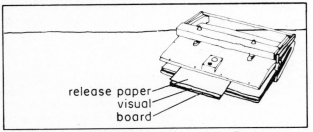

release paper
visual
board

by 10-inch work on regular mounting board; longer if necessary for larger (thicker) sizes.

6 COOL UNDER WEIGHT. Remove work carefully without bending or flexing it, and place under metal weight until cool.

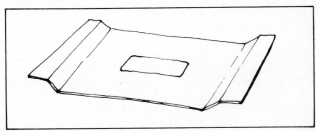

TO REMOVE MATERIALS MOUNTED WITH REMOVABLE TISSUE. Replace mounted material in carrier of release paper and place in press preheated to 200°F. Lower the platen so it rests on material for one minute. DO NOT LOCK THE PRESS CLOSED! Remove from press and immediately lift one corner of the visual, slowly peeling from the tissue. Reheating mounted sections may be necessary if peeling becomes difficult.

mounting and laminating images **5**

DRY BACKING CLOTH

Visual media like maps, charts, floor plans, etc., can be backed with this remarkable cloth (Seal Chartex) for added strength and preservation. This white, pliable fabric contains low temperature adhesive on one side. It bonds during cooling cycle. Can be folded, creased, rolled, and used as hinges in book form. Dry backing cloth comes in sheet sizes from 8-by 10-inch to 18-by 24-inch, and in rolls from 36-inch by 25-feet to 42-inch by 100-feet.

Instructions

1 WARM UP PRESS. The recommended temperature for general mounting work is 180°F. Set that temperature on the press and allow the unit to stabilize at that heat.

2 REDUCE MOISTURE. All visuals should be pre-dried in the heated press to reduce moisture levels. Position the work in a carrier of Kraft, or other smooth porous paper, and place in the heated press for 45 seconds. Open press momentarily and repeat cycle for 30 additional seconds.

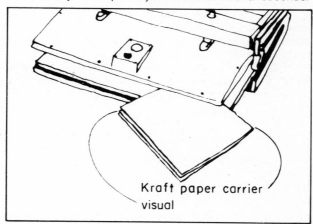

Kraft paper carrier
visual

3 TACK CLOTH TO VISUAL. Place pre-dried work FACE DOWN on a clean surface and cover with dry backing cloth, adhesive side (smooth surface) down. Cover one edge with Seal Release Paper and tack the single edge of cloth to one visual edge in a 3-inch continuous line through the release

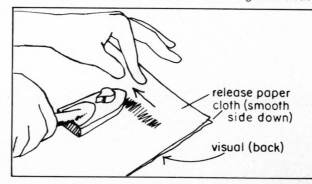

release paper
cloth (smooth side down)

visual (back)

paper. Trim to size as necessary. If backing work is larger than the press platen, eliminate all tacking procedures if possible. Also, begin press "bites" in the center first, working to outside edges successively. If tacking is necessary, complete Step 3 above and press the tacked edge first, working toward "free" edges.

4 BOND CLOTH IN PRESS. Insert work into protective carrier, like release paper, and place in press. Lock press closed for 20 to 30 seconds.

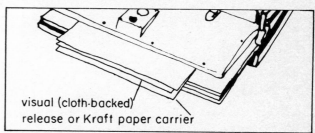

visual (cloth-backed)
release or Kraft paper carrier

5 COOL UNDER WEIGHT. Since the adhesive bonds while cooling, all work must be placed under weight until cool for proper adhesion.

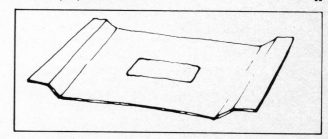

TO REMOVE DRY BACKING CLOTH, replace mounted material in a carrier of release paper and place in press preheated to 200°F. Lower the platen so it rests on the material for about one minute. DO NOT LOCK THE PRESS CLOSED! Remove from press and carefully peel away the cloth. ∎

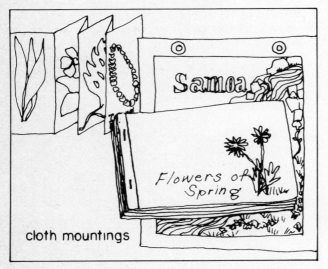

cloth mountings

Visual media such as charts, maps, posters, and similar instructional materials requiring a cloth backing for support or preservation; wet mounting on cloth could be the answer. This cloth-mounting technique is an age-old process that dates back to centuries ago when Far Eastern countries protected and preserved paintings and scrolls on cloth.

Cloth, usually unbleached muslin, wallpaper adhesive (wheat-paste flour), brush, and a mounting surface are the basic items for wet mounting on cloth.

The mounting surface may be any flat, waterproof surface (table, drawing board, etc.) sufficiently large enough to accommodate the material to be mounted. The mounting surface should also be able to accept tacks or staples.

Preparation of Material to be Mounted

The materials to be mounted should be colorfast. A quick check with a clean damp cloth on a surface corner will reveal if the material is colorfast. If it is not, thoroughly spray the material with a clear plastic spray (Krylon is one brand name) to set the ink surface and protect it from moisture.

beetle

soak cloth

mix paste

Preparation of Cloth for Mounting

First, place the mounting cloth in water so that it will be completely saturated by the time it is to be used. Next, mix the paste. Use the bristles of the brush to get an even, smooth, lump-free paste mixture. If the paste thickens after standing, add additional water (for additional strength, add a small amount of glue size to the paste mixture).

The mixing of the wheat paste is greatly facilitated by the use of a flour sieve. A combination sieve and storage bottle may be made from a canning jar. Puncture holes in the metal lid so that the paste flour can be shaken out easily during the mixing of the paste. A circular piece of cardboard placed under the perforated lid will keep the flour clean during storage.

Stretching the cloth properly is important. A definite attempt should be made to square the thread pattern with the surface on which the cloth is being stretched. After the cloth is thoroughly soaked in water, wring out the excess moisture and proceed with the following steps in the stretching process. (Before beginning the procedure, be sure that the mounting surface is clean and free of all foreign matter).

INSTRUCTION—CLOTH STRETCHING

1 Establish one corner, and either staple (using a staple gun) or thumbtack the corner of the cloth to the corner of the mounting board.

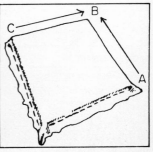

mounting and laminating images

2 Allowing a little excess of the cloth to extend over the edge of the board, stretch the edge of the cloth to the second corner. Try to keep the thread pattern parallel to the edge of the board.

3 In a similar manner, stretch the second edge of cloth to the third corner.

4 Thumbtack these two established edges at intervals of 3 to 4 inches. Draw the final corner of cloth to the fourth corner, and tack it in place temporarily. Starting on the long remaining side AB on corner A adjacent to the already adhered edge, draw the cloth tightly and staple it at intervals of 3 to 4 inches. Do the same to the remaining side BC, always keeping in mind that the thread pattern should be parallel to edges of the board.

INSTRUCTIONS—MOUNTING VISUAL

1 Place the visual on the stretched cloth, positioning it as desired and using light pencil marks to indicate the corners.

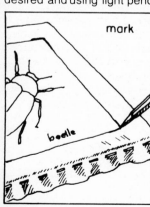
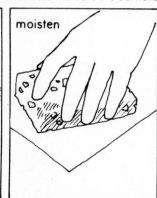

2 Now lay the visual facedown on a clean, dry surface and thoroughly moisten the paper surface until it lies absolutely flat with no wrinkles or folds in evidence. At this time there will be some evidence of a slight expansion of the paper material.

3 Apply the paste evenly on the muslin over the entire area idicated by pencil marks. It is best to go slightly beyond the area to be used.

4 Sponge off all excess moisture from the back of the paper material, and place it faceup, positioned according to the original marks indicating the corners.

5 Working from the center of the visual, gently rub out wrinkles so that the material will lie smooth and flat against the muslin surface.

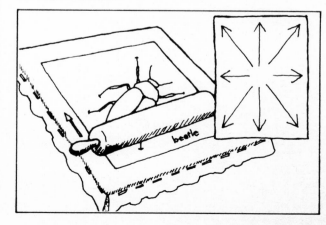

6 Place the rolling pin in the center parallel to the longest dimension of the visual. With light pressure, roll from the center to the two nearest edges.

7 Next, roll from the center to the two remaining edges. This forms a + shape. Again, place the rolling pin in the center and roll to each corner as indicated. This forms an X shape.

8 To complete the mounting process, cover the edges of the visual with strips of newsprint. Start with the rolling pin in the center and roll in an outward direction all along the edges. This squeezes out any excess paste onto the newsprint, which can then be discarded.

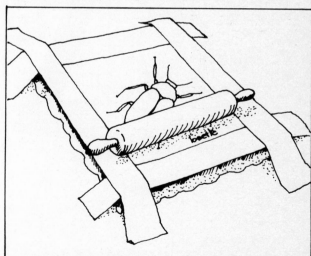

9 Next, check to see that there are no folds or wrinkles. If there is evidence of excess paste under any section of the visual, reroll that area. Finally, with a damp sponge, wipe off any excess paste from the surface of the visual as well as from the marginal cloth areas. Let the material dry. When it is completely dry, remove carefully from the mounting board and finish the edges as desired.

Finishing and Displaying Mounts

There are a number of ways to finish the edges of mounted materials. Cutting the cloth flush with the edge of the visual is the easiest method. However, if pinking shears are used, there will be less danger of the cloth unraveling. Taping the edge with cloth or plastic tape prevents raveling and gives added strength.

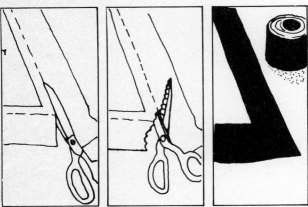

One of the most common ways for displaying mounts is to suspend the mount on a dowel rod. A variety of gummed-back picture hangers are available to fasten to the back of the mount. Eyelets (grommets) may be placed directly in the mounted material with the use of an eyelet punch.◀

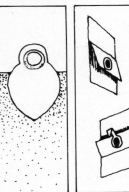
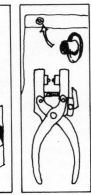

Cold laminating acetate is a transparent film with a pressure-sensitive adhesive backing that permanently bonds on contact to most dry surfaces, without heat. Acetate can be applied to photographs, clippings, valuable documents, charts, signs, and any materials requiring a permanent protective acetate covering. Nationwide Adhesive Products also carries a matte acetate that will accept pencil, ball-point pen, typewriter notations, etc.

Three techniques for laminating with cold laminating acetate will be discussed here; hand, clipboard, and machine applications.

Hand Application

1 Cut the acetate to the desired size. If the material is to be laminated on both sides and a transparent margin is desired, cut the acetate large enough to allow for such a margin. Separate the backing sheet from the acetate at one of the corners with the point of a cutting knife or by "flicking" a corner with a finger as illustrated.

2 Peel back the acetate sheet, and position the visual as desired on the backing sheet. *Or* completely peel off the

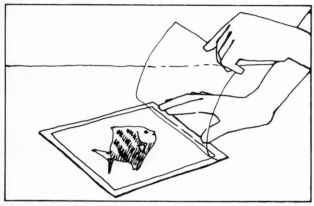

acetate, and position the visual on the backing sheet. With the "sticky" side of the acetate down, bend the acetate in a U shape and gently lower it down onto the face of the visual, pressing it down in a down and outward direction.

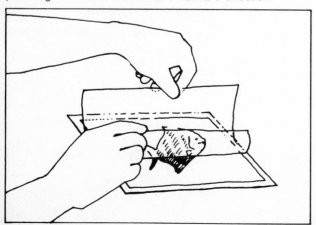

3 Turn the visual over onto a smooth, clean surface so that the acetate side is down. Using firm pressure, rub the entire surface down with your hand or a flat, smooth object—like the smooth side of a pocket comb or a ruler.

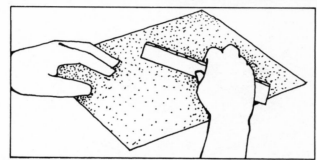

4 Trim the laminated visual to the desired size.

Clipboard Application

1 Insert the acetate unit (acetate and backing sheet) into the clipboard clamp. Separate the acetate sheet from the backing, and peel back to the clamp.

2 Lay the free end of the acetate over the top of the clamp. Position the visual or item(s) to be laminated on the backing sheet.

3 Roll the acetate back down. The clipboard assures accurate alignment. Lightly rub the finished lamination with your hand or a flat, smooth object.

Cold Acetate Laminator

Here is a technique for laminating a variety of materials. This laminating process involves a pressure-sensitive acetate and a cold-type laminating machine. Machines are available which can laminate materials up to 20 inches wide by any length and will accept materials from a few thousandths of an inch to ⅛-inch thick. This process can be used to laminate valuable documents, records, photographs, signs, flash cards, illustrations, and so forth. Projection or display transparencies can also be made using this process (see page 127 to 129).

INSTRUCTIONS
1 With the machine turned off, insert an edge of the acetate paper (backing sheet down) through the front opening until stopped by the machine rollers. Holding the acetate flat, push the switch to "nip" momentarily until about ¼-inch of the acetate enters the rollers.

2 Separate the paper backing sheet from the acetate as illustrated, and peel back to rest on the machine. Insert the materials to be laminated on top of the backing paper, face side up, and slide gently into the nip at the rollers.

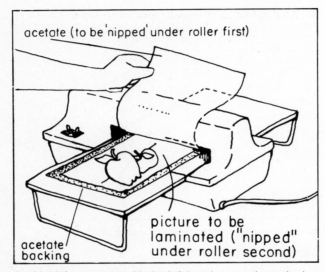

acetate (to be 'nipped' under roller first)

acetate backing

picture to be laminated ("nipped" under roller second)

3 Hold the acetate with the left hand as nearly vertical as practical, and flip the switch to start the rollers moving. The machine will pull the acetate, materials, and backing sheet through to the discharge shelf at the rear.

4 Trim the laminated materials to size and remove the backing paper. ◥

Heat laminating acetate is a tough polyester film with adhesive on one side specifically developed for use with a heat laminator or a dry mounting press. This acetate is available in two finishes; gloss and matte. Glossy laminating acetate makes colors come alive. You can write on the surface of the acetate with color marking pencils or pens. When a non-reflective surface is desired, matte-finish acetate should be used.

Heat laminating acetate is useful in protecting, preserving, and adding usefulness to such things as charts, maps, drawings, photographs, posters, etc. It makes visual media air-tight, water-proof, and smearproof. This acetate is available in rolls, and special laminating pouches (see page 109).

Four types of laminating machines and their laminating acetates are included in this section.

Heat Acetate Laminator-Acetate Roll

The heat acetate laminator laminates acetate to one or both sides of paper, cardboard, film, certain flat specimens, etc. Machines are available to laminate materials from 3 to 60 inches wide, any length.

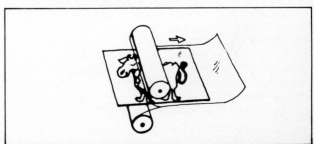

LAMINATING PAPER OR CARDBOARD SHEETS

1 Simply push a button or switch to set the heating unit of the machine in operation. A light will indicate when the machine is ready for lamination.

2 Push the control that starts the roller moving, and insert the material to be laminated. It will be discharged at the back of the machine sealed between two layers of transparent plastic film. Use the machine's cutter to cut the laminated material where desired. Material can be run through a second time if additional protection is required.

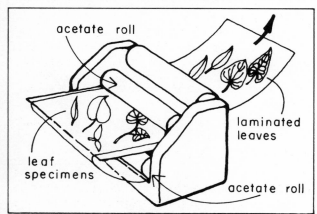

LAMINATING FLAT SPECIMENS OR SMALL SHEETS

When laminating flat specimens or small printed sheets, thread the bottom laminating roll as illustrated. This will permit the film to serve as a conveyer. Or, if preferred, the material to be laminated can be fed directly into the machine without changing the threading of the film as suggested. Specimens such as leaves and insects should be dried out before lamination.

Heat Acetate Laminator—Acetate Pouch

The Seal acetate pouch laminating system makes it possible to seal any paper or card from wallet-size to 8½-by-14-inches in precut plastic pouches of tough, transparent polyester. There are two types of pouches; a single-sided pouch for filing or displaying one side of a visual, and a two-sided pouch for items requiring acetate on both sides.

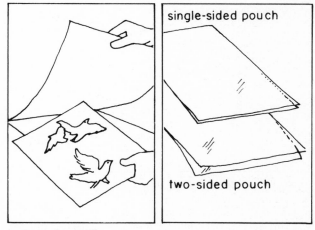

INSTRUCTIONS

1 Place the item or items to be laminated in the appropriate type and size of pouch. You can position materials accurately before inserting them in the machine. Frequently, you can arrange several items so they fit into one pouch.

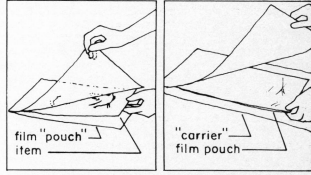

2 Place the loaded pouch inside the special Seal carrier.

3 Feed the carrier into the machine until the roller grabs hold.

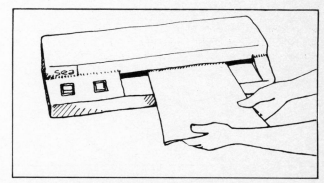

4 Let the carrier cool for about 45 to 60 seconds, then remove laminated material.

Dry Mounting Press Laminating

Any dry mounting press can be used to laminate visual media with heat laminating acetate. Laminating protects, preserves, and adds usefulness to such things as charts, maps, drawings, posters, signs, etc.

INSTRUCTIONS

1 INCREASE PRESSURE OF PRESS. Laminating requires more pressure than dry mounting (tissue). Increase press pressure by placing a ¼-inch masonite board under the sponge pad. The board should be approximately the same size as the pad.

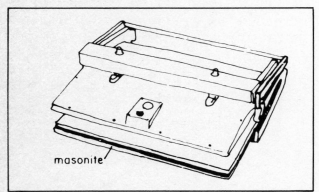

masonite

2 WARM UP PRESS. Set the temperature at 275° to 325° F, depending on the type of laminating to be done, and allow the press to warm up.

3 PRE-DRY MATERIAL IF NECESSARY. If the relative humidity is over 50 per cent, it is best to dry the material. Insert in a carrier of Kraft or other porous paper and place in the press. Dry for 45 seconds to 5 minutes, depending on the material and humidity. The press should be open momentarily every 45 to 60 seconds during drying.

4 COVER WITH LAMINATING ACETATE. Cut a piece of acetate large enough to cover the material with some to spare. Place the acetate with the dull (adhesive) side

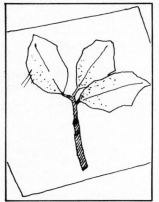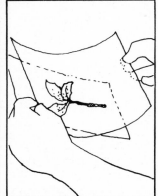

against the surface of the material to be laminated. Smooth out the acetate with your hand or a piece of lint-free fabric. NOTE: if the material is thin, like a single sheet of paper, it will curl when laminated on one side only. To prevent this, enclose the material in the acetate so that both sides are laminated at the same time. For two-sided laminations, use 325°F for 60 seconds.

5 SEAL IN PRESS. Enclose the acetate-covered material in a carrier of Seal release paper because if the adhesive side of the acetate comes into direct contact with the platen of the press, it will stick to the hot surface. Insert the work in the press and leave for 60 seconds. In some cases, this may not be enough time. If there are still small areas that have not sealed completely (these will show up as blisters), trim the edges and place the work back in the press for another 60 seconds.

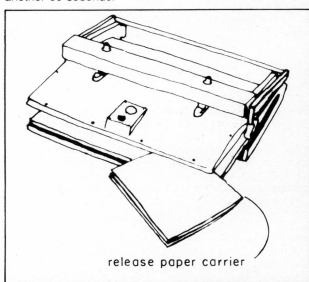

release paper carrier

6 COOL UNDER METAL WEIGHT (Seal Weight). Remove work and place under a weight to cool for a minimum of 30 seconds.

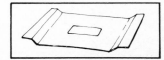

7 TRIM OFF EXCESS ACETATE. Remove the "overhang" of acetate around the edges with scissors, knife blade, or paper cutter.

Laminating Materials Wider Than Roll Width

You can sectionally laminate both pliable and non-pliable materials in widths wider than the acetate roll in either of the following ways.

Butt-Laminating. Follow standard laminating procedure. Apply full width of acetate, lining it up parallel with edge of material. After removing from press and cooling, place another strip of acetate alongside laminated section. Rub down slowly with side of hands to build up static electricity which will create tendency for temporary adhesion while preparing to replace in press. Follow this procedure as often as necessary until complete surface is laminated. Seams are practically unnoticeable.

Overlap-Laminating. This method is not as exacting as butt-laminating, but it is much faster, and in many cases, perfectly acceptable. Simply place one width over the other instead of next to it. An overlap of about ⅛- to ¼-inch is common.

SPECIAL EFFECTS LAMINATING

Exciting special effects can be created with heat laminating acetate that can be added to photographs, posters, signs, etc. A "crinkle" effect can be created by cutting a piece of acetate larger than the surface to which the special effect is to be added. Next, roll the acetate up in your hand until it is well wrinkled. Straighten the acetate out and place it over the surface (dull side down). Then just follow the basic laminating instructions. You'll create an exciting texture effect.

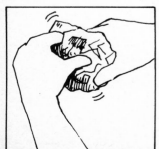

The "crinkle" effect can even become more exciting by sprinkling assorted wax crayon shavings over the surface

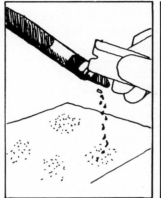

to which the special effect is to be added. Then, follow the crinkling and basic laminating instructions.

Here is still another "crinkle" effect. After hand-crinkling the acetate, spray the dull side with transparent or opaque aerosol-can colors. Allow the colors to dry. Next, follow the basic laminating instructions.

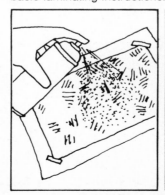

LAMINATING FRAGILE MATERIALS

Fragile materials such as leaves, ferns, butterflies, etc., can be laminated to illustration board to create effective displays. You need not mount them first. Leaves must be pre-dried. Place the leaves between paper towels and put both in a carrier of Kraft paper in the press at 275°F for 15 seconds. First, position the materials on the illustration board as desired. Next, lay a sheet of acetate over the arrangement and place in press at 275°F for 30 to 60 seconds (being sure to use a protective carrier, like Seal release paper). This will seal the materials to the board.▫

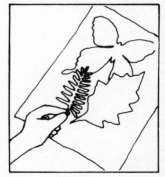
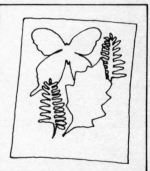

Thermocopy Machine Laminating

Many flat printed materials, such as valuable documents, photographs, and printed instructions, can have a special acetate laminated to their surfaces through use of a thermocopy machine. The acetate is designed to provide a protective covering and a surface to be written on, erased, and reused.

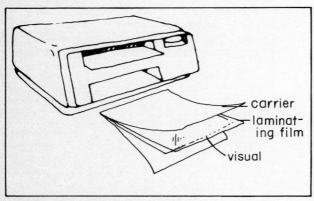

3M LAMINATING INSTRUCTIONS
The 3M company manufactures a laminating film that is designed to be used in thermocopy machines as illustrated here.

1 Assemble materials as illustrated. Make certain the original to be laminated is not folded, creased, or crumpled. All the necessary materials are in the box containing the film.

2 Set the speed control of the thermocopy machine at the slowest speed (darkest setting), and insert the materials into the machine. When laminating several sheets without interruption, gradually turn the dial to a faster (lighter) setting.

VIEWLEX (VIEWFAX) INSTRUCTIONS
Vieiew manufactures a laminating sheet for use in its thermocopy machines. Here are the instructions:

1 Assemble materials as illustrated, and place in a carrier screen. Insert assembled materials into the machine.

2 Follow step 2 of the 3M instructions.

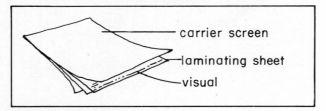

Laminating Both Sides of Original
If lamination is required for both sides of the original, simply repeat the aforementioned steps on the reverse side of the original, using a second sheet of film.

Laminating Materials Smaller than Laminating Film (Viewlex)
If the original is smaller than the sheet of laminating film (e.g., business or membership card, photograph), the interleaf sheet must be placed underneath the original. Failure to do this will cause the film to laminate to the carrier screen. ◣

mounting and laminating images

SOURCES

Selected publications and audiovisual media have been annotated and sourced here to supplement the contents of this section. The figures in parentheses at the end of each entry (O8) indicate the coded address source for the procurement of the reference. Complete addresses are listed under *Out-of-Town* sources at the end of this section.

Eboch, Sidney C.: OPERATING AUDIOVISUAL EQUIPMENT, 2d ed., Chandler Publishing, 1968.
This manual includes instructions for mounting materials for opaque projection and for preparing handmade slides and overhead projection transparencies. (O9)
SEAL INSTRUCTIONS BOOKLET, Seal Inc.
Illustrated instructions on dry mounting and heat laminating. (O30)

DRY MOUNTING, 35mm filmstrip, 51 frames, sound, color, Educational Media, 1967.
Use of dry mounting press and various types of tissue. (O12)
DRY MOUNTING AND LAMINATING PICTURES, *16mm film, ten minutes, sound, color, BFA.*
Illustrates dry mounting and plastic lamination methods using a dry mounting press, tacking iron, and household iron. (O2)
DRY MOUNTING INSTRUCTIONAL MATERIALS: BASIC TECHNIQUES, *16mm film, five minutes, sound, color, University of Iowa, 1965.*

Presents the basic dry mounting techniques that involve dry mounting tissue and Fotoflat. (O22)
DRY MOUNTING INSTRUCTIONAL MATERIALS: CLOTH BACKING, *16mm film, five minutes, sound, color, University of Iowa, 1965.*
Shows what Chartex backing cloth is, how it is applied with a dry mounting press, and some of the ways it can be used in preparing instructional materials. (O22)
DRY MOUNTING INSTRUCTIONAL MATERIALS: CREATIVE APPLICATIONS, *16mm film, seven minutes, sound, color, University of Iowa, 1969.*
Demonstrates some possibilities for use of the dry mounting press as a creative tool. (O22)
DRY MOUNTING INSTRUCTIONAL MATERIALS: DISPLAY AND USE, *16mm film, five minutes, sound, color, University of Iowa, 1965.*
Illustrates various classroom uses of instructional materials prepared with the dry mounting press. (O22)
DRY MOUNTING INSTRUCTIONAL MATERIALS: SPECIAL TECHNIQUES, *16mm film, five minutes, sound, color, University of Iowa, 1965.*
Illustrates special applications and processes utilizing a variety of dry mounting materials and techniques. (O22)
DRY MOUNTING INSTRUCTIONAL MATERIALS: USING IDEAS, *16mm film, eight minutes, sound, color. University of Iowa, 1969.*
Shows ways in which the dry mounting process can be put to use in the classroom, once you have mastered the technique. (O22)
DRY MOUNT YOUR TEACHING PICTURES, *16mm film, ten minutes, sound, b and w, McGraw-Hill films, 1958.*
Shows the step-by-step procedure for using dry mounting tissue and an ordinary iron in mounting pictures. (O26)
LAMINATING, *35mm filmstrip, 49 frames, sound, color, Educational Media, 1967.*
Covers step-by-step laminating of conventional items with the dry mounting press. Explains processes for laminating very large items. (O12)
PASSE PARTOUT FRAMING, *16mm film, ten minutes, sound, b and w or color, Indiana University, 1957.*
Framing flat and object materials using a transparent cover, a picture, a cardboard backing, and a tape binding. (O21)
TAPES, HINGING AND STORING, *35mm filmstrip, 39 frames, sound, color, Educational Media, 1967.*
Treats a variety of adhesive materials for classroom use. Included are edging and binding tapes, and special polyesters used in hinging. (O12)
WET MOUNTING PICTORIAL MATERIALS, *16mm film, twelve minutes, sound, b and w or color, Indiana University, 1952.*
Demonstrates, step-by-step, the mounting of pictorial materials on cloth using the wet mounting method. Methods of displaying and using mounted materials as turnover charts, opaque projection strips, and wall charts. (O21)

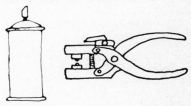

Most of the equipment and materials included in this section are available from local sources; such sources are indicated (L), and can be located in the *Yellow Pages* of the telephone directory. Items not readily available locally can be purchased directly, or purchase information obtained from the sources indicated (O).

ADHESIVE PEN, ADHESIVE STICK, DOUBLE-COATED ADHESIVE TAPE (L1, L6, O6, O27)
COLD ACETATE LAMINATOR (L2, L5, O8, O28, O32)
COLD LAMINATING ACETATE (L2, L5, O8, O28, O32)
DOUBLE-COATED ADHESIVE MOUNT (L1, L6, O13)
DRY MOUNTING PRESSES (L1, L2, L4, L5, O4, O6, O15, O30)
DRY MOUNTING TISSUE AND DRY BACKING CLOTH (L1, L2, L4, L5, O3, O6, O30)
FOAM TAPE (L1, L3, L6, O3, O10, O14)
HEAT ACETATE LAMINATORS (L1, L2, O17, O20, O23, O30)
HEAT LAMINATING ACETATE (dry mounting press) (L1, L2, L4, O3, O6, O23, O30)
HEAT LAMINATING ACETATE (pouches) (L1, L2, O23, O30)
HEAT LAMINATING ACETATE (rolls) (L1, L2, L4, O6, O15, O17, O30)
PINS (display, map, and pushpin) (L1, L4, L6, O3, O6, O15)
PLIABLE PLASTIC ADHESIVE (L1, L6, O5, O16)
RUBBER CEMENT (standard, pressure-sensitive, and aerosol can) (L1, L4, L6, O3, O6, O10, O15)

SCOTCH BRAND ADHESIVE #567 (L1, L5, L6)
TAPE EDGER (L1, L4, O7, O19, O29)
THERMOCOPY MACHINES (L2, O11, O18, O31)
WAX ADHESIVE STICK (L1, L6, O1, O10, O24, O25)

Addresses

LOCAL SOURCES (See Yellow Pages)

L1 - Artists' Materials and Supply Stores
L2 - Audio-Visual Equipment and Supply Stores
L3 - Building and Hardware Supply Stores
L4 - Drafting Equipment And Supply Stores
L5 - Photographic Equipment and Supply Stores
L6 - Stationers' Stores

OUT-OF-TOWN SOURCES

O1 - BECKLEY-CARDY CO., 1900 N, Narragansett, Chicago, IL 60639
O2 - BFA EDUCATIONAL MEDIA, 2211 Michigan Age., Santa Monica, CA 90404
O3 - DICK BLICK, P. O. Box 1267, Galesburg, IL 61401
O4 - BOGEN PHOTO CORP., P. O. Box 448, Englewood, NJ 07631
O5 - BROOKS MFG. CO., Box 41195B, Cincinnati, OH 45241
O6 - ARTHUR BROWN & BROTHER, INC., 2 West 46th St., New York, NY 10036
O7 - CHARLES BRUNNING CO., 1834 Walden Office Square, Schaumbrug, IL 60172
O8 - BURKE & JAMES, 690 Portland Ave., Rochester, NY 14621
O9 - CHANDLER PUBLISHING CO., 257 Park Ave. S., New York, NY 10010
O10 - DEMCO EDUCATIONAL CORP., Box 1488 Madison, WI 53701
O11 - A. B. DICK CO., 5700 West Touhy Ave., Chicago, IL 60648
O12 - EDUCATIONAL MEDIA LABS, 4101 S. Congress Ave., Austin, TX 78745
O13 - FALCON SAFETY PRODUCTS, INC., Mountainside, NJ 07092

O14 - SAM FLAX, 25 E. 28th St., New York, NY 10016
O15 - A. I. FRIEDMAN, INC., 25 W. 45th St., New York, NY 10036
O16 - GAYLORD BROS., INC., Box 8489, Stockton, CA 95208
O17 - GENERAL BINDING CORP., Northbrook, IL 60062
O18 - GESTETNER CORP., Gestetner Park, Yonkers, NY 10703
O19 - H. T. HERBERT CO., INC., 21-21 41st Ave., Long Island City, NY 11101
O20 - INDEX, INC., P. O. Box 239, Charlotte, NC 28230
O21 - INDIANA UNIVERSITY, Audio-Visual Center, Bloomington, IN 47401
O22 - UNIVERSITY OF IOWA, AV Center, C-5 East Hall, Iowa City, IA 52240
O23 - JACKSON-HIRSH, INC., 1400 Charing Cross Rd., Deerfield, IL 60015
O24 - LEA A-V SERVICE, 240 Audley Dr., Sun Prairie, WI 53590
O25 - LECTRO-STIK CORP., 3721 Broadway, Chicago, IL 60613
O26 - McGRAW-HILL FILMS, 1221 Avenue of the Americas, New York, NY 10020
O27 - NASCO, 901 Janesville Ave., Fort Atkinson, WI 53538
O28 - NATIONWIDE ADHESIVE PRODUCTS, INC., 19600 St. Clair, Cleveland, OH 44117
O29 - RIDGWAY'S, P. O. Box 36150, Houston, TX 77036
O30 - SEAL, INC., 251 Roosevelt Dr., Derby, CT 06418
O31 - 3M COMPANY, Visual Products Div., 3M Center, St. Paul, MI 55101
O32 - VALIANT INSTRUCTIONAL MATERIALS CORP., 237 Washington Ave., Hackensack, NJ 07601

simple display making

This section deals with the making of attractive, easy-to-make free-standing and hanging physical supports for posters, signs, information plaques, photographs, real objects, and other visual media requiring a display unit for viewing. Included here are patterns of attractive display units that can be traced and enlarged to any size. Most of the units can be made from a single piece of heavyweight cardboard.

Idea Sources

Base Materials

Free-Standing and Hanging Units

Sources

see display pattern: 6

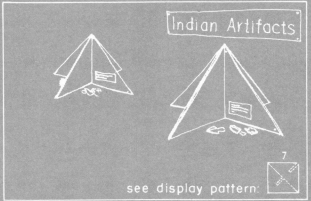

see display pattern: 7

Ideas for simple display units are all around us; in banks, restaurants, hotels, supermarkets, spirit stores, etc. Many of these display units are simple in design and equally easy to reproduce. Where possible, draw or trace a quick pattern of the display units you like. These patterns can be modified later to meet your display needs.

Simple display units, such as those included in this section, can be made from wood, metal, Plexiglas, mat board, etc. Four suitable base materials are briefly described here.

Mat Board

Heavyweight cardboard with or without textured (pebbled) surfaces. Ranges in thickness from 1/16 to 3/16 inch. Available in assorted colors and surfaces. A mat cutter (see page 21) is the recommended cutting tool.

Foam-cored Board

Foam-cored board with a smooth white surface (two sides). Combines strength with much lighter weight than an ordinary board. Resists moisture and remains rigid and strong during use because of its styrene foam-core center. An ideal base material for display making. The surface accepts markers, poster colors, inks, etc. Cuts easily with a razor blade. Available in 3/16- and ½-inch thickness.

Corrugated Board

An exciting material which has found a place in the making of display units. The board is made up of two layers of thin, strong paper welded together. The base layer, as shown in the accompanying visual, is flat; the second layer consists of a series of corrugations glued to the surface of the base layer. Available in assorted colors and sizes.

Plexiglas

A trade-named plastic sheeting which provides an excellent base material for simple display making. Cutting Plexiglas requires a special hand cutter or a power saw equipped with a special plastic-cutting blade. Folding or bending of Plexiglas is done by heating (with a special heating unit), or cutting at point of bending and cementing cut pieces with the recommended adhesive.

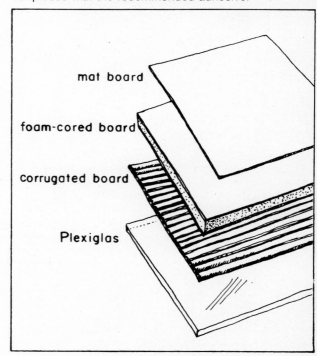

mat board

foam-cored board

corrugated board

Plexiglas

FREE-STANDING AND HANGING UNITS

The designs (patterns) of the free-standing and hanging display units included in this section have all been influenced by display units observed in banks, restaurants, hotels, etc. Not only are these units easy to make, most of them can be made from a single sheet of cardboard. The display patterns illustrated here can be enlarged to any size by grid

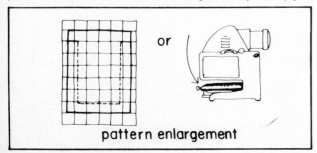

pattern enlargement

(see page 25) or by projection (see page 26). For suggested base (surface) materials from which the units can be made see page

Instructions

After you select the display unit you wish to make, it is recommended that you first practice with a sheet of paper; *cutting, scoring,* and *folding* as illustrated for the unit selected. This practice will give you a "feel" for making the unit.

1 Select the base material and the appropriate cutting tool.

2 Draw the exact size pattern on the base material. For accurate pattern lines, the use of a T square and triangle (page 18) are recommended. Where *scoring* is to be done on the back of the pattern, accurately draw the scoring lines on the back of the pattern as instructed.

3 Place the imaged pattern on a piece of protective cardboard (for protection of table) and follow the illustrated in-

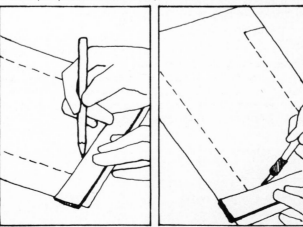

structions for *cutting* and *scoring* as illustrated for the pattern. Remember that *cutting* means cutting completely through the base material, and *scoring* means cutting only half-way through the material. For units requiring a cut-out groove (for joining two or more cut pieces together), the width of the cut-out groove must be equal to the thickness of the base material (if the base material is ⅛-inch thick, the cut groove must be ⅛-inch wide).

4 For cut pieces, join as illustrated; for a single piece, fold.

S.F. = score front
S.B. = score back
--- = cut

front — (cut out and remove)

<S.F. (bend back)

back — (insert in front) S.F. ∨

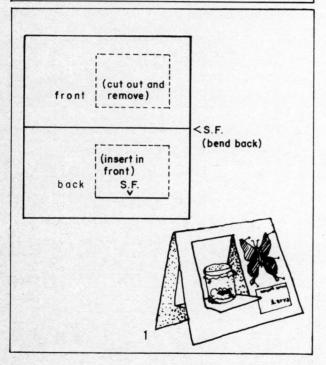

1

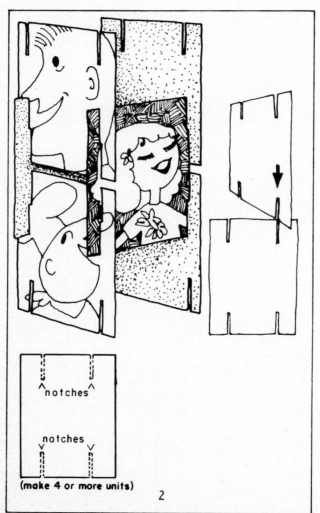

^notches^

notches ∨

(make 4 or more units)

2

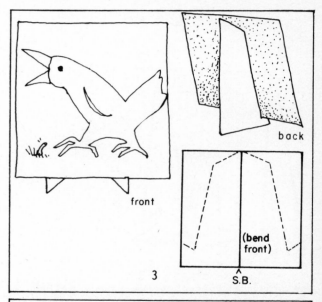

back

front

(bend front)

∧ S.B.

3

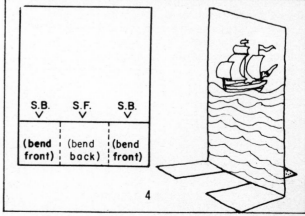

S.B. ∨ S.F. ∨ S.B. ∨

(bend front) | (bend back) | (bend front)

4

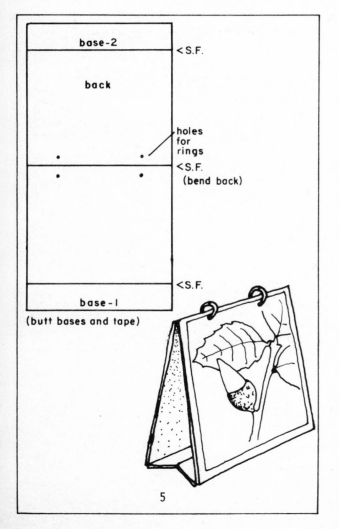

base-2

back

<S.F.

holes
for
rings
<S.F.
(bend back)

<S.F.

base-1

(butt bases and tape)

5

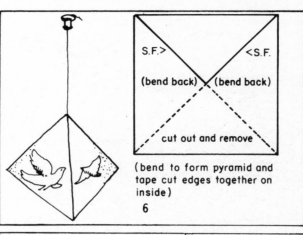

S.F.> <S.F.

(bend back) (bend back)

cut out and remove

(bend to form pyramid and
tape cut edges together on
inside)

6

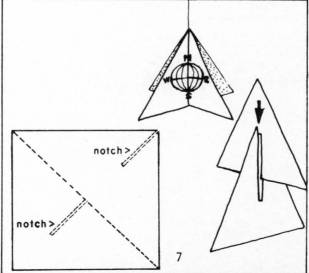

notch>

notch>

7

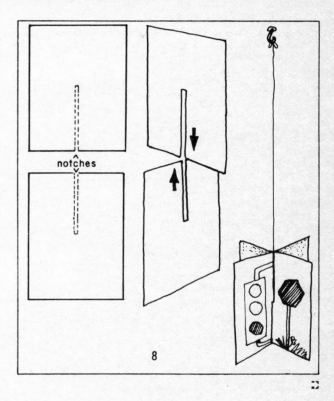

notches

8

119

DISPLAY PATTERNS

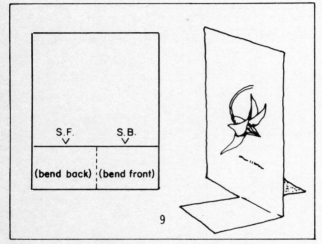

S.F. S.B.

(bend back) (bend front)

9

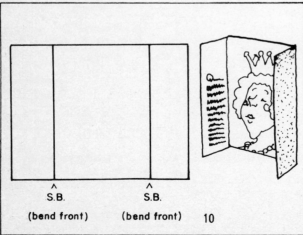

S.B. S.B.

(bend front) (bend front) 10

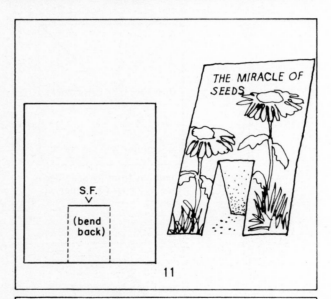

S.F.

(bend back)

11

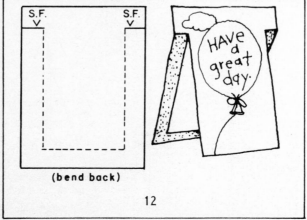

S.F. S.F.

(bend back)

12

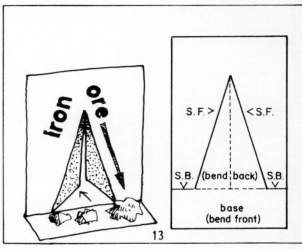

THE MIRACLE OF SEEDS

iron ore

S.F. > < S.F.

S.B. (bend back) S.B.

base
(bend front)

13

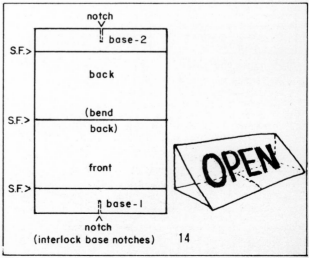

notch

base-2

S.F.>

back

S.F.>

(bend back)

front

S.F.>

base-1

notch
(interlock base notches)

14

120

SOURCES

Selected publications and audiovisual media have been annotated and sourced here to supplement the contents of this section. The figures in parentheses at the end of each entry (O8) indicate the coded address source for the procurement of the reference. Complete addresses are listed under *Out-of Town* sources at the end of this section.

BETTER BULLETIN BOARD DISPLAYS, University of Texas at Austin, 1961.
Deals with bulletin board ideas, resources, and construction. (O15)

Coplan, Kate, and Constance Rosenthal: GUIDE TO BETTER BULLETIN BOARDS, Oceana Publications, 1970.
Suggestions for the design and preparation of exciting bulletin boards. (O12)

EDUCATIONAL DISPLAYS AND EXHIBITS, University of Texas at Austin, 1965.
A handbook on guidelines, ideas, and production for displays and bulletin boards. (O15)

Garvey, Mona: TEACHING DISPLAYS: THEIR PURPOSE, CONSTRUCTION, AND USE, Shoe String, 1972.
A handbook to help teachers develop display ideas and techniques which can be applied to any subject at any level. (O13)

GOOD WORK BULLETIN BOARDS BOOK, Trend Enterprises.
Contains a collection of exciting bulletin board ideas for displaying student work, with an abundance of clever figures and display arrangements. (O16)

Horn, George F.: POSTERS: DESIGNING, MAKING, REPRODUCTION, Davis Publications, 1966.
Contains all the elements for successful poster making. (O6)

——: VISUAL COMMUNICATION: BULLETIN BOARDS, EXHIBITS, VISUAL AIDS, Davis Publications, 1973.
Covers planning, designing, and making visual media for use in the classroom, library, school, and community. (O6)

INSTRUCTIONAL DISPLAY BOARDS, University of Texas at Austin, 1968.
Explains the use and making of felt, hook and loop, magnetic, and peg boards. (O15)

Morland, John E.: PREPARATION OF INEXPENSIVE TEACHING MATERIALS, Chandler, 1973.
Contains instructions for preparing display and other modern teaching materials. (O5)

Randall, Reino, and Edward C. Haines: BULLETIN BOARDS AND DISPLAY, Davis Publications, 1961.
Combines basic design with imaginative use of materials for making bulletin boards and displays. (O6)

TREND'S IDEA BOOK, Trend Enterprises.
A basic bulletin board guide that presents practical suggestions for planning and making teachable bulletin boards. (O16)

Warren, Jefferson T.,: EXHIBIT METHODS, Sterling, 1972.
Photographic examples of successful exhibits with instructions for the design and construction of exhibits. (O14)

BETTER BULLETIN BOARDS, *16mm film, thirteen minutes, sound, b and w or color, Indiana University, 1956.*
The creation and use of bulletin boards for various purposes. Covers placement, size, design, lettering, and instructional applications. (O9)

BULLETIN BOARDS AND DISPLAY, *35mm filmstrips (2), 36 frames each, color, BFA, 1966.*
Shows good bulletin board design as an effective educational tool. Includes illustrations of layouts and designs, background materials, and fastening materials. (O2)

BULLETIN BOARDS: AN EFFECTIVE TEACHING DEVICE, *16mm film, eleven minutes, sound, color, BFA, 1956.*
Gives suggestions for the planning and organization of creatively designed bulletin boards. (O2)

CHALKBOARDS AND FLANNEL BOARDS, *35m filmstrips (4), 30 frames each, color, BFA, 1967.*
A set of four filmstrips that deal with the care, use, and construction of chalkboards and flannel boards. (O2)

ELECTRIC BOARDS FOR LEARNING, *16mm film, six minutes, sound, b and w, University of Iowa, 1965.*
Introduces various types of electric boards, shows their construction, and suggests a variety of uses for these boards. (O10)

EXCITING BULLETIN BOARDS, *35mm filmstrips (2), 40 frames each, sound, color, McGraw-Hill films, 1963.*
Shows color, lettering, and three-dimensional bulletin board materials. (O11)

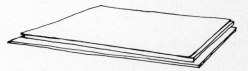

Most of the materials included in this section are available from local sources; such sources are indicated (L), and can be located in the *Yellow Pages* of the telephone directory. Items not readily available locally can be purchased directly, or purchase information obtained from the sources indicated (O).

CORRUGATED BOARD (L1, L4, O1, O3, O4, O8)
FOAM-CORED BOARD (L1, L2, O3, O4, O8, O17)
MAT BOARD (L1, L5, O3, O4, O8)
PLEXIGLAS (L2, L4, L5, O3, O7)

Addresses

LOCAL SOURCES (See Yellow Pages)

L1 - Artists' Materials and Supply Stores
L2 - Building and Hardware Supply Stores
L3 - Plexiglas Suppliers
L4 - Hobby/Crafts Supply Stores
L5 - Stationers' Stores

OUT-OF-TOWN SOURCES

O1 - BEMISS-JASON CORP., 3250 Ash St., Palo Alto, CA 94306
O2 - BFA EDUCATIONAL MEDIA, 2211 Michigan Ave., Santa Monica, CA 90404
O3 - DICK BLICK, P. O. Box 1267, Galesburg, IL 61401
O4 - ARTHUR BROWN & BROTHER, INC., 2 West 46th St., New York, NY 10036

O5 - CHANDLER PUBLISHING CO., 257 Park Ave. S., New York, NY 10010

O6 - DAVIS PUBLICATIONS, INC., 50 Portland St., Worcester, MA 01608

O7 - HAWAII PLASTICS CORP., 568 Dillingham Blvd., Honolulu, HI 96817.

O8 - SAM FLAX, 25 E. 28th St., New York, NY 10016

O9 - INDIANA UNIVERSITY, Audio-Visual Center, Bloomington, IN 47401

O10 - UNIVERSITY OF IOWA, AV Center, C-5 East Hall, Iowa City, IA 52240

O11 - McGRAW-HILL FILMS, 1221 Avenue of the Americas, New York, NY 10020

O12 - OCEANA PUBLICATIONS, 733 Plymouth Rd., Claremont, CA 91711

O13 - SHOE STRING PRESS, INC., 995 Sherman Ave., Hamden, CT 06514

O14 - Sterling Publishing Co., Inc., 419 Park Ave., New York, NY 10016

O15 - THE UNIVERSITY OF TEXAS at Austin, Instructional Media Center, Drawer W, University Station, Austin, TX 78712

O16 - TREND ENTERPRISES, INC., P. O. Box 3073, St. Paul, MN 55165

O17 - VISUAL PLANNING DIVISION, MPC, North Main St., Champlain, NY 12919

Transparencies, as treated in this section, deal with two basic formats; the large transparency for overhead projection or display, and slides of 3 ¼-by 4-inch and 2-by 2-inch formats. In this section, techniques for preparing transparencies range from just drawing or tracing on clear acetate to transferring images from original art to acetate with an electronic scanning machine. All the techniques here have been selected for inclusion because of their uniqueness and simplicity in preparation.

There are many different ways to prepare transparencies for study and display. They can be as simple as drawing or tracing on clear acetate, or as sophisticated as full-color electronic transparent prints. They can also be prepared on most copying machines such as thermocopy, diazo, and Xerographic.

Unfortunately, just tracing or transferring images from printed sources (books, magazines, newspapers, etc.) and converting them without modifications into a transparency seldom assures a good transparency. Converting images to an effective visual medium usually requires some modification. Here are some basic considerations or guidelines for preparing 8½-by 10½-inch transparencies.

Planning The Transparency

The transparency should tell its story with visual impact. Here are some guidelines for planning the transparency so that it does have that visual impact.

ESTABLISH THE IDEA

Carefully consider the exact message you want to get through to your audience. Make every possible effort to limit the message to *one* basic idea that is as clear-cut and independent as possible. Next, select a primary image (visual) of this idea. Think of this image as your "star" performer. Since no "star" performer can get over the message alone, determine the secondary elements in your idea that will establish the environment in which the idea will be established. These secondary elements may take the form of other images, symbols, and lettering. Sources of ideas to assist you at this stage of the planning include catalogs of commercial transparencies and filmstrips, and even good transparencies that already exist.

ROUGHING OUT THE IDEA—KEEPING IT SIMPLE
This is where your idea starts to develop into a visual message. Once you have your idea in mind, make a "blueprint." Start by drawing, freehand or tracing, from your visual source (see page 2 for ideas), a rough sketch of all elements of your idea. Position images (visuals) and lettering in such a way that your "performers" are in their proper places.

The visual format illustrated here is a suggested starting point for good design. Although both horizontal and vertical formats are acceptable, the horizontal is usually considered the best. However, you should use the format which best suits your particular needs. For placement of all elements of the transparency, it is recommended that titles (A) should

generally be at the top of the original, and the rest of the elements (B) in the upper two-thirds for better visibility. The focal point of interest (C) should be as near the center as possible. Now is the time to experiment with the "rough." Is everything you wish to get across in the design? Are the elements centered and well-balanced? Is the message simple and to the point? Are the images instantly recognizable? At this point also, some thought should be given to the use of color later on during the actual preparation of the transparency.

transparencies for study and display

Preparing The Transparency Original

The guidelines here apply to originals prepared on 8½-by 11-inch white bond paper, tracing paper, or transparent or translucent acetate. These originals can be used to produce thermocopy, Xerographic, diazo, or electronic stencil transparencies. The guidelines also apply to the preparation of direct image transparencies.

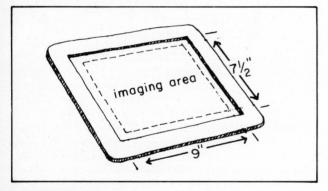

Imaging Area

If a regular transparency mount is used with 8½-by 10½-inch film, the acutal area in which imaging and lettering is to be done measures about 7½-by 9-inch. While the total imaging area will be projected on the screen, it is recommended that all imaging be kept within ¼-to ½-inch of the 7½-by 9-inch dimension.

IMAGE SIZE

While not a great deal has been written as to image (visual) size standards, visibility tests continue to support the recommendation that images should be no smaller than *one-fourth* the total height of the image area.

LETTER SIZE

Even though the transparency is to be projected to a super-size on a screen, the original size of the letters used on the transparency is important. The letters used will be seen in a size relative to the entire projected image. A good rule of thumb is never to use letters smaller than three-sixteenths of an inch high. The chart illustrated here lists letter size as related to viewing distance.

LETTER SIZE

Viewing Distance	Minimum Size
64 feet	2-inch
32 feet	1-inch
16 feet	½-inch
8 feet	¼-inch

Letters make words, and words make sentences. The manner in which these elements are used influences the message being presented. Where possible, limit the original to one point or comparison. Break paragraphs into sentences, and sentences into phrases and key words. Use a maximum of six or seven lines of copy (lettering) and six or seven words per line. Organize letters in straight lines only; stacked or stair-stepped letters impair readability. ◣

TRACE OR DRAW, THEN PROJECT; just that simple for making direct image transparencies for projection or display. This is perhaps the simplest way to make transparencies. Clear or matte (frosted) acetate and any one of the acetate imaging tools (pencil, pen, or marker) are needed to prepare a direct image transparency.

Clear or Prepared Acetate Transparency

When visuals cannot be removed from their original source (book, magazine, newspaper, etc.) and when copying equipment is not available, tracings of visuals can be made directly on clear or prepared acetate. If the original to be traced is the approximate size, then the instructions that follow will be sufficient. If the original is too small, see pages 25 to 29 for instructions on enlarging visuals. If the original is too large, see pages 27 to 29 for instructions on reducing visuals.

Images in black or color line can be projected on the screen by drawing directly on most clear or prepared acetate with a variety of pens, pencils, and markers. The instructions that follow are for the preparation of transparencies on clear or prepared acetate:

125

INSTRUCTIONS

Clear acetate is one of several types of transparent plastics or acetates (reprocessed x-ray film and color acetate are other examples). Prepared acetate is recommended when ink is used, because it has a special coating on both sides that will accept inks, watercolors, poster paints, and dyes without crawling.

1 Attach, where possible, a sheet of acetate to the surface of the visual to be traced. Place a sheet of protective paper (any clean sheet of paper will do) over the portion of the acetate where the hands or fingers might come in contact with the acetate. Oil residue from hands and fingers may be deposited on the surface of the acetate; this may prevent the surface from accepting the ink. In that not all clear acetates will accept ink, talcum powder or pumice can be rubbed over the surface. This will provide the "tooth" necessary to accept and hold the ink line.

2 If a quick, temporary image is desired, draw on the acetate with an opaque or transparent color marking pencil (transparent color pencil will project in color) or with a nylon- or felt-point pen containing a nonpermanent image

(water-base) ink. If a more permanent image is desired, draw on the acetate with India or acetate ink and pen; technical fountain, reservoir, crow quill, and Hunt Bowl Pointed pens are recommended for drawing on clear or prepared acetate.

3 To add color, use nylon-point pens for fine-line color and felt-point pens for broad-line color. See pages 46 to 48 for other coloring techniques.

4 Mount, if desired, for projection. See pages 146 to 149 for tips on mounting techniques.

5 To remove unwanted marking pencil or water-base image lines, use a damp piece of cloth.

6 If lettering is desired, consult the chart on page 54 for recommended lettering techniques on acetates.

Matte (Frosted) Acetate Transparency

INSTRUCTIONS

Matte acetate has a finely etched surface (dull side) which is ideal for accepting India ink, color drawing, and lead pencil lines.

1 Attach, where possible, a sheet of acetate to the surface of the visual to be traced. Place a sheet of protective paper

(any clean sheet of paper will do) over the portion of the acetate where the hands and fingers might come in contact with the acetate. Oil residue from hands and fingers may be deposited on the surface of the acetate; this may prevent the surface from accepting the ink or pencil line.

2 If an ink line is desired, draw directly on the acetate with India ink and pen. Technical fountain, reservoir, crow quill,

and Hunt Bowl Pointed pens are recommended. If a pencil line (black or color) is desired, use a transparent color marking pencil.

IMAGE TRANSFER TRANSPARENCIES

COLD LAMINATING ACETATE IMAGE TRANSFER TRANSPARENCY

3 To remove unwanted ink or pencil lines, use a water- or isopropyl alcohol-dampened cloth to gently remove the lines.

4 Spray the matte (dull) side of the film with clear plastic spray. Hold the spray can about 10 inches above the

acetate, and spray back and forth to apply an even coat of plastic. The use of a larger piece of protective paper placed under the acetate while spraying is recommended. Another method is to pass the acetate through a heat laminating machine; this will seal in the image while making it more transparent. See page 131 for use of the heat laminator. ◣

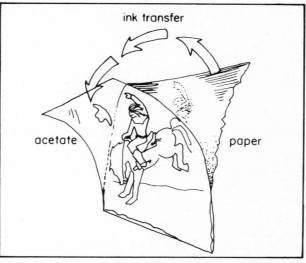

ink transfer

acetate

paper

Image transfer transparencies are almost "magic." Color or black and white images (pictures) printed on clay-coated magazine paper can be made into transparencies for projection or display without photographic or special equipment. The "magic" is "lifting" the image off the magazine page and transferring it to clear acetate.

Five techniques for preparing image transfer transparencies have been selected for inclusion here. Each technique has its own uniqueness, and should be fun to try.

Projection or display transparencies, in full color or black and white, can be made with cold laminating acetate (pressure-sensitive adhesive on one side) and printed pages from most magazines. Basically, the process of image transfer with cold laminating acetate is much the same as laminating with this acetate (see page 106). Once the magazine page has been laminated with acetate, water soaking, drying, and plastic spraying turns the laminated visual into a transparency suitable for projection or display.

Three methods for preparing image transfer transparencies with cold laminating acetate are included here; hand application, clipboard application, and cold acetate laminator application.

Instructions—Hand Application

1 CHECK FOR CLAY COATING. Moisten your finger and rub it on an unprinted section of the magazine; if a chalky substance remains on your finger, the paper is clay coated and suitable for image transfer. Next, trim the desired portion of the page larger than the area intended for transfer.

2 CUT ACETATE. Cut a piece of cold laminating acetate slightly larger than the image for transfer. Next, separate the backing sheet from the acetate at one corner with the point of a cutting knife or by "flicking" a corner with a finger as illustrated. ▚

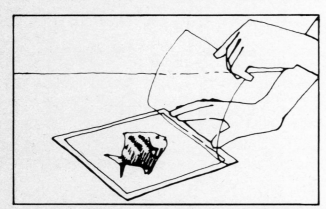

3 POSITION ACETATE ON MAGAZINE PAGE. Peel back the acetate sheet, and position the magazine as desired on the backing sheet. Or completely peel off the acetate, and

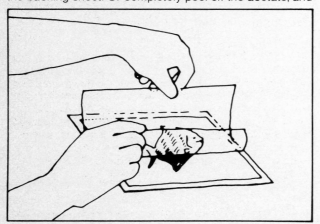

position the visual on the backing sheet. With the "sticky" side of the acetate down, bend the acetate in a U shape and gently lower it down onto the face of the visual, pressing it down in a down and outward direction. Turn the "sandwich" (acetate and visual) over onto a smooth, clean surface so that the acetate side is down. Using a firm pressure, rub the

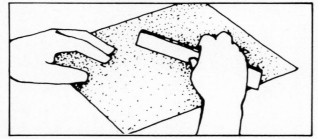

entire surface down with your hand or a flat, smooth object—like the smooth side of a pocket comb or a ruler. Trim off any excess paper.

4 SOAK IN SOAPY WATER. Place the "sandwich" into a pan of soapy water. The soap will speed up soaking time. Allow the paper to be completely saturated with water. Thicker paper will require longer soaking time.

5 PEEL PAPER AWAY AND WASH ACETATE. Gently peel the paper from the acetate. When the paper has been removed, a milky chalk still remains on the image transfer. Gently wash this off with a ball of cotton or soft tissue and plenty of soapy water.

6 AIR- OR TOWEL-DRY ACETATE. Hang up the transparency to dry. Allow about 30 minutes for this step. Or, dry by blotting with paper towels. When dry, the transfer side of the acetate will have a frosty appearance.

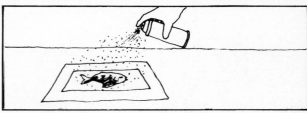

7 SPRAY TO SEAL IMAGE. Place the transparency down on a large piece of protective paper (frosted side of transparency up). To make this surface more transparent and to protect it, spray with a clear plastic spray (Krylon is one brand name). Hold the spray can about 10 inches above the transparency, and spray back and forth to apply an even coating of plastic. Allow it to dry thoroughly.

8 MOUNT FOR PROTECTION OR DISPLAY. Mount transparency on a regular mount (see page 145), or if the transparency is of an odd size, it is easy to cut special mounts from 8- or 10-ply cardboard.

transparencies for study and display 7

Instructions—Clipboard Application

Follow Steps 1 and 2 for Hand Application.

3 INSERT ACETATE IN CLIPBOARD. Insert the cut acetate into the clipboard. Separate the acetate sheet from the backing, and peel back to clamp. Lay the free end of the acetate over the top of the clamp.

4 POSITION VISUAL AND APPLY ACETATE. Position the magazine page on the backing sheet. Carefully lower the acetate sheet down onto the visual. Holding the visual to the backing sheet while lowering the acetate is recommended. Unclip, and turn laminated visual on clipboard. Using a firm pressure, rub the entire surface down with your hand or a flat, smooth object—like the smooth side of a pocket comb or a ruler.

Follow Steps 4, 5, 6, 7, and 8 for Hand Application. ◼

Instructions—Cold Acetate Laminator Application

A description of this type of acetate laminator is on page

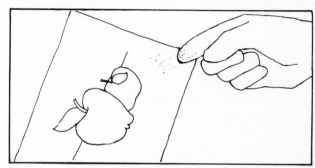

1 CHECK FOR CLAY COATING. Moisten your finger and rub it on an unprinted section of the magazine page; if a chalky substance remains on your finger, the paper is clay coated and suitable for image transfer.

2 INSERT ACETATE UNIT INTO MACHINE. With the machine turned off, insert an edge of the acetate unit (backing sheet down) through the front opening until stopped by the machine rollers. Holding the acetate unit flat, push the switch to "nip" momentarily until about ¼-inch of the acetate unit enters the rollers. Separate the paper backing sheet from the acetate, and peel back to rest on the machine.

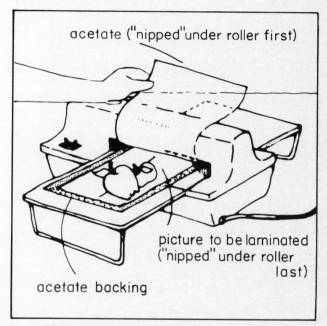

acetate ("nipped" under roller first)

picture to be laminated ("nipped" under roller last)

acetate backing

3 INSERT VISUAL INTO ACETATE UNIT. Position the visual (face up) on the backing sheet, and slide gently into the nip at the rollers. Hold the acetate with the left hand as nearly vertical as practical, and flip the switch to start the rollers moving. The machine will pull the acetate, visual, and backing sheet through to the discharge shelf at the rear.

4 TRIM VISUAL AND REMOVE BACKING SHEET. Trim laminated visual, and remove backing sheet.

Follow Steps 4, 5, 6, 7, and 8 for Hand Application. ◼

RUBBER CEMENT IMAGE TRANSFER
TRANSPARENCY

Inexpensive, full color or black and white transparencies for projection or display can be made from most magazines. This do-it-yourself technique for transferring magazine images to acetate is fun, and easy to do. In addition to magazine pages, all that you need are clear acetate sheets, steel wool, rubber cement, a 2-inch wide brush, ordinary tap water, and clear plastic spray (Krylon).

Instructions

1 CHECK FOR CLAY COATING. Moisten your finger and rub it on an unprinted section of the magazine page; if a chalky substance remains on your finger, the paper is clay

coated and suitable for image transfer. Next, trim the desired portion of the page larger than the area intended for transfer.

2 CUT AND ETCH ACETATE. Cut a piece of acetate (use 0.005-inch thick for best results) slightly larger than image for transfer. Next, lightly etch one side of the acetate with a

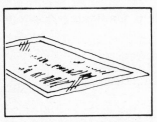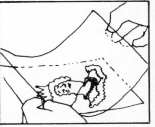

piece of fine-grade steel wool. Remove any etching dust that remains on the acetate.

3 APPLY RUBBER CEMENT TO ACETATE. First, thin rubber cement with rubber cement thinner (solvent), so that it will run freely from the brush. Next, apply a thin, even coat of rubber cement to the etched surface of the acetate.

4 APPLY RUBBER CEMENT TO MAGAZINE PAGE. Apply a thin, even coat of rubber cement to the SURFACE of the magazine page. TO ASSURE BETTER ADHESION OF BOTH SURFACES (acetate and magazine page), brush the rubber cement at 90° angles to each other. Allow both surfaces to thoroughly dry before contact.

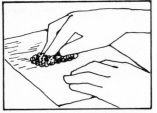

5 POSITION ACETATE ON MAGAZINE PAGE. Lay the magazine page (face up) on a smooth, clean surface. Grasp the acetate at two edges and bend into a U shape (cement coated side down). Carefully lower onto the center of the magazine page. Be sure the two coated surfaces make initial contact at the center. Firmly press down the two edges of acetate until both cemented surfaces are completely in contact. Next, with the fingers, press the two surfaces together with a firm pressure going from the center out in all directions. This should help eliminate air pockets. To assure absolute contact, turn the "sandwich" over on a clean, smooth surface so that the back side of the visual is up. With a new razor blade held at an angle, draw with a firm pressure from the center outward in all directions. Be sure the entire surface is pressed into contact by this method.

6 SOAK IN SOAPY WATER. Place the "sandwich" into a pan of soapy water. The soap will speed up soaking time. Allow the paper to be completely saturated with water. Thicker paper will require longer time in the water.

7 PEEL PAPER AWAY AND WASH ACETATE. Gently peel the paper from the acetate. Care must be taken along the edges of the "Sandwich" not to tear any rubber cement that might cling to the paper edge. If any paper fiber remains on the rubber cement surface, rub over it gently with the fingertip. It will generally release and wash off. When the paper has been removed, a milky chalk still remains on the image transfer. Gently wash this off with a ball of cotton or soft tissue and plenty of soapy water. Excess water may be removed from the transparency by blotting with a paper towel.

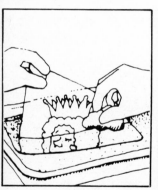

8 AIR- OR TOWEL-DRY ACETATE. Hang up the transparency to dry. Allow about 30 minutes for this step. Or, dry by blotting with paper towels. When dry, the rubber cemented side of the transparency will have a frosty appearance.

9 SPRAY TO SEAL IMAGE. Place the transparency down on a smooth, dry surface with the rubber cemented side up. Tape down the four corners. To make this surface more transparent and to protect the surface, spray this side with a clear plastic spray (Krylon). Hold the spray can about 10 inches above the transparency, and spray back and forth to apply an even coating of plastic. Allow it to dry thoroughly.

10 ADDED PROTECTION. Even though the rubber cement surface has been protected by plastic spray, it is still susceptible to damage. It is best to cover it with a piece of clear acetate for protection.

11 MOUNT FOR PROJECTION OR DISPLAY. Mount transparency on a regular mount (see page 145), or if the transparency is of an odd size, it is easy to cut special mounts from 8- or 10-ply cardboard. ◣

Inexpensive, full color or black and white transparencies can be made from most magazines and a heat laminator. Making transparencies with this machine is much the same as regular heat laminating (see page 108). Image transfer starts to take place when the adhesive surface of the acetate is heat-pressured to the surface of the magazine

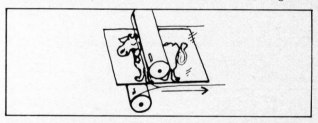

page as it passes through the laminator. Soaking in water, washing, drying, and re-laminating follows. The results, a transparent image on acetate ready for projection or display.

Since most heat laminators laminate both sides of a magazine simultaneously, it is possible to make two transparencies at one time. ⠶

Instructions

1 CHECK FOR CLAY COATING. Select two magazine pages for image transfer. To check for clay coating, moisten your finger and rub it on an unprinted section of the magazine page; if a chalky substance remains on your finger, the paper is clay coated and suitable for image transfer.

2 ASSEMBLE AND LAMINATE MAGAZINE PAGES. Since two transparencies can be made at the same time, place two magazine pages back to back and pass them through the heated rollers of the laminator. A thin laminating film is applied to both outer page surfaces.

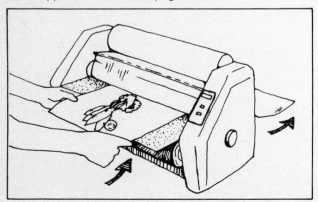

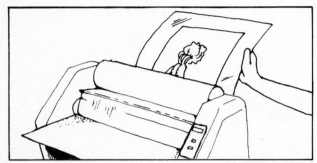

3 TRIM ACETATE EDGES FOR SEPARATION. Trim all four edges of the laminated pages enough to allow for separation of the two pages.

4 SOAK IN SOAPY WATER. Place laminated pages in soapy water, containing a little liquid soap. This softens the clay between the paper and the acetate. Let the work soak for about three minutes to loosen the acetate from the page. Some papers may require a longer soaking period.

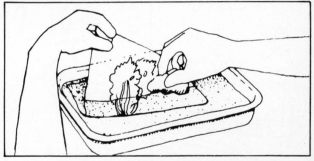

5 PEEL PAPER AWAY AND WASH ACETATE. Peel the page, which is now blank, from the acetate. The image is now embedded in the adhesive side of the acetate. In most cases, the page will simply fall away after soaking. If the page does not separate easily, rub the paper off firmly but gently with your fingers under water. Rinse the transparency in clean water.

6 DRY THE TRANSPARENCY. The transparency may be dried by blotting with paper towels, or it may be air-dried by hanging it up.

DRY MOUNTING PRESS IMAGE TRANSFER TRANSPARENCY

7 LAMINATE A SECOND TIME. After the transparency is completely dry, pass it back through the laminator. This will protect the transferred ink image and add more support to the transparency.

8 MOUNT TRANSPARENCY FOR SUPPORT. Mount the transparency to any one of the variety of mounts (see page 145).

Inexpensive, full color or black and white transparencies can be made from most magazines, a dry mounting press, and Seal's Seal-lamin film. Under heat and pressure, this film literally lifts the ink image off the magazine page. Only magazines that are printed on clay coated paper can be used.

Instructions

1 INCREASE PRESSURE AND WARM UP PRESS. Place a ¼-inch masonite board under the green thick pad of the press. Set the temperature at 300° F and allow the press to warm up.

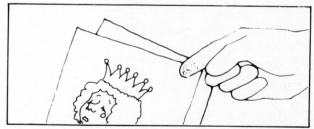

2 CHECK FOR CLAY COATING. Moisten your finger and rub it on an unprinted section of the magazine page; if a chalky substance remains on your finger, the paper is clay coated and suitable for image transfer.

3 PRE-DRY MAGAZINE PAGE. The magazine page should be pre-dried in the heated press to reduce moisture level. Position the page in a carrier of Kraft, or other smooth porous paper, and place in heated press for 45 seconds. Open press momentarily and repeat cycle for 30 additional seconds.

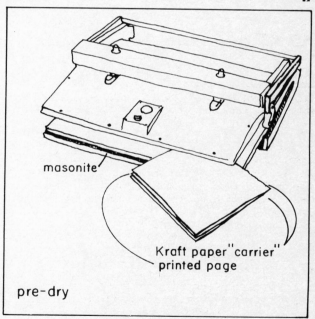

masonite

Kraft paper "carrier"
printed page

pre-dry

4 COVER WITH SEAL-LAMIN FILM. Place magazine page face up on a sheet of Kraft paper slightly smaller than the page. This will absorb any excess moisture still in the material. Overlap material with a piece of film, adhesive (dull) side down.

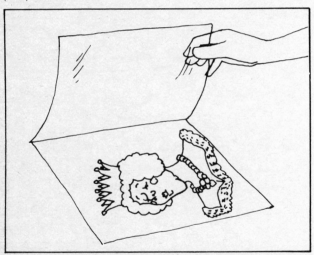

5 SEAL IN PRESS. Insert work in carrier of Seal release paper and place in the press for 60 seconds. If there are any incomplete areas (these will show up as blisters), put the work back in the press for 45 to 60 seconds.

 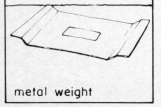

release paper carrier | metal weight

6 REMOVE WORK. Remove and cool under Seal weight for 30 seconds. Carefully take work out of carrier. The excess film around the edges may be stuck to the release paper. If you pull too hard, the film will wrinkle, which could cause a poor transparency.

7 SOAK IN LUKEWARM WATER. Place the work in a pan of lukewarm water to which a packet of Seal Tonic (or any mild liquid detergent) has been added. Let the work soak for about three minutes to loosen the film from the page.

8 PEEL PAPER AWAY. Peel the page, which is now blank, from the film. The image is now embedded in the adhesive side of the film. In most cases, the page will simply fall away. If the page does not separate easily, rub the paper off firmly but gently with your fingers under water.

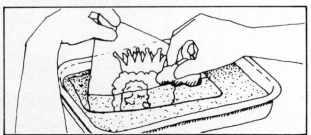

9 WIPE CLEAN AND SPRAY. Remove excess clay residue from the transparency by wiping the film gently with a wet sponge or soft cloth. Always rub in one direction to avoid wrinkling. Blot with a paper towel and allow to dry completely. Then spray the frosted side with a clear plastic, such as Krylon.

To protect the transparency, attach it to a transparency mount (see page 146).

transparencies for study and display 7

TRANSFER FILM IMAGE TRANSFER TRANSPARENCY

With this do-it-yourself transfer film and a dry mounting press, you can make full color or black and white transparencies for projection or display out of most magazines.

To make your own transfer film, use a transparent or frosted film (acetate) that meets the requirement for critical film register and remains stable under high heat temperatures. This type of film is available from art supply and drafting supply stores.

To make your own transfer film, spray one side of the film with three light coats of clear acrylic spray. Alternate the

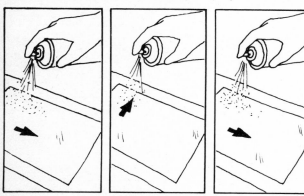

direction in which the spray is applied between coats. Allow the sprayed surface to dry between each application, and make sure the entire surface is evenly covered. The film now has a relatively unstable clear plastic surface, with a stable base. When heat is applied, during image transfer, the plastic coating softens and functions as an adhesive in much the same way as heat laminating film works.

Instructions

1 INCREASE PRESSURE AND WARM UP PRESS. Place a ¼-inch masonite board under the green thick pad of the press. Set the temperature at 300°F and allow the press to warm up.

2 CHECK FOR CLAY COATING. Moisten your fingertip and rub it over an unprinted section of the magazine page; if a chalky substance remains on your finger, the paper is clay coated and suitable for image transfer.

3 PRE-DRY MAGAZINE PAGE. The magazine page should be pre-dried in the heated press to reduce moisture level. Position the page in carrier of Kraft, or other smooth

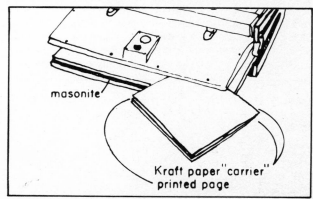

masonite

Kraft paper "carrier" printed page

porous paper, and place in heated press for 45 seconds. Open press momentarily and repeat cycle for 30 additional seconds.

4 COVER WITH TRANSFER FILM. Place magazine page face up on a sheet of Kraft paper the size of the magazine page. This will absorb any excess moisture still in the page. Cover the page with a sheet of transfer film (coated side down).

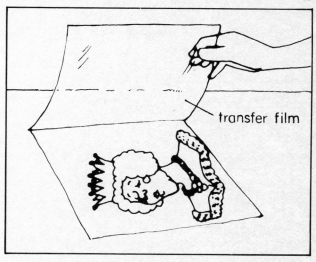

transfer film

5 SEAL IN PRESS. Insert work in a carrier of Seal release paper (Kraft paper also works) and place in the press for 60 seconds. If there are any incomplete areas (these will show up as blisters), put the work back in the press for 45 to 60 seconds.

 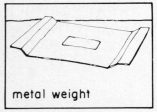

release paper carrier | metal weight

6 REMOVE WORK. Remove and cool under Seal weight for 30 seconds. Carefully take work out of carrier.

7 SOAK IN SOAPY WATER. Place the laminated page in a pan of soapy water for about three minutes to loosen film from the page. Thicker paper will require longer soaking time.

8 PEEL PAPER AWAY AND WASH FILM. Peel the page, which is now blank, from the film. The image is now embedded in the coated side of the film. In most cases, the page will simply fall away. If the page does not separate easily, rub the paper off firmly but gently with your fingers under water.

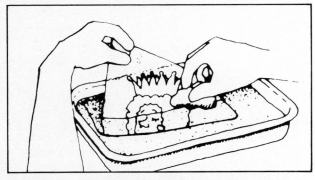

9 WIPE CLEAN AND SPRAY. Remove any excess clay residue from the transparency by wiping the film gently with a wet sponge or soft cloth. Blot with paper towels and allow to completely dry. To spray, place the transparency down on a large piece of protective paper (frosted side of transparency up), and spray with clear plastic spray (Krylon is one brand name). Hold the spray can about 10 inches above the transparency, and spray back and forth to apply an even coating of plastic. Allow it to dry completely.

10 MOUNT FOR PROJECTION OR DISPLAY. Mount transparency on a regular mount (see page146), or if the transparency is of an odd size, it is easy to cut special mounts from 8- or 10-ply cardboard. ∎

transparencies for study and display

THERMOCOPY TRANSPARENCIES

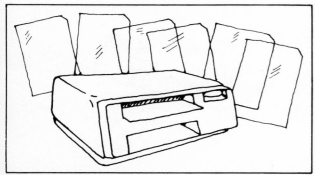

The thermocopy process, also known as thermal transfer, thermal copy, dry heat, and infrared, is the only copying process in which exposure and development are simultaneous. It is one of the simplest in both construction and operation. Only one step is involved: the insertion of a specially coated film and the original together into the exposure opening of the copying machine. The image is transferred from the original to the film in about four seconds. What actually takes place during this process is this: when the original (fully opaque or translucent) is passed through the machine, the heat from the light source (infrared) penetrates through the thermocopy film to the original, which is made up of images containing some metallic substance and whose colors are visible to infrared light. The image areas absorb the heat from the infrared light; thus the "hot" image of the original forms an image on the film at the point of image contact.

Handmade Originals

Creating originals for the thermocopy process is both easy and fun. Discussed here are two techniques for preparing handmade originals.

Marking Devices

Basic to preparing originals are marking devices that produce lines that can be produced by the thermocopy process. Marking devices include a #2 lead pencil, 3M black marking pen, India ink and pen, and typewriter with a carbon ribbon.

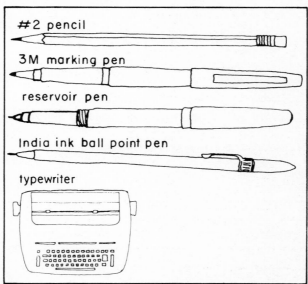

Paper Surfaces

Three paper surfaces that work best for preparing handmade originals are bond paper, guide sheet, and graph paper. The blue lines of graph paper will not reproduce when using a thermocopy machine.

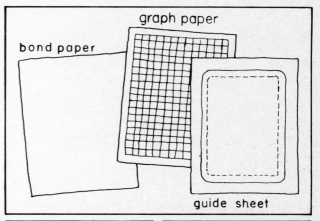

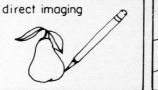

INSTRUCTIONS: DIRECT IMAGE ON PAPER
Art and lettering can be done directly on any of the papers and with the marking devices recommended.

INSTRUCTIONS: PASTE-UP IMAGE ON PAPER
Art from clip art books (see page 12), newspapers, magazines, etc., can be mounted directly on any of the papers recommended with small pieces of transparent tape.

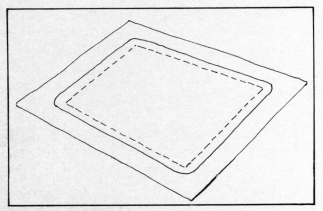

Thermocopy Guide Sheet

Here is a valuable aid for preparing art and lettering for the thermocopy process. This guide sheet, designed by the author, can be easily made by tracing the inside opening of the transparency mount to be used directly on a spirit

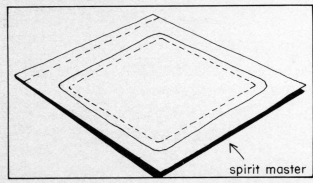

spirit master

master. Next, draw a broken line ½ inch from the solid line (do all art and lettering within this broken line). Make white

paper copies from this master with the spirit duplicator(Ditto machine). Guide sheets can be used to draw or trace on, or can be used for paste-up art and lettering or for typing. The

guidelines will not reproduce when passed through the thermocopy machine—only the art and lettering.

INSTRUCTIONS FOR MAKING TRANSPARENCIES

1 Place a sheet of thermocopy film, with the notch in the upper right-hand corner (away from the operator), on top of the original (printed side up).

2 Set the exposure dial as indicated by the manufacturer of the film. Feed the film and original into the machine. *Light lines on the transparency can be darkened by running the film only through the machine a second time.*

3 Retrieve the film and original, and separate. Mount the transparency if desired.

Helpful Techniques for Enhancing Finish Transparencies

1 To add color, see page 46 .

2 To add lettering, see the "Lettering Selection Chart," page 54 .

3 To mount, see page146 .

4 To add "motion," see page 50 .

transparencies for study and display 7

TRANSPAREX FILM TRANSPARENCY

ESCOTHERM COLOR-ON FILM TRANSPARENCY

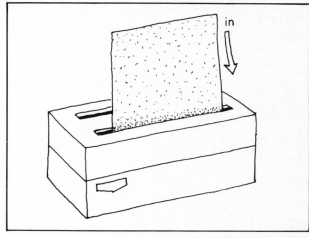

Transparex film, developed by Agfa-Gevaert, produces transparencies in six brilliant colors (red, yellow, green, blue, black, and opaque white). This process involves selecting the desired color of film, running it through any thermocopy machine with an original (see page 137 for preparation of original), and washing in ordinary tap water. Result: a clean, sharp color transparency ready for projection.

Instructions

1 Combine original art (face up) with the emulsion side of the film, and insert in the special Transparex carrier. Insert assembled units in any thermocopy machine, and expose at the recommended setting.

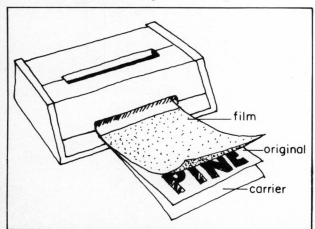

2 Separate the exposed film from the original, and insert in one of the Transparex processors. If a processor is not

available, processing can be done by hand-washing with a soft sponge and ordinary tap water.

3 Remove processed film processor.

Arkwright's Escotherm Color-On transparency is a thermocopy film that produces a frosted image on a clear acetate base. The frosted image projects as a black on white (clear) background or can be hand-colored with up to ten easy-to-use wipe-on colors.

Like other types of thermocopy film, Escotherm requires an original suitable for the thermocopy process. See page 137 for instructions on preparing thermocopy originals. Also, originals to be copied may be photographs (except Polaroid) or any printed, typed, drawn, or written materials, on one or both sides of the paper, halftone or line originals.

Instructions

1 *Testing:* As a test, place a sheet of thermocopy paper (buff side up) on top of the original and run through the thermocopy machine. A faint but readable copy indicates the

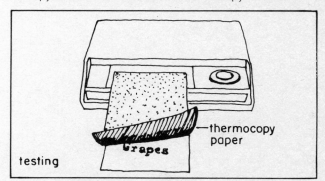

best setting for charging the original. Test sheets eliminate unnecessary film waste.

2 *Charging the Original:* Use the speed setting determined by running the test sheet. Place the charging sheet, dark side up, on top of the original. Run through the copy

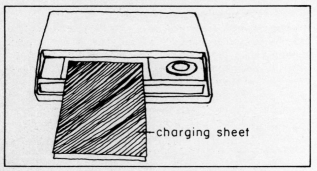

machine once. Registration for this step is not important. For black negative film or Color-On film, charge twice using the same charging sheet. Discard the charging sheet after charging the original

3 *Printing Film:* Place the film over the charged original with the clipped corner at the upper right, and pass through the copier.

4 *Applying Colors:* Apply Escotherm Applicolors to images (visuals, letters, etc.) with a Q-tip. Colors wipe off non-image areas with facial tissue moistened with water. ▪

The diazo process is not new; it dates back to World War I when a serious shortage of photographic papers and films pointed up the need for a substitute reproduction process.

This process works on the principle of ultraviolet light passing through a translucent or transparent original (master), which destroys the chemical coating on the film (foil), except where an opaque image (line, letter, etc.) has blocked the light. The exposed film is developed, and the remaining chemical is converted to a visible image.

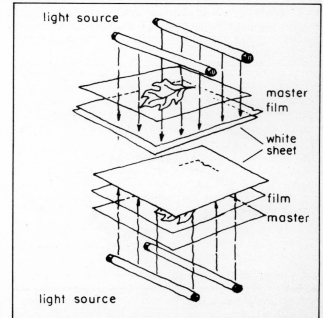

Diazo transparencies project in vivid colors far superior to those of many other techniques for producing projectables. For persons interested, additional history and information on the diazo process can be obtained from manufacturers and suppliers of diazo equipment and materials.

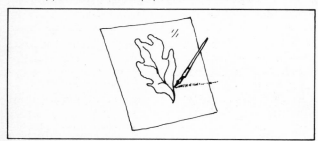

Preparation of Transparency Originals

Diazo originals, or "masters," are usually "line" artwork. However, soft lead pencils can be used to create shading or special effects. Any well-prepared *translucent* original can be used, such as an ink or pencil drawing on tracing paper or matte acetate, carbon-backed typewritten material, or photographic film positives. Transparency quality depends upon the relative image opacity and base translucency of the original.

TRANSFER OF ORIGINAL OPAQUE IMAGES

If the proposed transparency is printed, drawn, lettered, or typed on an opaque base (paper, cardboard, etc.), it can be transferred to a translucent or transparent base in one of the following ways:

1 It can be photographed, and a positive-transparent film can be made from the negative (enlargement or reduction of the original can be made this way).

2 A direct-positive reproducible print can be made on Kodak Auto-Positive paper or film, thereby eliminating the photographic negative.

3 Translucent or transparent-base originals can be made with thermocopy (see page 137) or Xerographic (see page 143) copying machines.

Monochrome Transparencies

Monochrome (single-color) transparencies are made by contacting the master on diazo film. Here are the instructions:

1 Place the appropriate-color diazo film in contact with the handmade or commercial master, face to face. The face side (sensitized) of the diazo film is found by locating the notch in the upper right-hand corner of the film. Use the interleaf sheet, if white or with a white side, as a backup to the master during exposure. Place the white side of the sheet behind the film.

2 To expose (if the light source of the diazo machine is *above* the exposure stage), follow the foregoing instructions; then insert assembled materials in the machine (master on top of film), and expose the recommended time. To expose (if the light source of the diazo machine is *below* the exposure stage), follow the foregoing instructions; then insert the assembled materials (film on top of master), and expose the recommended time.

3 After exposure, separate the film from the master and interleaf sheet. Roll the film with the sensitized (emulsion) side in, and place it in a large-mouth gallon-size jar or insert it in the developing unit of the diazo machine, if it has one. If

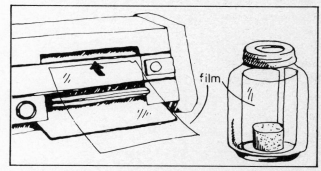

a large jar is used, soak a sponge or paper towel with strong ammonia water (28 percent is recommended) and place it in the jar. The ammonia can also be placed in a container as illustrated.

4 Mount, if desired, for protection. See page 145 for tips on mounting.

Here is a technique for producing a high-quality image of printed and visual material on both a stencil and a sheet of transparent film at the same time. The original can be anything from a page from a book to drawings, or even paste-up artwork that includes photographic halftones. The electronic stencil-cutting machine produces a stencil and a finished transparency for immediate projection.

Instructions

The Gestetner Corporation has prepared a booklet, *How to Make a Paste-Up Layout for Your Gestefax,* which contains instructions and illustrations for preparing artwork for the electronic stencil cutter. Refer to pages 35 to 36 for tips on paste-up techniques.

1 Carefully separate the stencil from the backing sheet, starting at a point approximately 3 inches from the top right side of the stencil. Peel just enough of the stencil to insert a ruler.

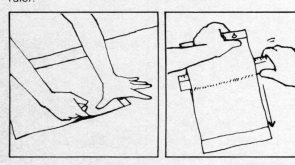

2 Insert, with care, a ruler in the opening created between the stencil and the backing sheet. Gently push the ruler to the opposite side of the stencil; then move the ruler downward about 11 inches. This will create a "pocket" in which the film is inserted.

3 Place a sheet of clear acetate (Gestetner Corporation's Gestefax transparency film is designed especially for this technique) in the "pocket" of the stencil. Thermocopy and most clear acetate film can also be used.

4 Attach the original (art, lettering, etc.) to the left-side drum of the stencil cutter.

5 Attach a stencil, with the film inserted, to the right-side drum. Use recommended machine settings for the type of original being reproduced. Start the machine.

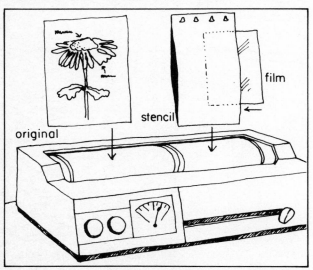

6 After the stencil has been cut, detach from the stencil drum and remove the film. It is now ready for immediate use.

7 To add color, see pages 46 to 48. To mount or mask, see pages 145 to 148. To add lettering, see page 54 for recommended lettering techniques. To add "motion," see page 50.

8 The "cut" stencil can be attached to a stencil duplicator, and hundreds of paper copies can be made. ∎

transparencies for study and display

XEROGRAPHIC TRANSPARENCIES

Overhead projection or display transparencies can be made in any Xerox office copier as easily and simply as making a regular paper copy.

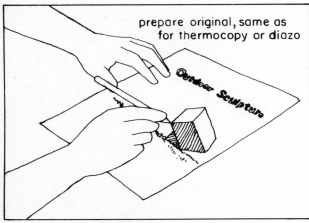

prepare original, same as for thermocopy or diazo

There are several producers and distributors of Xerographic film. However, Arkwright's Xerographic film and process will be discussed here. Xerographic film from Arkwright comes in 8½- by 11- and 8½- by 14-inch clear, red, yellow, blue, and green sheets.

Operating Instructions

Xerox Models 914, 420, 720, 2400, 3100, 3600-1, 4000, and 7000:
1 Fan the film sheets to allow for easy feeding and handling.

2 Place a supply of sheets (approximately ten to fifteen) into the loading tray with the white opaque strip facing up.

3 Make prints in the normal way with the pressure lever and temperature control at the same setting as used for paper. If the print is too light, pump up the toner to the desired darkness level.

4 If fusion is not adequate, go to the next highest heat setting (use this setting when making future transparencies).

Xerox Models 813, 660, and 330:

1 Fan the film sheets to allow for easy feeding and handling.

2 Load the tray with an opaque white strip feeding into the machine, but with the strip facing down.

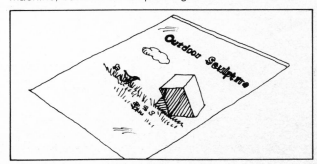

3 Put the dial setting on 1 after loading the tray.

4 Make prints in the normal way.

HELPFUL TIPS

Corrections
If changes are necessary after printing, delete image areas with tetrachloroethylene. New data can be added with marking pens or markers.

Removal of Oil Residue
The light oil residue on transparencies imaged in certain models will disappear eventually, but may be removed immediately by gently wiping both sides with paper tissue.

Print Quality
Always check that the copier is making clean, sharp black images on paper. The quality of the transparency will only be as good as that being produced on paper. ▪

The 3M brand "Color-Key" system produces fine-quality color transparencies for overhead projection and displays. The system involves a two-film process: a negative, and then a color positive. For the visual media designer/producer requiring quick, accurate color transparencies, "Color-Key" is one good solution.

Instructions

1 The original can be a drawing, hand lettering, dry transfer lettering (see the "Lettering Selection Chart," page 54), etc., on clear acetate, tracing paper (vellum), or other thin translucent paper.

original

2 Make a "Color-Key" negative by exposing to an ultraviolet light source. Develop with 3M brand "Color-Key" developer. From this negative you can make a positive in any of the "Color-Key" colors.

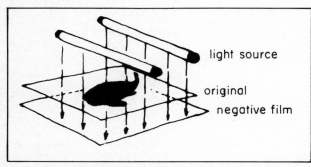

light source

original

negative film

3 Expose the negative to the desired sheet of color film.

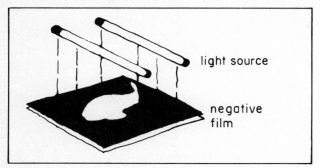

light source

negative film

4 Develop the color positive with 3M brand "Color-Key" developer. Swab, rinse, and blot dry.

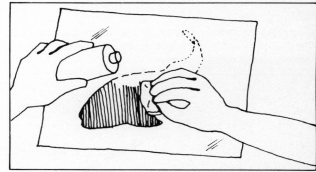

5 The results—an exact copy of the original on a clear film base in color.

transparencies for study and display

LARGE TRANSPARENCY MOUNTING

Large transparencies may be projected unmounted if the base (film) is thick enough to lie flat on the stage of the overhead projector. However, there are several good reasons for mounting transparencies. A mount will, for instance, block out light projecting around the edges of the transparency so that only the intended projection image area is seen on the projection screen. A mount also provides a solid base for easy handling, manipulation of overlays, and storing. Moreover, the surface of many mounts can be used to write notes related to the transparency.

Mounted transparencies can be projected horizontally or vertically. However, it is recommended that where possible the transparency should be produced and mounted horizontally so that full advantage can be taken of the most commonly used horizontal projection screens.

Careful consideration should be given to size, material, method of securing film to mount, and masking and hinging overlays when mounting large transparencies for projection. Since sizes of mounts and image areas have not yet been standardized, the recommended mount size is one that fits a standard letter-size file or can be carried in a briefcase.

Transparency Mounts

Mounts (frames) for overhead projection transparencies (projectuals) are available in a variety of formats and materials for reasons of economy and for various requirements.

Aperture (viewing area) sizes vary, depending upon film or projection equipment requirements, from 7½ by 9½ to 10 by 10 inches usually.

CARDBOARD MOUNT (PLAIN BACK)
A die-cut cardboard (pressboard) mount that is most popular because of its hard surface and durability.

CARDBOARD MOUNT (ADHESIVE BACK)
A sandwich-type cardboard mount with pressure-sensitive adhesive to permit the mounting of one or more "cells" inside. Place the mount open on a flat surface. Position the base "cell" on one side of the mount. Some mounts have

registration marks to assist in the registration of "cells." Fold the opposite side of the mount over so that it locks the base "cell" in place. Rub, with firm pressure around the top of the mount to assure good adhesion.

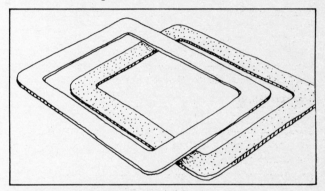

SOLID PLASTIC MOUNT
A permanent-type solid plastic mount in white or colors that resists warping caused by extreme changes in humidity. The mount is reusable and accepts mounting tape and staples.

TRANSPARENT PLASTIC MOUNT
A self-contained transparent plastic mount with an opaque border. No mounting or masking is required, unless overlays are desired. Lettering, writing, coloring, etc., are done directly on the surface of the mount.

HANDMADE MOUNT
Almost any opaque material with a fair degree of thickness can be used to make a mount. Regular manila file folders are ideal for mounts. Openings 7½ by 9½ inches, or the size desired, can be cut in one or both sides of the folder. Other materials such as chipboard and posterboard can be used as long as the material is stiff enough to hold the transparency. ◢

Mounting Base Transparency

Finished transparencies can be projected unmounted (un-framed). However, there are several advantages to mounting transparencies: the mount blocks light around the edge of the visual, adds rigidity for both handling and storage, and provides a convenient border for writing lecture notes. Here is a simple procedure for framing or mounting the base transparency:

1 Lay the mount upside down on a flat surface.

2 Center the transparency *face down* on the mount.

3 Tape all four sides.

ATTACHING OVERLAYS WITH TAPE
Overlays can help simplify complicated concepts and allow you to build your presentation step by step. Here is a simple procedure for adding overlays:

transparencies for study and display

1 Lay the mounted transparency right side up on a flat surface.

2 Center the first overlay, and tape (or use transparency hinges) along one edge of the mount. If all the overlays follow the same sequence, you can attach all the overlays on the same edge.

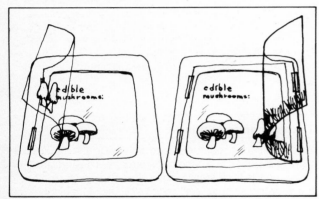

3 Center the second overlay over the first, and tape along the other edge.

It is generally recommended to limit the number of overlays to four.

ATTACHING OVERLAYS WITH TRANSPARENCY HINGES
To hinge overlays with overhead transparency hinges, remove the paper backing from the first hinge and follow these instructions:

1 Position the hinge, adhesive side up, under the film at the center position on the edge which is to be hinged. The bottom of the film is pressed onto the adhesive.

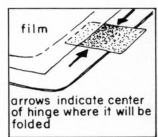

> **film**
> **arrows indicate center of hinge where it will be folded**

2 Then fold the hinge over, pressing it against the top of the film. The film is now sandwiched firmly between the two adhesive sides of the hinge.

3 Insert two staples through each hinge, or stack of hinges if other sequential overlays are used. An overhead transparency stapler is recommended since an ordinary

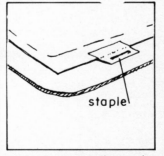

staple

stapler with standard staples may not penetrate the overlay and mount. Three hinges are recommended for each overlay.

ATTACHING MASKS

Sliding Masks
Sliding masks, made of cardboard, overhead transparency plastic mask, or other opaque material, can be used to achieve a controlled-pace presentation. The projection screen at the beginning of the presentation is dark; then, as

the mask slides off the mount, the image is revealed to the viewers. The track for the mask can be made from two pieces of cardboard and stapled to the mount as illustrated, or commercial overhead transparency plastic tracks can be purchased. An overhead transparency stapler is recommended for attaching tracks to the mount, since an ordinary stapler with standard staples may not penetrate the track and mount.

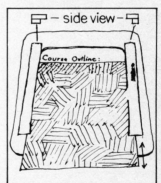

> **side view**
> **Course Outline:**

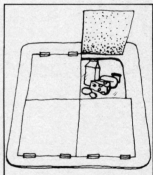

Spot Masks
Spot masks (or *barn door* masks) are designed to reveal a selected portion of a transparency. Masks can be cut into any shape desired and attached in much the same way as any of the other masks included in this section. Among the materials that can be used for spot masks are cardboard, file folder, and overhead transparency plastic mask.

Folding Masks

Folding masks, also known as accordion-pleat masks, are excellent for progressive disclosure of projected material. Strips of cardboard, cut the correct size, can be hinged together with pressure-sensitive tape and hinged to the edge of the mount; or simply fold an opaque sheet of heavy paper in strips the correct width and hinge to the mount. To use the folding mask, lift each fold or section as required to disclose another part of the image area. Notes and cues can be made on each fold.

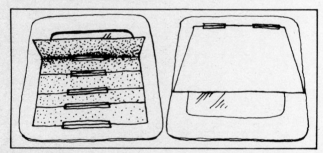

Hinged Masks

A progressive disclosure can be achieved by masking all or a portion of the transparency with an opaque sheet, such as cardboard or an overhead transparency plastic mask. Instructions for hinging masks and attaching overlays are the same and can be found on page 147.

Transparency Stapler

A heavy-duty stapler which is especially modified for attaching overlays to transparency mounts. It uses heavy, wide-faced steel staples designed for transparency mounting.

Transparency Plastic Track

Specially designed "tracks" for use with transparency cardboard or plastic mounts. Tracks are stapled or taped to transparency mount, and masks are then inserted. Masks will then slide easily along the tracks, allowing the desired areas to be blocked out at any desired moment.

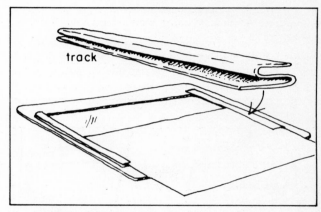

Transparency Hinge

Pressure-sensitized, metallized polyester film squares for hinging overlays to a base transparency. They are adhered to overlays to form small hinges and are then stapled to the transparency mount (see page 147). The hinges are extraordinarily strong and can be folded at least 12,000 times without breaking. They are packaged in a "pop-up" dispenser box.

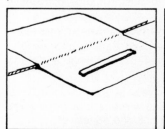 

Transparency Hinging Tape

Made of the same material as transparency hinges. Designed for hinging a complete side of a transparency and

DIRECT IMAGE SLIDES

for mounting a transparency on a mount and for use where a need for an indestructible tape is required. Tape is available in ½- or ¾-inch width.

Transparency Envelope

A large transparent plastic or heavypaper envelope for protecting overhead transparencies when stored. Some envelopes are hole-punched for insertion in loose-leaf notebooks.

Transparency Album

Especially designed for storage and protection of overhead transparencies. Each pocket page holds one transparency.

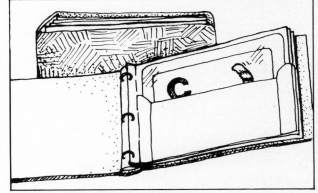

Transparency Carrying Case

Vinyl case for storing or transporting overhead transparencies.

Metal Transparency Cabinet

Metal cabinet designed for storing audio records or fifty transparencies.

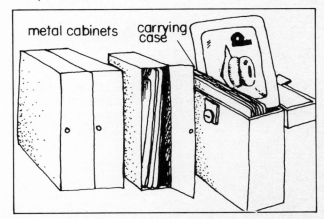

metal cabinets   carrying case

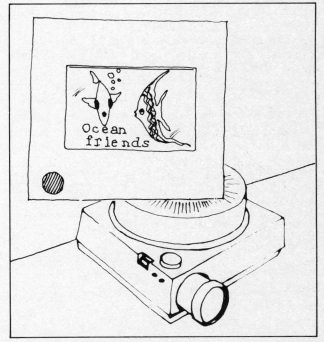

TRACE OR DRAW, MOUNT, THEN PROJECT; just that simple for making 2-by 2-inch direct image slides. This is perhaps the simplest way to make slides. Transparencies for overhead projection can also be made with this method (see page 125). Clear or prepared acetate, any one of the acetate imaging tools (pencil, pen, or marker), and slide mounts are all that is needed to make direct image slides.

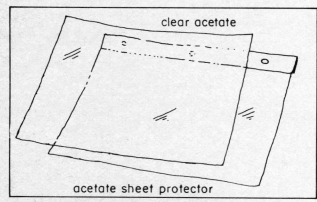

clear acetate

acetate sheet protector

CLEAR ACETATE is an all-purpose transparent cellulose acetate sheet that can be used much like an ordinary sheet of paper for drawing or tracing. The surface will accept several of the imaging tools (see Imaging Selection Chart on page 11). Clear acetate is available in sheets and rolls. Acetate sheet protectors for 3-hole or multi-hole binders can also be used for slide making. These protectors are usually available from stationers', office, and art supply stores. PREPARED ACETATE is a crystal acetate (plastic) with a special coating on both sides that will accept poster paints, watercolors, inks, and dyes without crawling. Available in both sheets and pads.

Due to the small image area of the slide, images that are traced or drawn must also be small. Small visuals are everywhere; in magazines, newspapers, books, dictionaries, the YELLOW pages, etc. Start a collection of small images. Not only can they be used to make direct image slides, they can be modified (see Section 2) for preparing other visual media.

Instructions

The Slide Guide Sheet on page 155 has been designed for direct image, thermocopy, and Xerographic slide making. This guide sheet should not be removed from the handbook. It may be photocopied (Xerographic or thermocopy) or traced if its use is better facilitated by reproducing.

1 Attach a sheet (for many slides) or a 2-inch wide strip (for a few slides) of acetate to the guide sheet. To secure the acetate to the guide sheet, punch holes at two edges of the acetate and mount a 1-inch piece of adhesive tape over each hole. Press tape firmly in place at each hole. Position the acetate to cover the number of slides you wish to make.

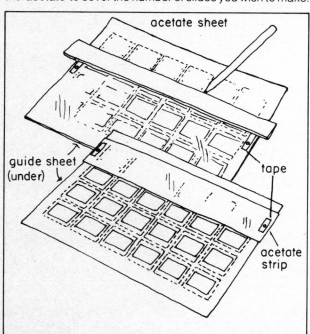

acetate sheet

guide sheet (under)

tape

acetate strip

2 First, select the appropriate imaging tool. For regular acetate, use overhead transparency projection pens or transparent or opaque color marking pencils. The pens will render a sharper image line. For prepared acetate, any of the imaging tools will work, including pen and drawing inks. Next, trace the outer (broken) line for each slide to be made. A ruler or T square and triangle are recommended for tracing the straight lines (see page 18). Make a very small dot at the four corners of the inner solid lined rectangle. This is the area in which you will draw or trace images.

3 Remove acetate from guide sheet and draw or trace directly on the acetate, staying within the four small dots.

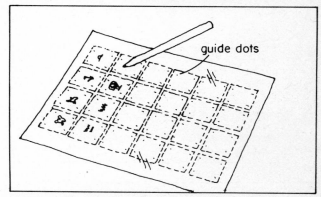

guide dots

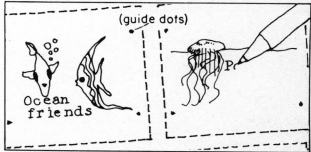

(guide dots)

Ocean friends

THERMOCOPY SLIDES

4 Carefully cut out each transparency on the line traced in Step 2. Scissors or any of the straight edge cutting tools can be used for the cutting.

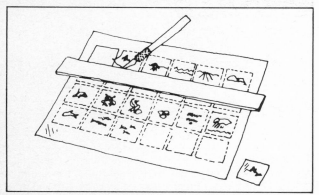

5 Mount cut transparencies in slide mounts. The Slide Guide Sheet was designed for use with mounts like Kodak Ready-mounts or similar designed mounts. See page 159 for information on other slide mounts that can be used. Mounting instructions can be found on page 160 .

TO ADD LETTERING TO SLIDES, see the Lettering Selection Chart on page 54 .

TO ADD COLOR, see page 46 .

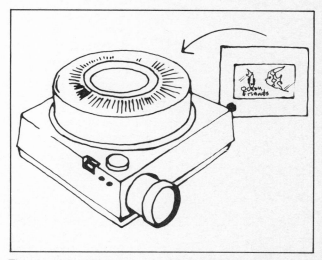

Thermocopy slides are actually miniature thermocopy transparencies (see page 137). With the exception of using a special slide guide sheet, making thermocopy slides is the same as making large thermocopy transparencies. Reading over the material on Thermocopy Transparencies first will be helpful in making these simple slides.

Instructions

The Slide Guide Sheet on page 155 has been designed for direct image, thermocopy, and Xerographic slide making. This guide sheet should be traced; not removed from the handbook. Should a number of these guide sheets be required, a spirit master can be made for reproducing paper copies (see page 34).

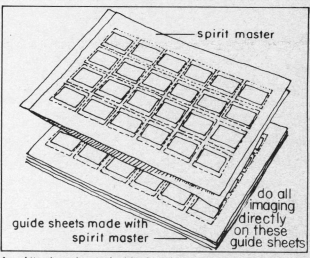

spirit master

guide sheets made with spirit master

do all imaging directly on these guide sheets

1 Attach a sheet of white bond paper to the guide sheet. To secure the paper to the guide sheet, punch holes at two edges of the paper and mount a 1-inch piece of adhesive tape over each hole. Press tape firmly into place at each hole.

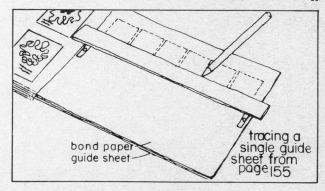

bond paper guide sheet

tracing a single guide sheet from page 155

2 With a colored pencil or pen, NOT BLACK, retrace the inside solid lined rectangle for the number of slides to be made. Wtih a lead pencil, India ink and pen, or any other "faxable" imaging tool, retrace the outer broken line for each slide to be made. This line will be cut out later. Remove traced guide sheet from Slide Guide Sheet.

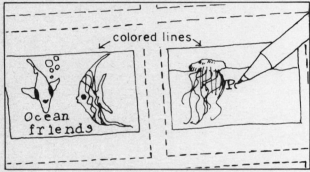

3 Do all imaging and lettering within the inside solid line for each slide. FOR IMAGES, you can draw or trace directly with lead pencil or India ink and pen, or use clip art (see page 12). FOR LETTERING, hand or typewritten letters

can be used. For more professional lettering, see Lettering Selection Chart on page 54.

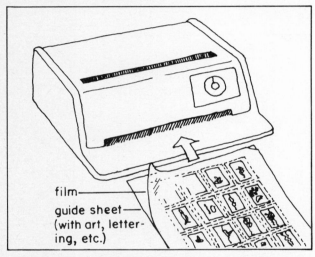

4 Place a sheet of thermocopy film, with the notch in the upper righthand corner (away from the operator), on top of the imaged guide sheet (image side up).

5 Set the exposure (speed) dial as instructed by the manufacturer of the film. Feed the film and original (guide sheet) into the machine. Retrieve the film and original, and separate. LIGHT IMAGES ON THE TRANSPARENCY CAN BE DARKENED BY RUNNING THE FILM ONLY THROUGH THE MACHINE A SECOND TIME.

6 Carefully cut out each transparency on the line traced in Step 2. Scissors or any of the straight edge cutting tools can be used for the cutting.

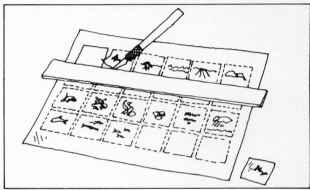

7 Mount transparencies in slide mounts. The Slide Guide Sheet was designed for use with mounts like Kodak Readymounts or similar designed mounts. See page 159 for information on other mounts that can be used. Mounting instructions can be found on page 160.

TO ADD COLOR TO SLIDES, see pages 46 to 48.

transparencies for study and display

XEROGRAPHIC SLIDES

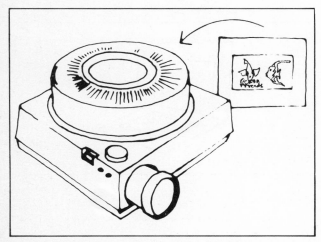

Xerographic slides are actually miniature Xerographic transparencies (see page 143). With the exception of using a special slide guide sheet, making Xerographic slides is the same as making large Xerographic transparencies. Reading over the material on Xerographic Transparencies first will be helpful in making these simple slides.

Instructions

The Slide Guide Sheet on page 155 has been designed for direct image, thermocopy, and Xerographic slide making. This guide sheet should be traced, not removed from the handbook. Should a number of these guide sheets be required, Xerox copies can be made from the handbook.

1 Attach a sheet of white bond paper to the guide sheet. To secure the paper to the guide sheet, punch holes at two

edges of the paper and mount a 1-inch piece of adhesive tape over each hole. Press tape firmly into place at each hole.

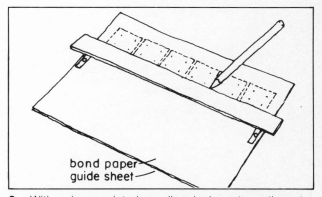

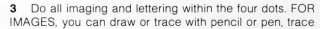

bond paper guide sheet

2 With a sharp-pointed pencil and ruler, retrace the outer broken line for each slide to be made. Next, make a very small dot at the four corners of the inner solid lined rectangle. This is the area in which you will do the imaging. Remove traced guide sheet from handbook.

3 Do all imaging and lettering within the four dots. FOR IMAGES, you can draw or trace with pencil or pen, trace

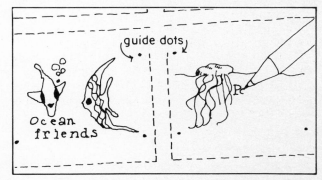

symbol templates, or use clip, dry transfer, or cut-out acetate art. FOR LETTERING, hand or typewritten letters can be used. For more professional lettering, see Lettering Selection chart on page 54. After imaging and lettering have been completed, erase all pencil dots.

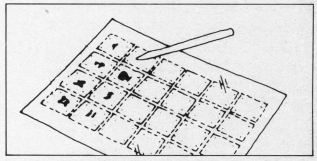

4 To make slide with various Xerox machines, follow the instructions on page 143. Retrieve the film and original, and separate.

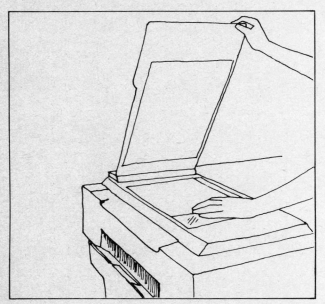

5 Carefully cut out each transparency on the line traced in Step 2. Scissors or any of the straight edge cutting tools can be used for the cutting.

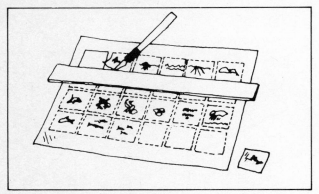

6 Mount transparencies in slide mounts. The Slide Guide Sheet was designed for use with mounts like Kodak Ready-Mounts or similar designed mounts. See page 159 for information on other mounts that can be used. Mounting instructions can be found on page 159.

SLIDE GUIDE SHEET FOR DIRECT IMAGE, THERMOCOPY, AND XEROGRAPHIC SLIDES

Image Area ——————

Cut Line - - - - - -

155

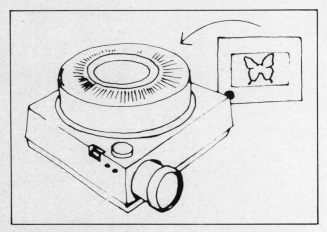

Instant 35mm slides can be made in 60 seconds with Starex's Instaslide film. The film has unusual adaptations. It makes positive slides from color or black and white negatives. Negatives can be made from color or black and white positives. No darkroom or chemicals are required for making these instant slides.

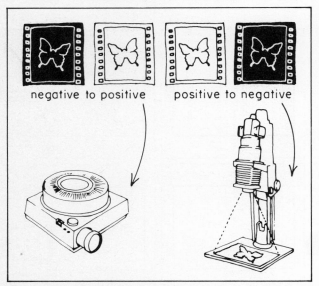

negative to positive   positive to negative

Instructions for Making 35mm (2-by 2-inch) Slides (Instaslide System)

1 Cut Instaslide film to 35mm (1½-inch) length. Place negative to be copied into white half of the printing frame (dull side of film up).

2 Place cut Instaslide film (emulsion side up) in the gray half of the printing frame. The emulsion side of both pieces of film will be facing each other.

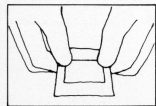

3 Insert locked printing frame into projector slot with the original negative (white half) closest to the projector's light source.

4 Turn the projector lamp on and expose as recommended.

5 Remove the printing frame from the projector. Separate the frame halves and remove the exposed Instaslide film.

6 Place exposed film (with emulsion side down) between two sheets of lintless paper (ordinary bond). A pad of this paper is supplied in the Instaslide kit.

7 Use any hand iron (with the controls set for low or synthetic fabrics) to iron the "sandwich" lightly with a quick, rotary motion for approximately 1 or 2 seconds.

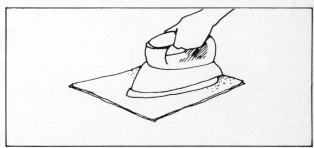

8 Remove film and insert into any slide mount (see page 159). The green tint will disappear after a few seconds. ∎

transparencies for study and display

KODAK VISUALMAKER SLIDES

is no larger than 8-by 8-inch. In addition, most three-dimensional objects that will fit into the same area, and are of moderate thickness can be photographed with equal ease. The copy photographed can, of course, be a part or section of a large piece of copy or a large object.

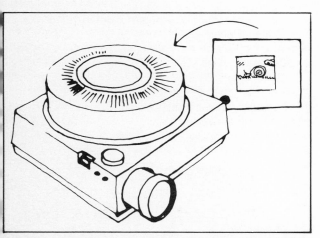

Perhaps the simplest method of all for making photographic 2-by 2-inch slides is the Kodak Ektagraphic Visualmaker slide system. This system consists of a kit that includes an Instamatic camera with flash attachment and two copy stands with built-in closeup lenses. With this slide making system you can make 2-by 2-inch color slides (with a 26.5mm square image area) from either Kodachrome-X film or Kodak Ektachrome-X film.

With the Kodak Visualmaker, no special skill is needed; no complicated equipment is involved. Even the time required between the exposure of the film and the return of mounted slides has been minimized, by provision of a special processing mailer, to less than one week.

With the Visualmaker a slide can easily be made of almost any piece of flat copy (printed, typed, drawn, or painted) that

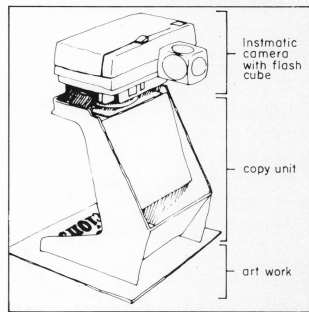

Instmatic camera with flash cube

copy unit

art work

Kodak has published two excellent publications specially dealing with the Visualmaker slide system; *Simple Copying Techniques With a Kodak Ektagraphic Visualmaker* (S-40) and *How to Use the Kodak Ektagraphic Visualmaker.* Both publications are recommended for making the most effective use of such a slide making system.

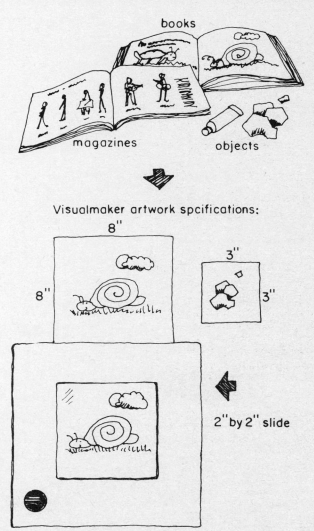

books

magazines

objects

Visualmaker artwork spcifications:

8"

8"

3"

3"

2" by 2" slide

POLAROID LAND PROJECTION TRANSPARENCIES

The Polaroid Corporation, makers of the Polaroid Land camera, has developed a transparency- (slide-) making system which produces a black and white slide on the spot. No darkroom or expensive equipment is required. All that is needed is a Polaroid Land camera and Polaroid Land projection film. This system is ideally suited for displaying information to a large audience, because the transparencies give a projected image of remarkable clarity and brilliance. At present there is a choice of films to make either linecopy

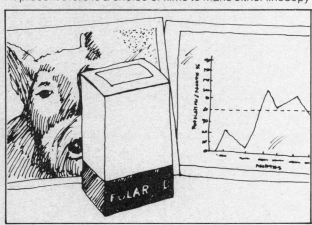

or continuous-tone slides. These slides can be projected as large as 20 feet square with a standard lantern slide projector. They can also be shown with overhead projectors or trimmed and mounted for use with 2¼- by 2¼-inch and 35mm projection equipment. Regardless of the projection method, there is no loss of resolution, detail, or tone.

Both Polaroid Land projection films are designed to be used with Polaroid MP-4 and MP-3 cameras and Polaroid roll-film cameras and backs (except the Model 80 series, J33, J66, and the "Swinger").

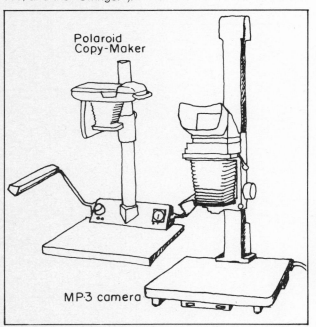

Type 146-L Film

This medium-speed, high-contrast, blue-sensitive film produces a fully developed, high-contrast transparency in thirty seconds. Eight-exposure roll. A 3¼- by 4¼-inch format sheet will produce one lantern-size slide or several 35mm-size slides. Film speed: 100 ASA, 21 DIN equivalent with tungsten lighting; 200 ASA, 24 DIN equivalent in daylight.

Type 46-L Film

This high-speed, medium-contrast panchromatic film produces a fully developed, continuous-tone transparency in two minutes. Eight-exposure roll. A 3¼- by 4¼-inch format sheet will produce one lantern slide or several 35mm-size slides. Film speed: 800 ASA, 30 DIN equivalent.

INSTRUCTIONS FOR EXPOSING AND PROCESSING FILMS

The instruction sheet included in the box of film will contain more detailed instructions than are included here.

1 *Exposure.* Snap it by exposing the film as recommended on the instruction sheet. Make certain the camera is held horizontal to the subject matter, because lantern slide projectors always take the slide in a horizontal position.

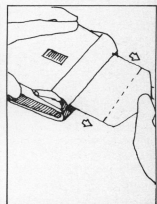

2 *Development.* Pull the tab slowly but steadily; the development will start. A fast pull can create small pinholes in the dark areas of the picture. Hesitation during a slow pull can cause streaks across the image area. Type 146-L film requires about fifteen seconds of development time at 70°F (21°C). Type 46-L film requires two minutes at 60°F and above.

SLIDE MOUNTING

3 *Development.* Lift out the positive transparency; the negative will remain in the camera. When the transparency is removed from the camera, the emulsion is soft and delicate, and so care must be exercised. For best results, start removal at the cutout slot in the upper right-hand corner near the cutter bar. Tear out diagonally, from the lower left. Do not allow the transparency to fall back against the negative. Do not touch the image side before hardening.

4 *Hardening.* Harden and stabilize the transparency in the Dippit. This should be done within one hour after removal from the camera. For best results, allow the transparency to dry in the air two or three minutes before dipping, or wave the transparency vigorously for ten to fifteen seconds. Here are instructions for using the Dippit:

a   Open the hinged cover of the Dippit and carefully slide in the transparency as far as it will go. Hold the film by the tab.

b   Close the cover of the Dippit. Make certain the film tab comes out through the slot in the cover. Turn the Dippit upside down and agitate for about twenty seconds (rock back and forth).

c   Turn the Dippit right side up. With the cover still closed, pull the film out with a rapid motion. The lips of the Dippit will squeegee excess liquid from the film. ◼

Usually slides are commercially processed and returned in cardboard mounts. If the slides are not subjected to rough handling or if they are stored in slide magazines or trays, cardboard mounts are satisfactory. For those making or processing their own slides, or wishing to provide a more permanent protection from dust, fingerprints, etc., a brief description of several types of mounts and accessories is included in this section.

2-by 2-Inch Slide Mounts

While 2- by 2-inch slide mounts have the same outer dimension (2 by 2 inches), the aperture (viewing area) differs to allow for the variety of film formats. Shown here are the more popular slide mounts with aperture dimensions indicated for each.

A 1 1/32 by 29/32 inches
B 29/32 by 20/32 inches
C 1½ by 1½ inches
D 1 1/16 by 1 1/16 inches

On the market today are several types of 2- by 2-inch slide mounts. Illustrated and discussed here are a select group of slide mounts.

■ Cardboard mount (permanent, heat-seal)

Mount with a slide heat mounting press (see page 161), electric hand iron, or dry mount tacking iron (see page 102).

■ Cardboard mount (permanent, adhesive-backed)

Seals in film upon contact. "Kalcor" is one brand name.

■ Cardboard mount (reusable)

Simply slip the film into the slot,

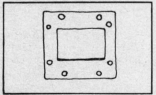 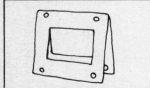

■ Plastic mount (permanent)

Requires a special slide hand mounting press (see page 161) for sealing film in permanently.

■ Plastic (reusable)

Requires no special mounting device. Mount has self-locking pins or seams that hold the film securely but is easy to open for reuse.

■ Metal mount (cover glass, mask, and metal frame)

Insert the film, mask, and two pieces of thin slide cover glass into the open end of the mount. The mount frame's three sides hold the slide securely without the need of tape.

■ Handmade glass mount (cover glass, mask, and slide binding tape)

An economical technique for mounting and binding all sizes of slides. Insert the film into a mask, and sandwich between two pieces of slide cover glass. Slide binding tape is used to bind the film, mask, and glass together.

slide label   thumb spot

SLIDE IDENTIFICATION AND "THUMB-SPOTTING"

Photo slide labels are ideal for properly identifying slides. These labels, available from Visual Planning, are designed for slide identification (see "Slide Mounting Accessories" for a description).

Slide "thumb-spotting" is a guide for accurate positioning of a slide in the projector or slide tray. Here are directions for "thumb-spotting:" After the slide has been mounted, turn so that it reads properly and place a thumb spot (commercial or hand-printed) in the lower lefthand corner of the mount.

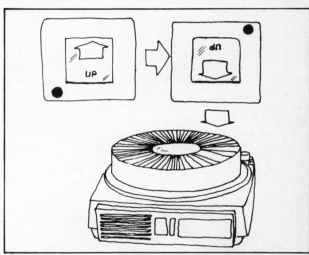

Commercial thumb spots (signal dots) are available for purchase. However, hand-printed spots can be made with a pencil eraser and ink stamp pad.

Slide Mounting Accessories

SLIDE MOUNTING PRESS

A hand-operated electric press for mounting all popular sizes of slides. Models are available for mounting 2- by 2-inch, 2¼- by 2¼-inch and 3¼- by 4-inch slides in cardboard mounts designed for heat mounting.

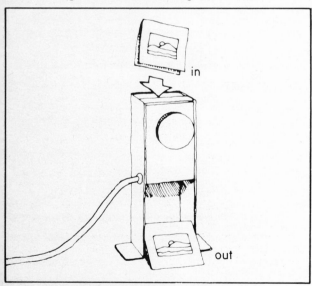

Instructions for Seary Presses

1 Place the film in a cardboard mount and fold.

2 Slip the folded mount in between heated pressure plates.

3 Squeeze the handles together like a pair of pliers. Press the locks, freeing the operator's hands for preparation of the next slide.

4 After two seconds, pull the release handle and the sealed slide drops out. Insert the next slide, and close the press while the right hand is still on the handle.

HAND MOUNTING PRESS

A hand mounting press designed for mounting permanent plastic slide mounts. The machine mounts the two halves and film in one operation.

SLIDE LABELS

A pressure-sensitive adhesive paper label with a printed red dot (thumb spot). the red dot is for correct placement of the slide into the projector or carrier (tray) (see page 160). Blank label space is for identification information that can be typed or written with pen, pencil, or ballpoint. Labels available in white and colors.

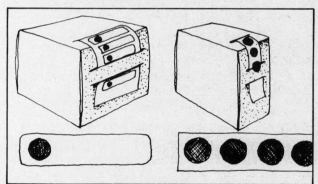

THUMB SPOTS (SIGNAL DOTS)

Self-sticking die-cut dots for use as thumb spots for slide mounts and other visual media requiring color-coded dot identification. Dots come in red, blue, green, gold, and silver—in a dispenser box. ◗

SOURCES

Selected publications and audiovisual media have been annotated and sourced here to supplement the contents of this section. The figures in parentheses at the end of each entry (O8) indicate the coded address source for the procurement of the reference. Complete addresses are listed under *Out-of-Town* sources at the end of this section.

BASIC PHOTOGRAPHY FOR THE GRAPHIC ARTS (No. Q-1), Eastman Kodak, 1974.
Deals with the making of line and halftone negatives, contacts and duplicates, screened paper prints, and offset lithographic plates for photomechanical reproduction. (O15)

Heward, William, and Jill Dardig; OVERHEAD TRANSPARENCIES: A GUIDE, Chartpak, 1974.
A booklet that deals with the design and preparation of overhead projection transparencies using rub-on and paste-up commercial materials. (O11)

"HOW-TO" GUIDE FOR DESIGN GRAPHICS (3M Color-Key), 3M Company.
A booklet on instructions and applications of the 3M Color-Key transparency system. (O41)

KODAK PHOTOGRAPHIC MATERIALS FOR THE GRAPHIC ARTS (No. Q-2), Eastman Kodak, 1973.
A booklet containing detailed data and information on using sensitized photographic materials in the preparation of visual media. (O15)

Krulik, Stephen, and Irwin Kaufman: HOW TO USE THE OVERHEAD PROJECTOR IN MATHEMATICS EDUCATION, National Council of Teachers of Mathematics, 1966.
Contains directions for making and storing overhead transparencies. (O31)

MAKING BLACK AND WHITE OR COLORED TRANSPARENCIES FOR OVERHEAD PROJECTION (No. S-7), Eastman Kodak, 1972.
Useful information on preparing overhead projectuals with Kodak films. (O15)

Minor, Ed, and Harvey Frye: TECHNIQUES FOR PRODUCING VISUAL INSTRUCTIONAL MEDIA, McGraw-Hill, 1977.
Section 8, Photographic Techniques, of this text is devoted to the preparation of transparencies ranging from high-contrast photographic to electronic stencil cutter. (O30)

OVERHEAD SYSTEM: PRODUCTION, IMPLEMENTATION AND UTILIZATION, University of Texas at Austin, 1967.
A handbook that deals with the design and preparation of overhead projection transparencies. (O40)

Rothschild, Norman: MAKING SLIDE DUPLICATES, TITLES, AND FILMSTRIPS, 3d. ed., American Photographic Book, 1973.
Illustrations and instructions for producing slides, filmstrips, and titles. (O2)

SIMPLE COPYING TECHNIQUES WITH A KODAK EKTAGRAPHIC VISUALMAKER (No. S-40), Eastman Kodak, 1973.
Complete illustrated instructions for making photographic slides with the Kodak Visualmaker slide system. (O15)

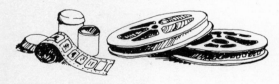

ADVANCED PRODUCTION TECHNIQUES, *35mm filmstrip, 51 frames, sound, color, Educational Media, 1968.*
Various color-producing processes are covered such as diazo, "color-lifting," and special color-yielding systems. (O18)

BASIC COPYING TECHNIQUES, *2-by 2-inch slides (78), sound (tape), color, Eastman Kodak Audio-Visual Library, 1972.*
A sound-slide set on basic photographic copying techniques designed mainly for the novice photographer. (O16)

BASIC EDUCATIONAL GRAPHICS, *Multimedia package, Scott Graphics, 1967.*
Deals with the application of basic graphic techniques in preparing overhead projectuals. Package is made up of overhead transparencies, filmstrips, sound disk, thermocopy masters, and manuals. (O35)

DIAZO TRANSPARENCY PRODUCTION, *16mm film, eleven minutes, sound, color, University of Iowa, 1964.*
Demonstrates exposing and developing diazo film. Shows techniques of applying letters, shading, inks, and cutouts to the master sheet. (O26)

DRY MOUNTING INSTRUCTIONAL MATERIALS: LAMINATING AND LIFTING, *16mm film, six minutes, sound, color, University of Iowa, 1965.*
Presents the concept of laminating flat instructional materials. One part of the film deals with picture "lifting" using the heat laminating process. (O26)

Pett, Dennis W.: COPYING AND DUPLICATING PROCESSES, *35mm filmstrips (6), sound, color, Indiana University, 1973.*
Six sound (audio cassette) filmstrips which include topics on copy and duplicating processes; carbon transfer, diazo copy, electrostatic copy, photocopy, screen stencil, and thermal copy. (O23)

PHOTOGRAPHIC SLIDES FOR INSTRUCTION, *16mm film, eleven minutes, sound, b and w or color, Indiana University, 1957.*
The preparation and use of slides made by the photographic process, including the use of Polaroid transparency film. (O23)

PLANNING THE PROJECTUAL, *35mm filmstrip, 47 frames, sound, color, Educational Media, 1968.*
Setting objectives and storyboarding, projectual composition, using color and overlays. (O18)

PREPARING PROJECTED MATERIALS, *16mm film, fifteen minutes, sound, color, BFA, 1965.*
Shows the use of projectors, 35mm cameras, Polaroid copying stand, and Thermofax copier. (O5)

PROJECTION IDEAS, II: DIAZO TRANSPARENCY PRODUCTION, *16mm film, eleven minutes, sound, color, University of Iowa, 1964.*
Demonstrates basic concepts of exposing and developing diazo film, and the step-by-step procedure for preparing a transparency. (O26)

PROJECTION IDEAS, III: DIRECT TRANSPARENCY PRODUCTION, *16mm film, five minutes, sound, color, University of Iowa, 1964.*
Introduces the production of hand-drawn and -lettered transparencies, primarily on acetate, and illustrates use of various pencil, pens, and lettering devices. (O26)

SIMPLE PROJECTUAL PRODUCTION, *35mm filmstrip, 40 frames, sound, color, Educational Media, 1968.*
Part A: techniques of preparing handmade projectuals. Part B: procedure for making heat transfer masters and production of heat transfer projectuals. (O18)

Most of the equipment and materials included in this section are available from local sources; such sources are indicated (L), and can be located in the *Yellow Pages* of the telephone directory. Items not readily available locally can be purchased directly, or purchase information obtained from the sources indicated (O).

CLEAR, PREPARED, AND MATTE ACETATE (L2, L2, L3, O6, O12, O35, O42)
COLD ACETATE LAMINATORS (L2, L5, O9, O30)
COLD LAMINATING ACETATE (L2, L5, L6, O9, O32)
DIAZO EQUIPMENT AND FILM (L2, L3, O7, O28, O35, O42)
DRY MOUNTING PRESSES (L1, L2, L5, O6, O8, O36)
ELECTRONIC STENCIL CUTTERS (L4, O10, O20, O34)
ELECTRONIC STENCIL FILM (L4, O20)
HEAT ACETATE LAMINATORS (L1, L2, O19, O22, O27, O36)
HEAT LAMINATING ACETATE (L1, L2, O19, O22, O27, O36)
INSTANT SLIDE EQUIPMENT AND FILM (L5, O38)
KODAK VISUALMAKER (L2, L5, O15)
LARGE TRANSPARENCY MOUNTS (cardboard) (L2, O12, O35, O38, O42)
LARGE TRANSPARENCY MOUNTS (solid plastic) (L2, O24, O35)
LARGE TRANSPARENCY MOUNTS (transparent) (L2, O6, O11)
OVERHEAD TRANSPARENCY ACCESSORIES (L2, O12, O35, O38, O42)
OVERHEAD TRANSPARENCY PROJECTION PENS (L1, L2, O6, O24, O35, O38, O42)
POLAROID TRANSPARENCY EQUIPMENT AND SUPPLIES(L2, L5, O33)
PROJECTORS (overhead and slide) (L2, L5, O4, O6, O35, O41)
SLIDE LABELS (L5, O42)
SLIDE MOUNTING PRESSES (L2, L5, O21, O37)
SLIDE MOUNTS (L2, L5, O9, O21)
SLIDE THUMB SPOTS (L5, O14, O21)
THERMOCOPY FILM (Escotherm) (L2, O3)
THERMOCOPY FILM (standard) (L2, O1, O10, O20, O29, O38, O39, O41)
THERMOCOPY FILM (Transparex) (L2, O1)

THERMOCOPY MACHINES (L2, L4, O10, O20, O38, O39, O41, O42)
3M BRAND COLOR-KEY FILM (L1, L3, O41)
TRANSPAREX FILM PROCESSORS (L2, O1)

Addresses

LOCAL SOURCES (See Yellow Pages)

L1 - Artists' Materials and Supply Stores
L2 - Audio-Visual Equipment and Supply Stores
L3 - Drafting Equipment and Supply Stores
L4 - Duplicating Equipment and Supply Stores
L5 - Photographic Equipment and Supply Stores
L6 - Stationers' Stores

OUT-OF-TOWN SOURCES

O1 - AGFA-GEVAERT, INC., 275 North St., Teterboro, NJ 07608
O2 - AMERICAN PHOTOGRAPHIC BOOK PUBLISHING CO., INC., 750 Zeckendorf Blvd., Garden City, NY 11530
O3 - ARKWRIGHT, Main St., Fiskeville, RI 02823
O4 - CHARLES BESELER CO., 8 Fernwood Rd., Florham Park, NJ 07932
O5 - BFA EDUCATIONAL MEDIA., 2211 Michigan Ave., Santa Monica, CA 90404
O6 - DICK BLICK, P. O. Box 1267, Galesburg, IL 61401
O7 - BLU-RAY, INC., P. O. Box 337, Essex, CT 06426
O8 - ARTHUR BROWN & BROTHER, INC., 2 West 46th St., New York, NY 10036
O9 - BURKE & JAMES, 690 Portland Ave., Rochester, NY 14621
O10 - A. B. DICK CO., 5700 West Touhy Ave., Chicago, IL 60648
O11 - CHARTPAK, One River Rd., Leeds, MA 01053
O12 - COLOR-STIK CO., 8 Fernwood Rd., Florham Park, NJ 07932
O13 - DEMCO EDUCATIONAL CORP., Box 1488, Madison, WI 53701
O14 - DENNISON MFG. CO., 300 Howard St., Framingham, MA 01701
O15 - EASTMAN KODAK CO., 343 State St., Rochester, NY 14650
O16 - EASTMAN KODAK CO., Audio-Visual Library Distribution, 343 State St., Rochester, NY 14650
O17 - EDUCATIONAL FILMSTRIPS, Box 1401, Huntsville, TX 77340

O18 - EDUCATIONAL MEDIA LABS, 4101 S. Congress Ave., Austin, TX 78745
O19 - GENERAL BINDING CORP., Northbrook, IL 60062
O20 - GESTETNER CORP., Gestetner Park, Yonkers, NY 10703
O21 - THE HIGHSMITH CO., INC., Box 25, Fort Atkinson, WI 53538
O22 - INDEX, INC., P. O. Box 239, Charlotte, NC 28230
O23 - INDIANA UNIVERSITY, Audio-Visual Center, Bloomington, IN 47401
O24 - THE INSTRUCTO CORP., 1635 N. 55th St., Paoli, PA 19301
O25 - INTERNATIONAL FILM BUREAU, INC., 332 S. Michigan Ave., Chicago, IL 60604
O26 - UNIVERSITY OF IOWA, AV Center, C-5 East Hall, Iowa City, IA 52240
O27 - JACKSON-HIRSH, INC., 1400 Charing Cross Rd., Deerfield, IL 60015
O28 - KEUFFEL & ESSER CO., Educational/Audiovisual Div., 20 Whippany Rd., Morristown, NJ 07960
O29 - LABELON CORP., 10 Chapin St., Canadaigua, NY 14424
O30 - McGRAW-HILL BOOK CO., 1221 Avenue of the Americas, New York, NY 10020
O31 - NATIONAL COUNCIL OF TEACHERS OF MATHEMATICS, 1906 Association Dr., Reston, VA 22091
O32 - NATIONWIDE ADHESIVE PRODUCTS, INC., 19600 St. Clair, Cleveland, OH 44117
O33 - POLAROID CORP., 549 Technology Square, Cambridge, MA 02139
O34 - RONEO VICKERS, INC., One Alsan Way, Little Ferry, NJ 07643
O35 - SCOTT GRAPHICS, INC., 195 Appleton St., Holyoke, MA 01040
O36 - SEAL, INC., 251 Roosevelt Dr., Derby, CT 06418
O37 - SEARY MFG. CO., 19 Nebraska Ave., Endicott, NY 13760
O38 - STAREX, INC., 655 Schyler Ave., Kearny, NJ 07032
O39 - TERSCH PRODUCTS, INC., Industrial Blvd., Rogers, MN 55374
O40 - THE UNIVERSITY OF TEXAS at Austin, Instructional Media Center, Drawer W, University Station, Austin, TX 78712
O41 - 3M COMAPNY, Visual Products Div., 3M Center, St. Paul, MI 55101
O42 - VISUAL PLANNING DIVISION, MPC, North Main St., Champlain, NY 12919